W9-CJN-774

EVERYMAN, I will go with thee,

and be thy guide,

In thy most need to go by thy side

Writing
of the 'Nineties
From Wilde to Beerbohm

EDITED WITH AN INTRODUCTION BY
DEREK STANFORD

DENT: LONDON
EVERYMAN'S LIBRARY
DUTTON: NEW YORK

All rights reserved
Made in Great Britain
at the
Aldine Press · Letchworth · Herts
for
J. M. DENT & SONS LTD
Aldine House · Bedford Street · London
© *Introduction, J. M. Dent & Sons Ltd, 1971*

This selection first included
in Everyman's Library 1971

NO. 773

ISBN: 0 460 00773 4

Contents

Hubert Crackanthorpe

G. S. Street

POEMS

Oscar Wilde

John Davidson

Francis Thompson

Ernest Rhys

W. B. Yeats

Norman Gale

Victor Plarr

Stephen Phillips

Herbert Horne

Arthur Symons

John Gray

Ernest Dowson

Theodore Peters

Lionel Johnson

Lord Alfred Douglas

Theodore Wratislaw

Aubrey Beardsley

PROSE POEMS AND CAMEOS

Oscar Wilde

Ernest Dowson

Max Beerbohm

Hubert Crackanthorpe

REVIEWS

Oscar Wilde

Richard Le Gallienne

Arthur Symons

Editor's Preface

The boundaries of my choice in this anthology of the Nineties are suggested by its sub-title: 'From Wilde to Beerbohm.' These two—the most popular and acclaimed authors of the period as they appear today—were separated by birth by eighteen years. I have therefore taken Wilde as representing the point of age and Beerbohm the point of youth—at least as to inclusion here.

Although I have called this collection *Writing of the 'Nineties*, I have exercised an editorial licence which I hope is not without justification. Thus, in the case of three authors (Wilde, Beerbohm and Symons) I have included work written *before* 1890 and *after* 1900, since although their best productions belong to the Nineties, their activities outside that decade constitute an important prelude and aftermath to its literature.

With Arthur Symons I had also to allow a temporal extension so that he might pronounce upon three of the leading spirits of the period—Wilde, Yeats and Dowson—beyond the bar of 1899. A like motive has additionally led me to include Lord Alfred Douglas' moving tribute to Wilde *The Dead Poet*, written in 1901 after his erstwhile friend's decease.

All other works in this collection were either written or appeared in magazines or book form in the years suggested by the title of the anthology. The dates of first publication in book form are given in the list of contents.

I wish to thank those publishers, executors and literary executors who have given their permissions for the publication of copyright material.

The Bodley Head have granted permission for the poems 'At the Rhymers' Club: I. The toast' and 'An Autobiography' by Ernest Rhys from *London and other Rhymes*, 1894; for the Editor's Apology and Chapters I and II from G. S. Street's *Autobiography of a Boy*, 1894; for the two poems by Victor Plarr, 'Epitaphium Citharistriæ' and 'Ad Cinerarium' from *In the Dorian Mood*, 1896; and for Sir Max Beerbohm's story 'Diminuendo' from *The Works of Max Beerbohm*, 1896. William Heinemann Ltd for two other works by Beerbohm, the essay 'Aubrey Beardsley' from *A*

Variety of Things, 1928, and 'L'Oiseau Bleu' from *Yet Again*, 1909; also for nineteen poems from *The Poems of Arthur Symons*, 1901, two of which are printed in Richard Le Gallienne's review of his 'Silhouettes', 1892, and one of which is included in my present introduction. Constable & Company Ltd for two of Arthur Symons's prose works, the story 'An Autumn City' from *Spiritual Adventures*, 1905, and the Introduction to *The Symbolist Movement in Literature*, 1908; also for Norman Gale's poem 'The Shaded Pool' from *A Country Muse*, 1892. The Richards Press for the three poems '*Ερος δ'αὐτε*', 'Odour' and 'Epitaph (Villon)' from *Poems by Theodore Wratislaw (1871–1933)*, 1935; and J. M. Dent & Sons Ltd for the two essays by Arthur Symons, 'An Artist in Attitudes: Oscar Wilde', and 'Ernest Dowson', and the review 'Mr W. B. Yeats' from *Studies in Prose and Verse*, 1904.

Edward Colman, executor of the Lord Alfred Douglas Literary Estate, has granted permission for four poems by Lord Alfred Douglas, 'A Song' from *Poems*, 1896, 'The Travelling Companion' from *The City of the Soul*, 1899, and 'The Dead Poet' and 'My Soul is like a Silent Nightingale' from *Sonnets*, 1909. The Society of Authors, as the literary representative of the Estate of Richard Le Gallienne, for 'John Gray: "Silverponts"', 'Arthur Symons: "Silhouettes"', and 'Lionel Johnson: "Poems"', from *Retrospective Reviews: A Literary Log*, 1896. The Prior Provincial of St Dominic's Priory, London, for the three poems, 'The Barber', 'Complaint' and 'Les Demoiselles de Sauve' by John Gray from *Silverpoints*, 1892; and Mr M. B. Yeats, Macmillan & Co., London, and the Macmillan Company, New York, for 'Down by the Salley Gardens' and 'The Man Who Dreamed of Faeryland' from *The Collected Poems of W. B. Yeats*, 1933, and for extracts from poems and plays printed in Arthur Symons's *Studies in Prose and Verse*, 1904.

D. S.

Select Bibliography

Since the bibliography of the 'Nineties is so extensive, this short list has been planned to supplement the titles of books given on the contents pages and in the prefatory notices to the individual authors. Titles given in these two places are not repeated in this bibliography.

INDIVIDUAL AUTHORS

AUBREY BEARDSLEY. WORKS. ART: *A Book of Fifty Drawings by Aubrey Beardsley*, 1897; *A Second Book of Fifty Drawings by Aubrey Beardsley*, 1899. Literature: Rev. John Gray (ed.), *Last Letters of Aubrey Beardsley*, 1915; R. A. Walker (ed.), *Letters from Aubrey Beardsley to Leonard Smithers*, 1937; *Under the Hill*, 1959; H. Maas, J. L. Duncan, W. G. Good (eds.), *The Letters of Aubrey Beardsley*, 1971. BIOGRAPHICAL AND CRITICAL: Arthur Symons, *Aubrey Beardsley*, 1898; Robert Ross, *Aubrey Beardsley*, 1908; Haldane Macfall, *Aubrey Beardsley: The Man and His Work*, 1928; Stanley Weintraub, *Beardsley: A Biography*, 1967; Brian Reade, *Beardsley*, 1967; Derek Stanford, *Aubrey Beardsley's Erotic Universe*, 1967; Brigid Brophy, *Black and White: A Portrait of Aubrey Beardsley*, 1968.

MAX BEERBOHM. WORKS. Literature: *The Happy Hypocrite*, 1897; *More*, 1899; *Yet Again*, 1909; *Zuleika Dobson*, 1911; *A Christmas Garland*, 1912; *Seven Men*, 1919; *And Even Now*, 1920; *Around Theatres*, 1924; *Max Beerbohm's Letters to Reggie Turner*, 1964; *More Theatres 1898–1903*, 1969. Art: *Caricatures of Twenty-Five Gentlemen*, 1896; *Poet's Corner*, 1904; *Rossetti and His Circle*, 1922. BIOGRAPHICAL AND CRITICAL: J. G. Riewald, *Sir Max Beerbohm: Man and Writer*, The Hague, 1953; S. N. Behrman, *Conversations with Max*, 1960; Lord David Cecil, *Max: A Biography*, 1964.

HUBERT CRACKANTHORPE. WORKS: *Sentimental Studies and a Set of Village Tales*, 1895; *Vignettes*, 1896; *Last Studies*, 1897.

JOHN DAVIDSON. WORKS. Plays: *Bruce*, 1886; *Smith*, 1888; *An Unhistorical Pastoral*, 1889; *A Romantic Farce*, 1889; *Scaramouch in Naxos*, 1889; *The Theatrocrat: A Tragic Play of Church and State*, 1905; *The Triumph of Mammon*, 1907; *Mammon and His Message*, 1908. Verse: *New Ballads*, 1897; *The Last Ballad*, 1899; *Holiday and Other Poems*, 1906; *The Testament of John Davidson*, 1908; *Fleet Street and Other Poems*, 1909; *John Davidson: A Selection of His Poems*, 1961. Prose: *Perfervid*, 1890; *Sentences and Paragraphs*, 1893; *A Random Itinerary and a Ballad*, 1894; *Baptist Lake*, 1894; *The Wonderful Mission of Earl Lavender*, 1895. BIOGRAPHICAL AND CRITICAL: Hayim Fineman, *John Davidson*, 1916; Priscilla Thoules, *Modern Poetic Drama*, 1934.

LORD ALFRED DOUGLAS. WORKS. Verse: *Collected Poems*, 1919; *Collected Satires*, 1926; *Complete Poems*, 1928. Prose: *Oscar Wilde and Myself*, 1914; *Autobiography*, 1929; *Oscar Wilde: A Summing-up*, 1940. BIOGRAPHICAL AND CRITICAL: William Freeman, *The Life of Lord Alfred Douglas*, 1948; Rupert Croft-Cooke, *Bosie: The Story of Lord Alfred Douglas, his Friends and Enemies*, 1963.

ERNEST DOWSON. WORKS. Verse: Desmond Flower (ed.), *The Poetical Works of Ernest Dowson*, 1967. Play: *Pierrot of the Minute*, 1896. Prose: *Adrian Rome* (with Arthur Moore), 1899; Mark Longaker (ed.), *The Stories of Ernest Dowson*, 1947; Desmond Flower and Henry Maas (ed.), *Letters of Ernest Dowson*. BIOGRAPHICAL AND CRITICAL: Victor Plarr, *Ernest Dowson: Reminiscences 1887–1897*, 1914; Mark Longaker, *Ernest Dowson*, 1944; Thomas Swann, *Ernest Dowson*, 1964.

NORMAN GALE. WORKS. Verse: *A Country Muse: New Series*, 1893; *Orchard Songs*, 1894; *Cricket Songs*, 1894; *Songs for Little People*, 1905; *A Book of Quatrains*, 1909; *Collected Poems*, 1919. Prose: *A June Romance*, 1892; *A Verdant Country* (with Alfred Hayes), 1893.

JOHN GRAY. WORKS. Verse: *Spiritual Poems*, 1896; *The Long Road*, 1926; *Poems*, 1931. Prose: *The Blackmailers* (with André Raffalovich), 1893; *Park: A Fantastic Story*, 1932. BIOGRAPHICAL AND CRITICAL: B. Sewell, *Two Friends: Canon Gray and Mr. Raffalovich*, 1963; Brocard Sewell, *Footnote to the Nineties: A Memoir of John Gray and André Raffalovich*, 1968.

HERBERT HORNE. WORKS. Prose: *Alessandro Filipepi* [Sandro Botticelli], 1908.

LIONEL JOHNSON. WORKS. Verse: Ian Fletcher (ed.), *The Complete Poems of Lionel Johnson*, 1953. Prose: *The Art of Thomas Hardy*, 1894; *Post Liminium*, 1911; Francis, Earl Russell (ed.), *Some Winchester Letters of Lionel Johnson*, 1919; *Reviews and Critical Papers*, 1921.

RICHARD LE GALLIENNE. WORKS. Verse: *My Ladies' Sonnets and Other Poems*, 1887; *Volumes in Folio*, 1889; *English Poems*, 1892; *Robert Louis Stevenson: An Elegy and Other Poems*, 1895. Prose: *Book Bills of Narcissus*, 1892; *The Religion of a Literary Man*, 1893; *George Meredith: Some Characteristics*, 1893; *Prose Fancies* (First and Second Series), 1895, 1896; *The Quest of the Golden Girl*, 1896; *The Romance of Zion Chapel*, 1898; *Young Lines*, 1898; *Rudyard Kipling: A Criticism*, 1900. BIOGRAPHICAL AND CRITICAL: R. Whittington Egan and G. Smeardon, *The Quest of the Golden Boy*, 1960.

WILLIAM THEODORE PETERS. WORKS. Verse: *Tutti-Frutti*, 1881; *The Tournament of Love*, 1894; *Posies out of Rings*, 1896.

STEPHEN PHILLIPS. WORKS. Verse: *Christ in Hades*, 1897; *New Poems*, 1908. Plays: *Paolo and Francesca*, 1900; *Herod*, 1901; *Ulysses*, 1902; *Nero*, 1906.

VICTOR GUSTAVE PLARR. WORKS. Prose: *Literary Etiquette*, 1903. Plays: *The Tragedy of Asgard*, 1905.

ERNEST RHYS. WORKS. Verse: *Welsh Ballads*, 1903. Prose: *English Lyric Poetry*, 1913.

GEORGE SLYTHE STREET. WORKS. Prose: *Miniatures and Moods*, 1893; *Episodes*, 1895; *Quales Ego*, 1896; *The Wise and the Wayward*, 1897; *Some Notes on a Struggling Genius*, 1898.

ARTHUR SYMONS. WORKS. Verse: *The Fool of the World and Other Poems*, 1906; *Knave of Hearts*, 1913. Prose: *An Introduction to the Study of Browning*, 1886; *Studies in Two Literatures*, 1897; *Plays, Acting and Music*, 1903; *Cities*, 1903; *Studies in Seven Arts*, 1906; *Cities of Italy*, 1907; *William Blake*, 1907; *The Romantic Movement in English Poetry*, 1909; *Figures of Several Centuries*, 1916; *Cities and Sea-coasts and Islands*, 1917; *Studies in the Elizabethan Drama*, New York, 1919; *Dramatis Personae*, New York, 1923; *Confessions: A Study in Pathology*, 1930. Play: *Tragedies*, 1916. BIOGRAPHICAL AND CRITICAL: T. Earle Welby, *Arthur Symons: A Critical Study*, 1925; Roger Lhombreaud, *Arthur Symons: A Critical Biography*, 1963; John M. Munro, *Arthur Symons*, N.Y., 1969.

FRANCIS THOMPSON. WORKS. Verse: *Poems*, 1893; *Sister Songs*, 1895. Prose: *Health and Holiness*, 1905; *St. Ignatius Loyola*, 1909; *The Works of Francis Thompson* (vols. I and II verse, vol. III prose), 1913. BIOGRAPHICAL AND CRITICAL: Everard Meynell, *The Life of Francis Thompson*, 1913.

OSCAR WILDE. WORKS: G. F. Maine (ed.), *The Works of Oscar Wilde*, 1948; *The Artist as Critic*, ed. Richard Ellmann, 1970. BIOGRAPHICAL AND CRITICAL: Robert Sherard, *Life of Oscar Wilde*, 1906; Robert Sherard, *The Real Oscar Wilde*, 1911; Vincent O'Sullivan, *Aspects of Oscar Wilde*, 1936; Frank Harris, *Oscar Wilde*, 1938; Hesketh Pearson, *Life of Oscar Wilde*, 1946; H. Montgomery Hyde, *The Trials of Oscar Wilde*, 1948; Vyvyan Holland, *Son of Oscar Wilde*, 1954; Philippe Jullian, *Oscar Wilde*, 1969.

THEODORE WRATISLAW. WORKS. Verse: *Caprices*, 1893; *Orchids*, 1896; John Gawsworth (ed.), *Selected Poems of Theodore Wratislaw*, 1935. Prose: *Swinburne: A Study*, 1900.

WILLIAM BUTLER YEATS. WORKS. Verse: *The Wanderings of Oisin and Other Poems*, 1889; *The Rose*, 1893; *The Wind Among the Reeds*,

1899; *In the Seven Woods*, 1903; *The Green Helmet*, 1910; *Collected Poems*, 1950. Plays: *The Countess Cathleen*, 1892; *The Land of Heart's Desire*, 1894. Prose: *John Sherman and Dhoya* (published under the pseudonym 'Ganconagh'), 1891; *The Celtic Twilight*, 1893; *The Secret Rose*, 1897; *Early Poems and Stories*, 1925; *Autobiographies*, 1926; Allan Wade (ed.), *The Letters of William Butler Yeats*, 1955; A. Norman Jeffares (ed.), *Yeats: Selected Prose*, 1964; A. Norman Jeffares (ed.), *Yeats: Selected Criticism*, 1964. BIOGRAPHICAL AND CRITICAL: Richard Ellmann, *Yeats: The Man and Masks*, 1948; A. Norman Jeffares, *W. B. Yeats: Man and Poet*, 1949; T. R. Henn, *The Lonely Tower: Studies in the Poetry of W. B. Yeats*, 1950.

WORKS OF GENERAL REFERENCE TO THE PERIOD

W. Hamilton, *The Aesthetic Movement in England*, 1882; W. G. Blaikie Murdoch, *The Renaissance of the Nineties*, 1911; J. M. Kennedy, *English Literature 1880–1905*, 1913; Holbrook Jackson, *The Eighteen Nineties*, 1913; Bernard Muddiman, *The Men of the Nineties*, 1920; E. T. Raymond, *Portraits of the Nineties*, 1921; Victor Starrett, *Etcetera*, 1923; Osbert Burdett, *The Beardsley Period*, 1925; A. J. A. Symons (ed.), *An Anthology of 'Nineties Verse*, 1928; R. L. Megroz, *Modern English Poetry 1882–1932*, 1933; J. Lewis May, *John Lane and the Nineties*, 1936; William Gaunt, *The Aesthetic Adventure*, 1945; Graham Hough, *The Last Romantics*, 1949. A. G. Lehmann, *The Symbolist Aesthetic in France 1885–1895*, 1950; Ruth Z. Temple, *The Critic's Alchemy: A Study of the Introduction of Symbolism into England*, New York, 1953; Katherine Mix, *A Study in Yellow: The Yellow Book and its Contributors*, 1960. Stanely Weintraub (ed.), *The Yellow Book: Quintessence of the Nineties*, New York, 1964; Stanley Weintraub (ed.), *The Savoy: Nineties Experiment*, University Park, Pa., 1965; Barbara Charlesworth, *Dark Passages: The Decadent Consciousness in Victorian Literature*, Madison, Wisc., 1965; Derek Stanford (ed.), *Poets of the Nineties: A Biographical Anthology*, 1965; Karl Beckson (ed.), *Aesthetes and Decadents of the 1890's: An Anthology of British Poetry and Prose*, New York, 1966; Derek Stanford (ed.), *Short Stories of the Nineties: A Biographical Anthology*, 1968; C. J. Dixon (ed.), *Fin de Siècle: Poetry of the Late Victorian Period 1860–1900*, 1968; R. V. Johnson, *Aestheticium*, 1969; John Dixon Hunt, *The Pre-Raphaelite Imagination 1848–1900*, 1968; Derek Stanford (ed.), *Critics of the Nineties: A Biographical Anthology*, 1970.

The *Textual Notes* and *Select Bibliography* in *The Complete Poems of Lionel Johnson*, ed. Ian Fletcher, 1953, contain a mass of biographical and bibliographical information on the period.

Introduction

In terms of literature and art, the Eighteen-Nineties in England appear as a vast terminus and junction. Into it run those Victorian ideas which were to cease with the century while alongside them one can distinguish fresher notions which, modified perhaps, have come to play a part in our own era. 'Here,' wrote Richard Le Gallienne, looking back on that decade of his prime, 'was not so much the ending of a century as the beginning of a new one.'

But before we look forward, let us look back to July 1879 when Laura Troubridge, daughter of a Colonel who had been A.D.C. to the old Queen, went with her cousin Charles to tea with Oscar Wilde at Keats House in Tite Street, Chelsea. Laura, who found Oscar 'quite delightful' and confessed herself 'awfully in love with him,' duly recorded her afternoon's impressions: 'great fun, lots of vague intense men, such duffers who amused us awfully. The room was a mass of white lilies, photographs of Mrs. Langtry, peacock-feather screens and coloured pots, pictures of various merit.'

These 'vague intense men' were aesthetes—disciples and satellites of Oscar Wilde, hierophant of the Aesthetic Movement, and high priest of the generation of the 'Nineties. Wilde, in his days at Magdalen College, Oxford, had sat at the feet of Walter Pater, a timorous Fellow of Brasenose. Pater, who lived rather like a hermit, expounded a discreetly worded philosophy of hedonism, but Wilde saw through the veiling decorum to the charge of ethical gunpowder within. Looking back on his brilliant lurid career from the darkness of Reading Gaol, Wilde spoke of Pater's first work *Studies in the History of the Renaissance* as 'that book which has had such a strange influence over my life.' Earlier, he described it in glowing terms as 'the golden book of spirit and sense, the Holy Writ of beauty,' adding, however, that it was 'the very flower of decadence,' and that 'the Last Trumpet should have sounded the moment it was written.'

Three years more and Wilde, on an American tour sponsored by the D'Oyly Carte Opera Company, was to deliver his full-length manifesto of aestheticism, *The English Renaissance of Art*, given first as a lecture in New York and reprinted in this anthology. The lecture may be thought of as a large-scale popularization of the ideas of Pater but the gist of it is given in the record of a conversation which its author had in Paris the following year with Coquelin, the great star of the Comédie Française:

'What is civilization, Mr. Wilde?'
'Love of beauty.'
'And what is beauty?'

'That which the middle-classes call ugly.'
'And what do the middle-classes call beauty?'
'It does not exist.'

The tone of dedication, the persiflage, and the transvaluation of bourgeois values—these are elements we meet time and time again in the literature of the 'Nineties. The irony is present in the epigraph affixed by Max Beerbohm to his *Works*, published in 1896 in his twenty-fourth year: 'I am utterly purposed I will not offend.' Max, with his 'sentiment of style,' could enjoy the ambiguity of the remark because he knew that—exemplary as was his composition from the point of verbal technique—he *did* offend the reader, morally speaking, by reason of his calculated levity of mind. And if the Aesthete was mocked by the solid Victorian intelligence—'We know that we are not Bunthorne, nor have we any taste for buffoonery, apart from the stage' wrote Frederick Harrison in the *Pall Mall Gazette* in 1882—then the Aesthetes were not slow in mocking back at all those conventions which the middle-class Philistine mentality endorsed.

We see Arthur Symons, for example, addressing 'A Word on Behalf of Patchouli' to the public when he came to write his Preface to the second edition of his volume of poems *Silhouettes*: 'An ingenious reviewer once described some verses of mine as "unwholesome," because, he said, they had "a faint smell of Patchouli about them." I am a little sorry he chose Patchouli, for that is not a particularly favourite scent with me. If he had only chosen Peau d'Espagne, which has a subtle meaning, or Lily of the Valley, with which I have associations . . .' Or turn to the same author's Epilogue in the eighth and last number of his magazine *The Savoy* (December 1896) and we find both the dedicated tone (with reference to art and beauty) and the overt contempt for the reading-public and popular opinion. 'Worst of all,' wrote Symons, looking back on the magazine's failure, 'we assumed that there were very many people in the world who cared for art, and really for art's sake. Comparatively few people care for art at all, and most of these care for it because they mistake it for something else.'

'Love of beauty' and 'care for art'—between the poles of these two ideas most of the characteristic writing of the 'Nineties finds a place. Another factor contributing to the advancement of this aesthetic viewpoint was the work of the Pre-Raphaelite poets and painters. In 1882 Dante Gabriel Rossetti had died, and in the February of the following year a large exhibition of his pictures covered the walls of Burlington House. It was on this occasion that F. H. W. Myers, a Fellow of Trinity College, Cambridge, later to be known as the author of the first extensive scientific approach to the phenomenon of spiritualism (*Human Personality and its Survival after Death*) wrote an admirably suggestive essay *Rossetti and the Religion of Beauty*. Rossetti's pictures he took to constitute 'the visible sign of the admission of a new strain of thought and emotion within the pale of our artistic hierarchy,' and Myers' study is important because it represents the acceptance by a solid Victorian humanistic mind of what had been thought previously as in part a fad or wayward affectation. But, under one form or another, it is the love or religion of beauty which is the keynote of Pre-Raphaelite art, and which the men of the 'Nineties were to interpret more individually.

Beauty of fact gave them realism—a vogue for Zola and Maupassant, those two French mentors of English fiction in the 'Nineties; the novels of George Moore, and the short stories of Hubert Crackanthorpe and those of his erstwhile tutor George Gissing. Beauty of the passing moment made for impressionism, whether in the painting and drawing of the New English Art Club (founded in 1886 and dominated by the example of Whistler) or in such a prizer of ephemerality as Arthur Symons, writing of the coming of the London dark or catching an evanescent charm in the following interior nocturne:

Pastel

The light of our cigarettes
Went and came in the gloom:
It was dark in the little room.

Dark and then, in the dark,
Sudden, a flash, a glow,
And a hand and a ring I know

And then, through the dark, a flush
Ruddy and vague, the grace
(A rose!) of her lyric face.

Curiously, too, this desire for beauty could result in a poetry diametrically opposed to the poetry of impressionism. If impressionism is one of the fruits of an extreme dedication to the present, then an equal dedication to the past produces traditionalism. The poet and critic Lionel Johnson wrote of Symons as 'a slave to impressionism, whether the impression be precious or not.' With 'a delicate Tory temperament,' the perfervid faith of a Roman convert, the ingrained habit of wide and deep reading, and a nature somewhat reclusive and inverted, Johnson was fitted to be the mouthpiece of anti-modernism, both in verse and prose. His poetry, so often concerned to 'mourn the death of beauty and the death of grace,' has behind its ordered façade the zeal of a high idealism. Johnson's reputation for learning was vast—vaster than his learning, which was certainly considerable—and his influence on the young poets of the time was a valuably chastening one. Yeats, who felt that he himself lacked the ballast of scholarship, reports how Johnson once said to him: 'Yeats, you need ten years in a library, but I have need of ten years in the wilderness.' Behind Johnson lay the authority—the magic, the charisma—of Cardinal Newman, and the precepts and teachings of the Fathers of the Church; behind Symons, the mystique of Verlaine and Mallarmé's poetics for an *élite*; behind Yeats, Irish mythology and folklore.

Two other poets complete the leading verse roles in the caste of the 'Nineties. Ernest Dowson, author of 'Cynara,' may be deemed to

represent that aspect of the religion or love of beauty most characteristic of the *fin-de-siècle* period as a whole, namely the beauty of love and
passion. Dowson, to quote from his most famous poem, 'was desolate
and sick of an old passion'; but no other poet, of like minor status, has
employed his stock of clichés with such neatness and grace; and if there
was a sparseness about his work, there was also a classical economy.

Behind Dowson's poetry, as indicated by the superscriptions to his
verses, stood the lyrical poets of Roman antiquity: Horace, Catullus,
Propertius. Behind the Scot, John Davidson, stood a figure of different
nature—that of the philosopher Nietzsche. 'Art,' wrote Marcel Schwob,
a French writer with whom many of the English poets were in sympathy, 'is opposed to general ideas, it describes only the individual,
wishes only for the unique.' But Davidson, the truculent exception,
was interested in ideas. His verse celebrated the beauty of the will, as in
the following assertive lines:

> I woke because I thought the time had come;
> Beyond my will there was no other cause;
> And everywhere I found myself at home
> Because I chose to be the thing I was.

These poets (with others, including Victor Plarr, Le Gallienne and
John Gray) were regular members of the Rhymers' Club, a *cénacle* of
youngish poets who, early in 1891, took to meeting about once a month
usually at the Cheshire Cheese in Fleet Street, and published collec-
tively two anthologies (*The Book of the Rhymers' Club*, 1892, and *The
Second Book of the Rhymers' Club*, 1894) which helped to create a taste
for 'pure' or 'aesthetic' poetry as distinct from 'mixed' didactic poetry
of the more ponderous Victorian masters. It is also historically signifi-
cant that the influence of these poets combined, as T. S. Eliot pointed
out, 'to insist upon the importance of *verse as speech*,' a prime concern
of much twentieth-century poetry. In place of the strident rhetoric with
which the Victorian poet sought to persuade his reading public, these
'poets of the Cheshire Cheese' substituted a conversational tone and
the sense of an 'audience fit though few.' A new register was to be
explored: intimate, elegant and urbane.

Mention of Yeats among these Rhymers' Club poets brings us to a
fresh topic—the movement referred to as the 'Celtic Twilight.'
Originally the title of a collection of folk tales by Yeats (published in
1893), it came later to stand for that aspect of the Irish cultural revival
which dwelt on the supernatural, the psychic and the mythological.
It could, in fact, be considered as the equivalent in the artistic field of
Irish Nationalism in the political. 'The Anglo-Saxons have taken our
lands . . . we have taken their language and have added beauty to it,'
Wilde told Irish compatriots during his American tour, whilst in his
essay *The Critic as Artist* he proclaimed that 'it is the Celt who leads
in Art.' Nor was it the Irish only who, at that time, appeared bathed in
the light of expectation and promise. Authors of Welsh, Cornish,
Highland Scot and Breton extraction felt themselves stirred by the
Time-Spirit. Was there to be some millennial revelation, the production,
say, of some sacred book?

The Celtic Twilight movement may be said to express that aspect of the cult of beauty represented by the beauty of the mystical and supernatural. Indeed, it opposed those three elements—the rationalistic, the materialistic and the scientific—which had dominated British thought since the founding of the Royal Society in 1662. *Avant-garde* the movement certainly was: modernist in a progressive sense, it certainly was not.

The theories of the Celtic Twilight contain many parallels with French Symbolism, the chief characteristic of which Arthur Symons was to describe as a 'revolt against exteriority, against rhetoric, against a materialist tradition.' His most important critical book *The Symbolist Movement in Literature*, 1899 (the Introduction to which is reprinted in this anthology) was dedicated to Yeats as 'the chief representative of that movement in your country.' Thd Celtic Twilight was, in fact, the one largely indigenous manifestation of Symbolism in these islands.

What the Celtic Twilight shared with the Symbolism derived from France—and, indeed, with all those other trends which stemmed from Rossetti's 'religion of beauty'—was one common point of view when contrasted with that of the earlier Victorians. Whereas the latter artists addressed themselves to the *conscience* of their public, it was to the *sensibility* of their audience that the men of the 'Nineties appealed. Neither logic nor fact but feeling became the new measure of this new art.

This appeal to sensation and feeling was something which Realism practised too. Symons, however, rejecting Realism in favour of Impressionism and Symbolism, spoke of Zola's mistake in 'trying to build in brick and mortar inside the covers of a book.' Instead he desired some less long-winded method which would render the author's communication in a style of immediacy. 'The Impressionist,' he wrote, 'would flash upon you [an] exact . . . image of what you have just seen, just as you have seen it. . . . The Symbolist would flash upon you the "soul" of that which can be apprehended only by the soul—the finer sense of things unseen, the deeper meaning of things evident.'

The above quotation is from an essay entitled *The Decadent Movement in Literature* with which Symons had associated Impressionism and Symbolism—two dogs without existing bad names. When the term Decadent meant anything specific beyond the desire of certain young men to shock the middle-classes, it referred either to a subtilizing Byzantine use of language or to a literature or art dominated by moral deliquescence. In Wilde's play *Salome*, written in French and described by Max Beerbohm as 'terribly corrupt,' in his poem *The Sphinx* ('a gigantic python crawling in the dark'), and in Beardsley's rococo and 'remarkable erotic romance' *Under the Hill*, we have a decadence of both style and subject—an 'ingenious deformation of the language,' 'perversity of form and perversity of matter.'

'I am the Empire at the time of the Decadence,' Paul Verlaine had written in an early sonnet, and the idea of a waning century as expressive of the waning human spirit fascinated these 'Nineties writers—'Fin-de-siècle, fin-du-monde!' as a character remarks in one of John Davidson's novels.

Yet from this seeming *cul-de-sac*, there were to develop two tendencies in twentieth-century writing: the alembicated novels of James Joyce and Henry Miller, and the fiction of perversity as represented by Gide, Genet, William Burroughs, and other authors of our present permissive age. In a similar fashion Symbolism transformed itself in the new era, its concern with the secret underside of the mind becoming focused upon the automatic subconscious vortex of the Surrealist writers and painters. Indeed, as Richard Le Gallienne claimed, 'those last ten years of the nineteenth century properly belong to the twentieth century, and, far from being decadent, except in certain limited manifestations, they were years of an immense and multifarious renaissance.'

DEREK STANFORD.

Seaford, 1971.

ESSAYS
PORTRAITS
MANIFESTOES

OSCAR FINGAL O'FLAHERTY WILLS WILDE
(1854-1900)

Oscar Wilde was born on 15 October 1854 in the Irish capital, and was educated first at Trinity College, Dublin and later at Magdalen College Oxford. From his mother he derived a strong histrionic vein and from his father a disposition to depravity. His self-dramatizing homosexual conduct led in 1895 to his receiving two years' imprisonment with hard labour. After his sentence he lived in Paris under the name of Sebastian Melmoth, dying there—a Roman convert—'beyond his means,' as he said, on 30 November 1900.

Poet, critic, novelist, short-storyist, dramatist and wit, Wilde was 'a man who stood in symbolical relationship to [his] own age' (*The Letters of Oscar Wilde*, ed. Rupert Hart-Davis, 1962), being both its arbiter and scapegoat; its jester, entertainer and tragic figure.

Wilde in this essay was concerned with the further beautifying of both life and art—the two activities which have been spoken of as Aestheticism.

The English Renaissance of Art

AMONG the many debts which we owe to the supreme aesthetic faculty of Goethe is that he was the first to teach us to define beauty in terms the most concrete possible, to realise it, I mean, always in its special manifestations. So, in the lecture which I have the honour to deliver before you, I will not try to give you any abstract definition of beauty—any such universal formula for it as was sought for by the philosophy of the eighteenth century—still less to communicate to you that which in its essence is incommunicable, the virtue by which a particular picture or poem affects us with a unique and special joy; but rather to point out to you the general ideas which characterise the great English Renaissance of Art in this century, to discover their source, as far as that is possible, and to estimate their future as far as that is possible.

I call it our English Renaissance because it is indeed a sort of new birth of the spirit of man, like the great Italian Renaissance of the fifteenth century, in its desire for a more gracious and

3

comely way of life, its passion for physical beauty, its exclusive
attention to form, its seeking for new subjects for poetry, new
forms of art, new intellectual and imaginative enjoyments: and I
call it our romantic movement because it is our most recent
expression of beauty.

It has been described as a mere revival of Greek modes of
thought, and again as a mere revival of mediaeval feeling. Rather
I would say that to these forms of the human spirit it has added
whatever of artistic value the intricacy and complexity and
experience of modern life can give: taking from the one its
clearness of vision and its sustained calm, from the other its
variety of expression and the mystery of its vision. For what, as
Goethe said, is the study of the ancients but a return to the real
world (for that is what they did); and what, said Mazzini, is
mediaevalism but individuality?

It is really from the union of Hellenism, in its breadth, its
sanity of purpose, its calm possession of beauty, with the adven-
tive, the intensified individualism, the passionate colour of the
romantic spirit, that springs the art of the nineteenth century in
England, as from the marriage of Faust and Helen of Troy
sprang the beautiful boy Euphorion.

Such expressions as 'classical' and 'romantic' are, it is true,
often apt to become the mere catchwords of schools. We must
always remember that art has only one sentence to utter: there
is for her only one high law, the law of form or harmony—yet
between the classical and romantic spirit we may say that there
lies this difference at least, that the one deals with the type and
the other with the exception. In the work produced under the
modern romantic spirit it is no longer the permanent, the essential truths of life that are treated of; it is the momentary situation
of the one, the momentary aspect of the other that art seeks to
render. In sculpture, which is the type of one spirit, the subject
predominates over the situation; in painting, which is the type
of the other, the situation predominates over the subject.

There are two spirits, then: the Hellenic spirit and the spirit of
romance may be taken as forming the essential elements of our
conscious intellectual tradition, of our permanent standard of
taste. As regards their origin, in art as in politics there is but one
origin for all revolutions, a desire on the part of man for a nobler
form of life, for a freer method and opportunity of expression.
Yet, I think that in estimating the sensuous and intellectual spirit
which presides over our English Renaissance, any attempt to
isolate it in any way from the progress and movement and social
life of the age that has produced it would be to rob it of its
true vitality, possibly to mistake its true meaning. And in

disengaging from the pursuits and passions of this crowded modern world those passions and pursuits which have to do with art and the love of art, we must take into account many great events of history which seem to be the most opposed to any such artistic feeling.

Alien then from any wild, political passion, or from the harsh voice of a rude people in revolt, as our English Renaissance must seem, in its passionate cult of pure beauty, its flawless devotion to form, its exclusive and sensitive nature, it is to the French Revolution that we must look for the most primary factor of its production, the first condition of its birth: that great Revolution of which we are all the children though the voices of some of us be often loud against it; that Revolution to which at a time when even such spiritis as Coleridge and Wordsworth lost heart in England, noble messages of love blown across seas came from your young Republic.

It is true that our modern sense of the continuity of history has shown us that neither in politics nor in nature are there revolutions ever but evolutions only, and that the prelude to that wild storm which swept over France in 1789 and made every king in Europe tremble for his throne, was first sounded in literature years before the Bastille fell and the Palace was taken. The way for those red scenes by Seine and Loire was paved by that critical spirit of Germany and England which accustomed men to bring all things to the test of reason or utility or both, while the discontent of the people in the streets of Paris was the echo that followed the life of Émile and of Werther. For Rousseau, by silent lake and mountain, had called humanity back to the golden age that still lies before us and preached a return to nature, in passionate eloquence whose music still lingers about our keen northern air. And Goethe and Scott had brought romance back again from the prison she had lain in for so many centuries— and what is romance but humanity?

Yet in the womb of the Revolution itself, and in the storm and terror of that wild time, tendencies were hidden away that the artistic Renaissance bent to her own service when the time came— a scientific tendency first, which has borne in our own day a brood of somewhat noisy Titans, yet in the sphere of poetry has not been unproductive of good. I do not mean merely in its adding to enthusiasm that intellectual basis which is its strength, or that more obvious influence about which Wordsworth was thinking when he said very nobly that poetry was merely the impassioned expression in the face of science, and that when science would put on a form of flesh and blood the poet would lend his divine spirit to aid the transfiguration. Nor do I dwell much on the great cosmical emotion and deep pantheism of science to which Shelley has given its first and Swinburne its latest glory of song, but rather on its influence on the artistic spirit in preserving that close observation and the sense of limitation as well as of clearness of vision which are the characteristics of the real artist.

The great and golden rule of art as well as of life, wrote William Blake, is that the more distinct, sharp and defined the boundary line, the more perfect is the work of art; and the less keen and sharp the greater is the evidence of weak imitation, plagiarism and bungling. 'Great inventors in all ages knew this— Michael Angelo and Albert Dürer are known by this and by this alone'; and another time he wrote, with all the simple directness of nineteenth-century prose, 'to generalise is to be an idiot.'

And this love of definite conception, this clearness of vision, this artistic sense of limit, is the characteristic of all great work and poetry; of the vision of Homer as of the vision of Dante, of Keats and William Morris as of Chaucer and Theocritus. It lies at the base of all noble, realistic and romantic work as opposed to the colourless and empty abstractions of our own eighteenth-century poets and of the classical dramatists of France, or of the vague spiritualities of the German sentimental school: opposed, too, to that spirit of transcendentalism which also was root and flower itself of the great Revolution, underlying the impassioned contemplation of Wordsworth and giving wings and fire to the eagle-like flight of Shelley, and which in the sphere of philosophy, though displaced by the materialism and positive-ness of our day, bequeathed two great schools of thought, the school of Newman to Oxford, the school of Emerson to America. Yet is this spirit of transcendentalism alien to the spirit of art. For the artist can accept no sphere of life in exchange for life itself. For him there is no escape from the bondage of the earth: there is not even the desire of escape.

He is indeed the only true realist: symbolism, which is the essence of the transcendental spirit, is alien to him. The meta-physical mind of Asia will create for itself the monstrous, many-breasted idol of Ephesus, but to the Greek, pure artist, that work is most instinct with spiritual life which conforms most clearly to the perfect facts of physical life.

'The storm of revolution,' as André Chenier said, 'blows out the torch of poetry.' It is not for some little time that the real influence of such a wild cataclysm of things is felt: at first the desire for equality seems to have produced personalities of more giant and Titan stature than the world had ever known before. Men heard the lyre of Byron and the legions of Napoleon; it was a period of measureless passions and of measureless despair; ambition, discontent, were the chords of life and art; the age was an age of revolt: a phase through which the human spirit must pass, but one in which it cannot rest. For the aim of culture is not rebellion but peace, the valley perilous where ignorant armies clash by night being no dwelling-place meet for her to whom the gods have assigned the fresh uplands and sunny heights and clear, untroubled air.

And soon that desire for perfection, which lay at the base of the Revolution, found in a young English poet its most complete and flawless realisation.

Phidias and the achievements of Greek art are foreshadowed in Homer: Dante prefigures for us the passion and colour and intensity of Italian painting: the modern love of landscape dates from Rousseau, and it is in Keats that one discerns the beginning of the artistic renaissance of England.

Byron was a rebel and Shelley a dreamer; but in the calmness and clearness of his vision, his perfect self-control, his unerring sense of beauty and his recognition of a separate realm for the imagination, Keats was the pure and serene artist, the forerunner of the pre-Raphaelite school, and so of the great romantic movement of which I am to speak.

Blake had indeed, before him, claimed for art a lofty, spiritual mission, and had striven to raise design to the ideal level of poetry and music, but the remoteness of his vision both in painting and poetry and the incompleteness of his technical powers had been adverse to any real influence. It is in Keats that the artistic spirit of this century first found its absolute incarnation.

And these pre-Raphaelites, what were they? If you ask nine-tenths of the British public what is the meaning of the word aesthetics, they will tell you it is the French for affectation or the German for a dado; and if you inquire about the pre-Raphaelites you will hear something about an eccentric lot of young men to whom a sort of divine crookedness and holy awkwardness in drawing were the chief objects to art. To know nothing about their great men is one of the necessary elements of English education.

As regards the pre-Raphaelites the story is simple enough. In the year 1847 a number of young men in London, poets and painters, passionate admirers of Keats all of them, formed the habit of meeting together for discussions on art, the result of such discussions being that the English Philistine public was roused suddenly from its ordinary apathy by hearing that there was in its midst a body of young men who had determined to revolutionise

English painting and poetry. They called themselves the pre-Raphaelite Brotherhood.

In England, then as now, it was enough for a man to try and produce any serious beautiful work to lose all his rights as a citizen; and besides this, the pre-Raphaelite Brotherhood—among whom the names of Dante Rossetti, Holman Hunt and Millais will be familiar to you—had on their side three things that the English public never forgives: youth, power and enthusiasm.

Satire, always as sterile as it is shameful and as impotent as it is insolent, paid them that usual homage which mediocrity pays to genius—doing, here as always, infinite harm to the public, blinding them to what is beautiful, teaching them that irreverence which is the source of all vileness and narrowness of life, but harming the artist not at all, rather confirming him in the perfect rightness of his work and ambition. For to disagree with three-fourths of the British public on all points is one of the first elements of sanity, one of the deepest consolations in all moments of spiritual doubt.

As regards the ideas these young men brought to the regeneration of English art, we may see at the base of their artistic creations a desire for a deeper spiritual value to be given to art as well as a more decorative value.

Pre-Raphaelites they called themselves; not that they imitated the early Italian masters at all, but that in their work, as opposed to the facile abstractions of Raphael, they found a stronger realism of imagination, a more careful realism of technique, a vision at once more fervent and more vivid, an individuality more intimate and more intense.

For it is not enough that a work of art should conform to the aesthetic demands of its age: there must be also about it, if it is to affect us with any permanent delight, the impress of a distinct individuality, an individuality remote from that of ordinary men, and coming near to us only by virtue of a certain newness and wonder in the work, and through channels whose very strangeness makes us more ready to give them welcome.

La personnalité, said one of the greatest of modern French critics, *voilà ce qui nous sauvera*.

But above all things was it a return to Nature—that formula which seems to suit so many and such diverse movements: they would draw and paint nothing but what they saw, they would try and imagine things as they really happened. Later there came to the old house by Blackfriars Bridge, where this young brotherhood used to meet and work, two young men from Oxford, Edward Burne-Jones and William Morris—the latter substituting for the simpler realism of the early days a more exquisite spirit of choice, a more faultless devotion to beauty, a more intense seeking for perfection: a master of all exquisite design and of all spiritual vision. It is of the school of Florence rather than of that of Venice that he is kinsman, feeling that the close imitation of Nature is a disturbing element in imaginative art. The visible aspect of modern life disturbs him not; rather is it for him to render eternal all that is beautiful in Greek, Italian, and Celtic legend. To Morris we owe poetry whose perfect precision and clearness of word and vision has not been excelled in the literature of our country, and by the revival of the decorative arts he has given to our individualised romantic movement the social idea and the social factor also.

But the revolution accomplished by this clique of young men, with Ruskin's faultless and fervent eloquence to help them, was not one of ideas merely but of execution, not one of conceptions but of creations.

For the great eras in the history of the development of all the arts have been eras not of increased feeling or enthusiasm in feeling for art, but of new technical improvements primarily and specially. The discovery of marble quarries in the purple ravines of Pentelicus and on the little low-lying hills of the island of Paros gave to the Greeks the opportunity for that intensified vitality of action, that more sensuous and simple humanism, to which the Egyptian sculptor working laboriously in the hard porphyry and rose-coloured granite of the desert could not attain. The splendour of the Venetian school began with the introduction of the new oil medium for painting. The progress in modern music has been due to the invention of new instruments entirely, and in no way to an increased consciousness on the part of the musician of any wider social aim. The critic may try and trace the deferred resolutions of Beethoven[1] to some sense of the incompleteness of the modern intellectual spirit, but the artist would have answered, as one of them did afterwards, 'Let them pick out the fifths and leave us at peace.'

And so it is in poetry also: all this love of curious French metres like the Ballade, the Villanelle, the Rondel; all this increased value laid on elaborate alliterations, and on curious words and refrains, such as you will find in Dante Rossetti and Swinburne, is merely the attempt to perfect flute and viol and

[1] As an instance of the inaccuracy of published reports of this lecture, it may be mentioned that all unauthorised versions give this passage as *The artist may trace the depressed revolution of Bunthorne simply to the lack of technical means*! [R.R.]

trumpet through which the spirit of the age and the lips of the poet may blow the music of their many messages.

And so it has been with this romantic movement of ours: it is a reaction against the empty conventional workmanship, the lax execution of previous poetry and painting, showing itself in the work of such men as Rossetti and Burne-Jones by a far greater splendour of colour, a far more intricate wonder of design than English imaginative art has shown before. In Rossetti's poetry and the poetry of Morris, Swinburne and Tennyson a perfect precision and choice of language, a style flawless and fearless, a seeking for all sweet and precious melodies and a sustaining consciousness of the musical value of each word are opposed to that value which is merely intellectual. In this respect they are one with the romantic movement of France of which not the least characteristic note was struck by Théophile Gautier's advice to the young poet to read his dictionary every day, as being the only book worth a poet's reading.

While, then, the material of workmanship is being thus elaborated and discovered to have in itself incommunicable and eternal qualities of its own, qualities entirely satisfying to the poetic sense and not needing for their aesthetic effect any lofty intellectual vision, any deep criticism of life or even any passionate human emotion at all, the spirit and the method of the poet's working—what people call his inspiration—have not escaped the controlling influence of the artistic spirit. Not that the imagination has lost its wings, but we have accustomed ourselves to count their innumerable pulsations, to estimate their limitless strength, to govern their ungovernable freedom.

To the Greeks this problem of the conditions of poetic production, and the places occupied by either spontaneity or self-consciousness in any artistic work, has a peculiar fascination. We find it in the mysticism of Plato and in the rationalism of Aristotle. We find it later in the Italian Renaissance agitating the minds of such men as Leonardo da Vinci. Schiller tried to adjust the balance between form and feeling, and Goethe to estimate the position of self-consciousness in art. Wordsworth's definition of poetry as 'emotion remembered in tranquillity' may be taken as an analysis of one of the stages through which all imaginative work has to pass; and in Keats's longing to be 'able to compose without this fever' (I quote from one of his letters), his desire to substitute for poetic ardour 'a more thoughtful and quiet power,' we may discern the most important moment in the evolution of that artistic life. The question made an early and strange appearance in your literature too; and I need not remind you how deeply the young poets of the French romantic movement were excited and stirred by Edgar Allan Poe's analysis of the workings of his own imagination in the creating of that supreme imaginative work which we know by the name of *The Raven*.

In the last century, when the intellectual and didactic element had intruded to such an extent into the kingdom which belongs to poetry, it was against the claims of the understanding that an artist like Goethe had to protest. 'The more incomprehensible to the understanding a poem is the better for it,' he said once, asserting the complete supremacy of the imagination in poetry as of reason in prose. But in this century it is rather against the claims of the emotional faculties, the claims of mere sentiment and feeling, that the artist must react. The simple utterance of joy is not poetry any more than a mere personal cry of pain, and the real experiences of the artist are always those which do not find their direct expression but are gathered up and absorbed into some artistic form which seems, from such real experiences, to be the farthest removed and the most alien.

'The heart contains passion but the imagination alone contains poetry,' says Charles Baudelaire. This too was the lesson that Théophile Gautier, most subtle of all modern critics, most fascinating of all modern poets, was never tired of teaching— 'Everybody is affected by a sunrise or a sunset.' The absolute distinction of the artist is not his capacity to feel nature so much as his power of rendering it. The entire subordination of all intellectual and emotional faculties to the vital and informing poetic principle is the surest sign of the strength of our Renaissance.

We have seen the artistic spirit working, first in the delightful and technical sphere of language, the sphere of expression as opposed to subject, then controlling the imagination of the poet in dealing with his subject. And now I would point out to you its operation in the choice of subject. The recognition of a separate realm for the artist, a consciousness of the absolute difference between the world of art and the world of real fact, between classic grace and absolute reality, forms not merely the essential element of any aesthetic charm but is the characteristic of all great imaginative work and of all great eras of artistic creation— of the age of Phidias as of the age of Michael Angelo, of the age of Sophocles as of the age of Goethe.

Art never harms itself by keeping aloof from the social problems of the day: rather, by so doing, it more completely realises for us that which we desire. For to most of us the real life is the life we do not lead, and thus, remaining more true to the essence of its own perfection, more jealous of its own unattainable beauty, is less likely to forget form in feeling or to accept the passion of creation as any substitute for the beauty of the created thing.

The artist is indeed the child of his own age, but the present will not be to him a whit more real than the past; for, like the philosopher of the Platonic vision, the poet is the spectator of all time and of all existence. For him no form is obsolete, no subject out of date; rather, whatever of life and passion the world has known, in desert of Judaea or in Arcadian valley, by the rivers of Troy or the rivers of Damascus, in the crowded and hideous streets of a modern city or by the pleasant ways of Camelot—all lies before him like an open scroll, all is still instinct with beautiful life. He will take of it what is salutary for his own spirit, no more; choosing some facts and rejecting others with the calm artistic control of one who is in possession of the secret of beauty.

There is indeed a poetical attitude to be adopted towards all things, but all things are not fit subjects for poetry. Into the secure and sacred house of Beauty the true artist will admit nothing that is harsh or disturbing, nothing that gives pain, nothing that is debatable, nothing about which men argue. He can steep himself, if he wishes, in the discussion of all the social problems of his day, poor-laws and local taxation, free trade and bimetallic currency, and the like; but when he writes on these subjects it will be, as Milton nobly expressed it, with his left hand, in prose and not in verse, in a pamphlet and not in a lyric. This exquisite spirit of artistic choice was not in Byron: Wordsworth had it not. In the work of both these men there is much that we have to reject, much that does not give us that sense of calm and perfect repose which should be the effect of all fine, imaginative work. But in Keats it seemed to have been incarnate, and in his lovely *Ode on a Grecian Urn* it found its more secure and faultless expression; in the pageant of the *Earthly Paradise* and the knights and ladies of Burne-Jones it is the one dominant note.

It is to no avail that the Muse of Poetry be called, even by such a clarion note as Whitman's, to migrate from Greece and Ionia and to placard REMOVED and TO LET on the rocks of the snowy Parnassus. Calliope's call is not yet closed, nor are the epics of Asia ended; the Sphinx is not yet silent, nor the fountain of Castaly dry. For art is very life itself and knows nothing of death; she is absolute truth and takes no care of fact; she sees (as I remember Mr. Swinburne insisting on at dinner) that Achilles is even now more actual and real than Wellington, not merely more noble and interesting as a type and figure but more positive and real.

Literature must rest always on a principle, and temporal considerations are no principle at all. For to the poet all times and places are one; the stuff he deals with is eternal and eternally the same: no theme is inept, no past or present preferable. The steam whistle will not affright him nor the flutes of Areadia weary him: for him there is but one time, the artistic moment; but one law, the law of form; but one land, the land of Beauty—a land removed indeed from the real world and yet more sensuous because more enduring; calm, yet with that calm which dwells in the faces of the Greek statues, the calm which comes not from the rejection but from the absorption of passion, the calm which despair and sorrow cannot disturb but intensify only. And so it comes that he who seems to stand most remote from his age is he who mirrors it best because he has stripped life of what is accidental and transitory, stripped of that 'mist of familiarity which makes life obscure to us.'

Those strange, wild-eyed sibyls fixed eternally in the whirlwind of ecstasy, those mighty-limbed and Titan prophets, labouring with the secret of the earth and the burden of mystery, that guard and glorify the chapel of Pope Sixtus at Rome—do they not tell us more of the real spirit of the Italian Renaissance, of the dream of Savonarola and of the sin of Borgia, than all the brawling boors and cooking women of Dutch art can teach us of the real spirit of the history of Holland?

And so in our own day, also, the two most vital tendencies of the nineteenth century—the democratic and pantheistic tendency and the tendency to value life for the sake of art—found their most complete and perfect utterance in the poetry of Shelley and Keats who, to the blind eyes of their own time, seemed to be as wanderers in the wilderness, preachers of vague or unreal things. And I remember once, in talking to Mr. Burne-Jones about modern science, his saying to me, 'the more materialistic science becomes, the more angels shall I paint: their wings are my protest in favour of the immortality of the soul.'

But these are the intellectual speculations that underlie art. Where in the arts themselves are we to find that breadth of human sympathy which is the condition of all noble work; where in the arts are we to look for what Mazzini would call the social ideas as opposed to the merely personal ideas? By virtue of what claim do I demand for the artist the love and loyalty of the men and women of the world? I think I can answer that.

Whatever spiritual message an artist brings to his aid is a matter for his own soul. He may bring judgment like Michael Angelo or peace like Angelico; he may come with mourning like the great Athenian or with mirth like the singer of Sicily; nor is it for us to do aught but accept his teaching, knowing that we cannot smite the bitter lips of Leopardi into laughter or burden with our discontent Goethe's serene calm. But for warrant of its truth such

message must have the flame of eloquence in the lips that speak
it, splendour and glory in the vision that is its witness, being
justified by one thing only—the flawless beauty and perfect form
of its expression: this indeed being the social idea, being the
meaning of joy in art.

Not laughter where none should laugh, nor the calling peace
where there is no peace; not in painting the subject ever, but the
pictorial charm only, the wonder of its colour, the satisfying
beauty of its design.

You have most of you seen, probably, that great masterpiece
of Rubens which hangs in the gallery of Brussels, that swift
and wonderful pageant of horse and rider arrested in its most
exquisite and fiery moment when the winds are caught in
crimson banner and the air lit by the gleam of armour and the
flash of plume. Well, that is joy in art, though that golden
hillside be trodden by the wounded feet of Christ and it is for
the death of the Son of Man that that gorgeous cavalcade is
passing.

But this restless modern intellectual spirit of ours is not receptive enough of the sensuous element of art; and so the real influence of the arts is hidden from many of us: only a few, escaping
from the tyranny of the soul, have learned the secret of those
high hours when thought is not.

And this indeed is the reason of the influence which Eastern
art is having on us in Europe, and of the fascination of all Japanese
work. While the Western world has been laying on art the intolerable burden of its own intellectual doubts and the spiritual
tragedy of its own sorrows, the East has always kept true to art's
primary and pictorial conditions.

In judging of a beautiful statue the aesthetic faculty is absolutely
and completely gratified by the splendid curves of those marble
lips that are dumb to our complaint, the noble modelling of those
limbs that are powerless to help us. In its primary aspect a
painting has no more spiritual message or meaning than an
exquisite fragment of Venetian glass or a blue tile from the wall of
Damascus: it is a beautifully coloured surface, nothing more.
The channels by which all noble imaginative work in painting
should touch, and do touch the soul, are not those of the truths of
life, nor metaphysical truths. But that pictorial charm which does
not depend on any literary reminiscence for its effect on the one
hand, nor is yet a mere result of communicable technical skill on
the other, comes of a certain inventive and creative handling of
colour. Nearly always in Dutch painting and often in the works
of Giorgione or Titian, it is entirely independent of anything
definitely poetical in the subject, a kind of form and choice in

workmanship which is itself entirely satisfying, and is (as the Greeks would say) an end in itself.

And so in poetry too, the real poetical quality, the joy of poetry, comes never from the subject but from an inventive handling of rhythmical language, from what Keats called the 'sensuous life of verse.' The element of song in the singing accompanied by the profound joy of motion, is so sweet that, while the incomplete lives of ordinary men bring no healing power with them, the thorn-crown of the poet will blossom into roses for our pleasure; for our delight his despair will gild its own thorns, and his pain, like Adonis, be beautiful in its agony; and when the poet's heart breaks it will break in music.

And health in art—what is that? It has nothing to do with a sane criticism of life. There is more health in Baudelaire than there is in [Kingsley]. Health is the artist's recognition of the limitations of the form in which he works. It is the honour and the homage which he gives to the material he uses—whether it be language with its glories, or marble or pigment with their glories—knowing that the true brotherhood of the arts consists not in their borrowing one another's method, but in their producing, each of them by its own individual means, each of them by keeping its objective limits, the same unique artistic delight. The delight is like that given to us by music—for music is the art in which form and matter are always one, the art whose subject cannot be separated from the method of its expression, the art which most completely realises the artistic ideal, and is the condition to which all the other arts are constantly aspiring.

And criticism—what place is that to have in our culture? Well, I think that the first duty of an art critic is to hold his tongue at all times, and upon all subjects: *C'est un grand advantage de n'avoir rien fait, mais il ne faut pas en abuser*.

It is only through the mystery of creation that one can gain any knowledge of the quality of created things. You have listened to *Patience* for a hundred nights and you have heard me for one only. It will make, no doubt, that satire more piquant by knowing something about the subject of it, but you must not judge of aestheticism by the satire of Mr. Gilbert. As little should you judge of the strength and splendour of sun or sea by the dust that dances in the beam, or the bubble that breaks on the wave, as take your critic for any sane test of art. For the artists, like the Greek gods, are revealed only to one another, as Emerson says somewhere; their real value and place time only can show. In this respect also omnipotence is with the ages. The true critic addresses not the artist ever but the public only. His work lies with them. Art can never have any other claim but her own perfection: it is for the critic to create for art the social aim, too, by teaching the people the spirit in which they are to approach all artistic work, the love they are to give it, the lesson they are to draw from it.

All these appeals to art to set herself more in harmony with modern progress and civilisation, and to make herself the mouth-piece for the voice of humanity, these appeals to art 'to have a mission,' are appeals which should be made to the public. The art which has fulfilled the conditions of beauty has fulfilled all conditions: it is for the critic to teach the people how to find in the calm of such art the highest expression of their own most stormy passions, 'I have no reverence,' said Keats, 'for the public, nor for anything in existence but the Eternal Being, the memory of great men and the principle of Beauty.'

Such then is the principle which I believe to be guiding and underlying our English Renaissance, a Renaissance many-sided and wonderful, productive of strong ambitions and lofty person-alities, yet for all its splendid achievements in poetry and in the decorative arts and in painting, for all the increased comeliness and grace of dress, and the furniture of houses and the like, not complete. For there can be no great sculpture without a beautiful national life, and the commercial spirit of England has killed that; no great drama without a noble national life, and the commercial spirit of England has killed that too.

It is not that the flawless serenity of marble cannot bear the burden of the modern intellectual spirit, or become instinct with the fire of romantic passion—the tomb of Duke Lorenzo and the chapel of the Medici show us that—but it is that, as Théophile Gautier used to say, the visible world is dead, *le monde a disparu.*

Nor is it again that the novel has killed the play, as some critics would persuade us—the romantic movement of France shows us that. The work of Balzac and of Hugo grew up side by side together; nay, more, were complementary to each other, though neither of them saw it. While all other forms of poetry may flourish in an ignoble age, the splendid individualism of the lyrist, fed by its own passion, and lit by its own power, may pass as a pillar of fire as well across the desert as across places that are pleasant. It is none the less glorious though no man follow it—nay, by the greater sublimity of its loneliness it may be quickened into loftier utterance and intensified into clearer song. From the mean squalor of the sordid life that limits him, the dreamer or the idyllist may soar on poesy's viewless wings, may traverse with fawn-skin and spear the moonlit heights of Cithaeron though Faun and Bassarid dance there no more. Like Keats he may wander through the old-world forests of Latmos, or stand like Morris on the galley's deck with the Viking when king and galley have long since passed away. But the drama is the meeting-place of art and life; it deals, as Mazzini said, not merely with man, but with social man, with man in his relation to God and to Humanity. It is the product of a period of great national united energy; it is impossible without a noble public, and belongs to such ages as the age of Elizabeth in London and of Pericles at Athens; it is part of such lofty moral and spiritual ardour as came to Greek after the defeat of the Persian fleet, and to Englishman after the wreck of the Armada of Spain.

Shelley felt how incomplete our movement was in this respect, and has shown in one great tragedy by what terror and pity he would have purified our age; but in spite of *The Cenci* the drama is one of the artistic forms through which the genius of the England of this century seeks in vain, to find outlet and expression. He has had no worthy imitators.

It is rather, perhaps, to you that we should turn to complete and perfect this great movement of ours, for there is something Hellenic in your air and world, something that has a quicker breath of the joy and power of Elizabeth's England about it than our ancient civilisation can give us. For you, at least, are young; 'no hungry generations tread you down,' and the past does not weary you with the intolerable burden of its memories nor mock you with the ruins of a beauty, the secret of whose creation you have lost. That very absence of tradition, which Mr. Ruskin thought would rob your rivers of their laughter and your flowers of their light, may be rather the source of your freedom and your strength.

To speak in literature with the perfect rectitude and insouciance of the movements of animals, and the unimpeachableness of the sentiment of trees in the woods and grass by the roadside, has been defined by one of your poets as a flawless triumph of art. It is a triumph which you above all nations may be destined to achieve. For the voices that have their dwelling in sea and mountain are not the chosen music of Liberty only: other messages are there in the wonder of wind-swept height and the majesty of silent deep—messages that, if you will but listen to them, may yield you the splendour of some new imagination, the marvel of some new beauty.

'I foresee,' said Goethe, 'the dawn of a new literature which all people may claim as their own, for all have contributed to its foundation.' If, then, this is so, and if the materials for a civilisation as great as that of Europe lie all around you, what profit, you will ask me, will all this study of our poets and painters be to you? I might answer that the intellect can be engaged without direct didactic object on an artistic and historical problem; that the demand of the intellect is merely to feel itself alive; that nothing which has ever interested men or women can cease to be a fit subject for culture.

I might remind you of what all Europe owes to the sorrow of a single Florentine in exile at Verona, or to the love of Petrarch by that little well in Southern France; nay, more, how even in this dull, materialistic age the simple expression of an old man's simple life, passed away from the clamour of great cities amid the lakes and misty hills of Cumberland, has opened out for England treasures of new joy compared with which the treasures of her luxury are as barren as the sea which she has made her highway, and as bitter as the fire which she would make her slave.

But I think it will bring you something besides this, something that is the knowledge of real strength in art: not that you should imitate the works of these men; but their artistic spirit, their artistic attitude, I think you should absorb that.

For in nations, as in individuals, if the passion for creation be not accompanied by the critical, the aesthetic faculty also, it will be sure to waste its strength aimlessly, failing perhaps in the artistic spirit of choice, or in the mistaking of feeling for form, or in the following of false ideals.

For the various spiritual forms of the imagination have a natural affinity with certain sensuous forms of art—and to discern the qualities of each art, to intensify as well its limitations as its powers of expression, is one of the aims that culture sets before us. It is not an increased moral sense, an increased moral super-vision that your literature needs. Indeed, one should never talk of a moral or an immoral poem—poems are either well written or badly written, that is all. And, indeed, any element of morals or implied reference to a standard of good or evil in art is often a sign of a certain incompleteness of vision, often a note of discord in the harmony of an imaginative creation; for all good work aims at a purely artistic effect. 'We must be careful,' said Goethe, 'not to be always looking for culture merely in what is obviously moral. Everything that is great promotes civilisation as soon as we are aware of it.'

But, as in your cities so in your literature, it is a permanent canon and standard of taste, an increased sensibility to beauty (if I may say so) that is lacking. All noble work is not national merely, but universal. The political independence of a nation must not be confused with any intellectual isolation. The spiritual freedom, indeed, your own generous lives and liberal air will give you. From us you will learn the classical restraint of form.

For all great art is delicate art, roughness having very little to do with strength, and harshness very little to do with power. 'The artist,' as Mr. Swinburne says, 'must be perfectly articulate.'

This limitation is for the artist perfect freedom: it is at once the origin and the sign of his strength. So that all the supreme masters of style—Dante, Sophocles, Shakespeare—are the supreme masters of spiritual and intellectual vision also.

Love art for its own sake, and then all things that you need will be added to you.

This devotion to beauty and to the creation of beautiful things is the test of all great civilised nations. Philosophy may teach us to bear with equanimity the misfortunes of our neighbours, and science resolve the moral sense into a secretion of sugar, but art is what makes the life of each citizen a sacrament and not a speculation, art is what makes the life of the whole race immortal.

For beauty is the only thing that time cannot harm. Philosophies fall away like sand, and creeds follow one another like the withered leaves of autumn; but what is beautiful is a joy for all seasons and a possession for all eternity.

Wars and the clash of armies and the meeting of men in battle by trampled field or leaguered city, and the rising of nations there must always be. But I think that art, by creating a common intellectual atmosphere between all countries, might—if it could not overshadow the world with the silver wings of peace—at least make men such brothers that they would not go out to slay one another for the whim or folly of some king or minister, as they do in Europe. Fraternity would come no more with the hands of Cain, nor Liberty betray freedom with the kiss of Anarchy; for national hatreds are always strongest where culture is lowest.

'How could I?' said Goethe, when reproached for not writing like Körner against the French. 'How could I, to whom barbarism and culture alone are of importance, hate a nation which is among the most cultivated of the earth, a nation to which I owe a great part of my own cultivation?'

Mighty empires, too, there must always be as long as personal ambition and the spirit of the age are one, but art at least is the only empire which a nation's enemies cannot take from her by conquest, but which is taken by submission only. The sovereignty of Greece and Rome is not yet passed away, though the gods of the one be dead and the eagles of the other tired.

And we in our Renaissance are seeking to create a sovereignty that will still be England's when her yellow leopards have grown weary of wars and the rose of her shield is crimsoned no more with the blood of battle; and you, too, absorbing into the generous

heart of a great people this pervading artistic spirit, will create
for yourselves such riches as you have never yet created, though
your land be a network of railways and your cities the harbours
for the galleys of the world.

I know, indeed, that the divine natural pre-science of beauty
which is the inalienable inheritance of Greek and Italian is not
our inheritance. For such an informing and presiding spirit of
art to shield us from all harsh and alien influences, we of the
Northern races must turn rather to that strained self-consciousness of our age which, as it is the key-note of all our romantic
art, must be the source of all or nearly all our culture. I mean that
intellectual curiosity of the nineteenth century which is always
looking for the secret of the life that still lingers round old and
bygone forms of culture. It takes from each what is serviceable
for the modern spirit—from Athens its wonder without its
worship, from Venice its splendour without its sin. The same
spirit is always analysing its own strength and its own weakness,
counting what it owes to East and to West, to the olive-trees of
Colonus and to the palm-trees of Lebanon, to Gethsemane and
to the garden of Proserpine.

And yet the truths of art cannot be taught: they are revealed
only, revealed to natures which have made themselves receptive
of all beautiful impressions by the study and worship of all
beautiful things. And hence the enormous importance given to
the decorative arts in our English Renaissance; hence all that
marvel of design that comes from the hand of Edward Burne-
Jones, all that weaving of tapestry and staining of glass, that
beautiful working in clay and metal and wood which we owe to
William Morris, the greatest handicraftsman we have had in
England since the fourteenth century.

So, in years to come there will be nothing in any man's house
which has not given delight to its maker and does not give delight
to its user. The children, like the children of Plato's perfect city,
will grow up 'in a simple atmosphere of all fair things'—I quote
from the passage in the *Republic*—'a simple atmosphere of all
fair things, where beauty, which is the spirit of art, will come on
eye and ear like a fresh breath of wind that brings health from a
clear upland, and insensibly and gradually draw the child's soul
into harmony with all knowledge and all wisdom, so that he will
love what is beautiful and good, and hate what is evil and ugly
(for they always go together) long before he knows the reason
why; and then when reason comes will kiss her on the cheek as a
friend.'

That is what Plato thought decorative art could do for a nation,
feeling that the secret not of philosophy merely but of all gracious

existence might be externally hidden from any one whose youth had been passed in uncomely and vulgar surroundings, and that the beauty of form and colour even, as he says, in the meanest vessels of the house, will find its way into the inmost places of the soul and lead the boy naturally to look for that divine harmony of spiritual life of which art was to him the material symbol and warrant.

Prelude indeed to all knowledge and all wisdom will this love of beautiful things be for us; yet there are times when wisdom becomes a burden and knowledge is one with sorrow: for as every body has its shadow so every soul has its scepticism. In such dread moments of discord and despair where should we, of this torn and troubled age, turn our steps if not to that secure house of beauty where there is always little forgetfulness, always a great joy; to that *città divina*, as the old Italian heresy called it, the divine city where one can stand, though only for a brief moment, apart from the division and terror of the world and the choice of the world too?

This is that *consolation des arts* which is the key-note of Gautier's poetry, the secret of modern life foreshadowed—as indeed what in our century is not?—by Goethe. You remember what he said to the German people: 'Only have the courage,' he said, 'to give yourselves up to your impressions, allow yourselves to be delighted, moved, elevated, nay instructed, inspired for something great.' The courage to give yourselves up to your impressions: yes, that is the secret of the artistic life—for while art has been defined as an escape from the tyranny of the senses, it is an escape rather from the tyranny of the soul. But only to those who worship her above all things does she ever reveal her true treasure: else will she be as powerless to aid you as the mutilated Venus of the Louvre was before the romantic but sceptical nature of Heine.

And indeed I think it would be impossible to overrate the gain that might follow if we had about us only what gave pleasure to the maker of it and gives pleasure to its user, that being the simplest of all rules about decoration. One thing, at least, I think it would do for us: there is no surer test of a great country than how near it stands to its own poets; but between the singers of our day and the workers to whom they would sing there seems to be an ever-widening and dividing chasm, a chasm which slander and mockery cannot traverse, but which is spanned by the luminous wings of love.

And of such love I think that the abiding presence in our houses of noble imaginative work would be the surest seed and preparation. I do not mean merely as regards that direct literary expression of art by which, from the little red-and-black cruse of oil or wine, a Greek boy could learn of the lionlike splendour of Achilles, of the strength of Hector and the beauty of Paris and the wonder of Helen, long before he stood and listened in crowded market-place or in theatre of marble; or by which an Italian child of the fifteenth century could know of the chastity of Lucrece and the death of Camilla from carven doorway and from painted chest. For the good we get from art is not what we learn from it; it is what we become through it. Its real influence will be in giving the mind that enthusiasm which is the secret of Hellenism, accustoming it to demand from art all that art can do in re-arranging the facts of common life for us—whether it be by giving the most spiritual interpretation of one's own moments of highest passion or the most sensuous expression of those thoughts that are the farthest removed from sense; in accustoming it to love the things of the imagination for their own sake, and to desire beauty and grace in all things. For he who does not love art in all things does not love it at all, and he who does not need art in all things does not need it at all.

I will not dwell here on what I am sure has delighted you all in our great Gothic cathedrals. I mean how the artist of that time, handicraftsman himself in stone or glass, found the best motives for his art, always ready for his hand and always beautiful, in the daily work of the artificers he saw around him—as in those lovely windows of Chartres—where the dyer dips in the vat and the potter sits at the wheel, and the weaver stands at the loom: real manufacturers these, workers with the hand, and entirely delight-ful to look at, not like the smug and vapid shopman of our time, who knows nothing of the web or vase he sells, except that he is charging you double its value and thinking you a fool for buying it. Nor can I but just note, in passing, the immense influence the decorative work of Greece and Italy had on its artists, the one teaching the sculptor that restraining influence of design which is the glory of the Parthenon, the other keeping painting always true to its primary, pictorial condition of noble colour which is the secret of the school of Venice; for I wish rather, in this lecture at least, to dwell on the effect that decorative art has on human life—on its social not its purely artistic effect.

There are two kinds of men in the world, two great creeds, two different forms of natures: men to whom the end of life is action, and men to whom the end of life is thought. As regards the latter, who seek for experience itself and not for the fruits of experience, who must burn always with one of the passions of this fiery-coloured world, who find life interesting not for its secret but for its situations, for its pulsations and not for its purpose; the passion for beauty engendered by the decorative arts will be to them more satisfying than any political or religious enthusiasm, any enthusiasm for humanity, any ecstasy or sorrow for love. For art comes to one professing primarily to give nothing but the highest quality to one's moments, and for those moments' sake. So far for those to whom the end of life is thought. As regards the others, who hold that life is inseparable from labour, to them should this movement be specially dear: for, if our days are barren without industry, industry without art is barbarism.

Hewers of wood and drawers of water there must be always indeed among us. Our modern machinery has not much lightened the labour of man after all: but at least let the pitcher that stands by the well be beautiful and surely the labour of the day will be lightened: let the wood be made receptive of some lovely form, some gracious design, and there will come no longer discontent but joy to the toiler. For what is decoration but the worker's expression of joy in his work? And not joy merely—that is a great thing yet not enough—but that opportunity of expressing his own individuality which, as it is the essence of all life, is the source of all art. 'I have tried,' I remember William Morris saying to me once, 'I have tried to make each of my workers an artist, and when I say an artist I mean a man.' For the worker then, handicraftsman of whatever kind he is, art is no longer to be a purple robe woven by a slave and thrown over the whitened body of a leprous king to hide and to adorn the sin of his luxury, but rather the beautiful and noble expression of a life that has in it something beautiful and noble.

And so you must seek out your workman and give him, as far as possible, the right surroundings, for remember that the real test and virtue of a workman is not his earnestness nor his industry even, but his power of design merely; and that 'design is not the offspring of idle fancy: it is the studied result of accumulative observation and delightful habit.' All the teaching in the world is of no avail if you do not surround your workman with happy influences and with beautiful things. It is impossible for him to have right ideas about colour unless he sees the lovely colours of Nature unspoiled; impossible for him to supply beautiful incident and action unless he sees beautiful incident and action in the world about him.

For to cultivate sympathy you must be among living things and thinking about them, and to cultivate admiration you must be among beautiful things and looking at them. 'The steel of Toledo and the silk of Genoa did but give strength to oppression and lustre to pride,' as Mr. Ruskin says; let it be for you to create an art that is made by the hands of the people for the joy of the people, to please the hearts of the people, too; an art that will be your expression of your delight in life. There is nothing 'in common life too mean, in common things too trivial to be ennobled by your touch'; nothing in life that art cannot sanctify.

You have heard, I think, a few of you, of two flowers connected with the aesthetic movement in England, and said (I assure you, erroneously) to be the food of some aesthetic young men. Well, let me tell you that the reason we love the lily and the sunflower, in spite of what Mr. Gilbert may tell you, is not for any vegetable fashion at all. It is because these two lovely flowers are in England the two most perfect models of design, the most naturally adapted for decorative art—the gaudy leonine beauty of the one and the precious loveliness of the other giving to the artist the most entire and perfect joy. And so with you: let there be no flower in your meadows that does not wreathe its tendrils around your pillows, no little leaf in your Titan forests that does not lend its form to design, no curving spray of wild rose of brier that does not live for ever in carven arch or window or marble, no bird in your air that is not giving the iridescent wonder of its colour, the exquisite curves of its wings in flight, to make more precious the preciousness of simple adornment.

We spend our days, each one of us, in looking for the secret of life. Well, the secret of life is in art.

ARTHUR WILLIAM SYMONS

(1865-1945)

Arthur Symons was born on 21 February 1865 at Milford Haven. He was the son of a Methodist minister but rejected his father's Christianity before he had completed his schooldays.

He settled in the 'nineties in Fountain Court, Temple, where for a while he shared chambers with Havelock Ellis and W. B. Yeats. He was married in 1901, and experienced a total nervous breakdown in 1908 from which he never fully recovered.

Symons was a great 'importer' of French literature into England, and has justly been described as 'a good minor poet, and excellent translator, a major critic' (*The Complete Poems of Lionel Johnson*, edited by Ian Fletcher, 1953). He was also an editor of courage and distinction, and it was he who edited the eight numbers of the periodical *The Savoy* (Jan.–Dec. 1896) published by Leonard Smithers, a prime source for Aubrey Beardsley illustrations.

The acerbity of tone sometimes evident in the following essay was probably the author's response to the witty remarks which Wilde had made at Symons's expense, of which 'An Egoist who had no Ego' (as reported by Frank Harris) was the cruellest.

An Artist in Attitudes: Oscar Wilde

WHEN the 'Ballad of Reading Gaol' was published, it seemed to some people that such a return to, or so startling a first acquaintance with, real things, was precisely what was most required to bring into relation, both with life and art, an extraordinary talent, so little in relation to matters of common experience, so fantastically alone in a region of intellectual abstractions. In this poem, where a style formed on other lines seems startled at finding itself used for such new purposes, we see a great spectacular intellect, to which, at last, pity and terror have come in their own person, and no longer as puppets in a play. In its sight, human life has always been something acted on the stage; a comedy in which it is the wise man's part to sit aside and laugh, but in which he may also disdainfully take part, as in a carnival, under any mask. The unbiassed, scornful intellect, to which humanity has never been a burden, comes now to be unable to sit aside and laugh, and it has worn and looked behind so many masks that there is nothing left desirable in illusion. Having seen, as the artist sees, further than morality, but with so partial an eyesight as to have overlooked it on the way, it has come at length to discover morality in the only way left possible, for itself. And, like most of those who, having 'thought themselves weary,' have made the adventure of putting thought into action, it has had to discover it sorrowfully, at its own incalculable expense. And now, having become so newly acquainted with what is pitiful, and what seems most unjust, in the arrangement of human affairs, it has gone, not unnaturally, to an extreme, and taken, on the one hand, humanitarianism, on the other realism, at more than their just valuation, in matters of art. It is that odd instinct of the intellect, the necessity of carrying things to their furthest point of development, to be more logical than either life or art, two very wayward and illogical things, in which conclusions do not always follow from premises.

Well, and nothing followed, after this turning-point, as it seemed, in a career. 'Whatever actually occurs is spoiled for art,' Oscar Wilde has said. One hoped, but he had known at least himself, from the beginning. Nothing followed. Wit remained, to the very end, the least personal form of speech, and thus the kindest refuge for one who had never loved facts in themselves. 'I am dying beyond my means' was the last word of his which was repeated to me.

His intellect was dramatic, and the whole man was not so much a personality as an attitude. Without being a sage, he maintained the attitude of a sage; without being a poet, he maintained the attitude of a poet; without being an artist, he maintained the attitude of an artist. And it was precisely in his attitudes that he was most sincere. They represented his intentions; they stood for the better, unrealised part of himself. Thus his attitude, towards life and towards art, was untouched by his conduct; his perfectly just and essentially dignified assertion of the artist's place in the world of thought and the place of beauty in the material world being in nowise invalidated by his own failure to create pure beauty or to become a quite honest artist. A talent so vividly at work as to be almost genius was incessantly urging him into action, mental action. Just as the appropriate word always came to his lips, so the appropriate attitude always found him ready to step into it, as into his own shadow. His mind was eminently reasonable, and if you look closely into his wit, you will find that it has always a basis of logic, though it may indeed most probably be supported by its apex at the instant in which he presents it to you. Of the purely poetical quality he had almost nothing; his style, even in prose, becomes insincere, a bewildering echo of Pater or of some French writer, whenever he tries to write beautifully. Such imagination as he had was like the flickering of light along an electric wire, struck by friction out of something direct and hard, and, after all, only on the surface.

'But then it is only the Philistine,' he has said, in his essay on Wainewright, 'who seeks to estimate a personality by the vulgar test of production. This young dandy sought to be somebody rather than to do something. He recognised that Life itself is an art, and has its modes of style no less than the arts that seek to express it.' 'Art never expresses anything but itself,' he has said, in another essay in the same book, so aptly called 'Intentions'; and that 'principle of his new aesthetics' does but complete his view of the function of life. Art and life are to be two things, absolutely apart, each a thing made to a pattern, not a natural, or, as he would take it to be, an accidental, growth. It is the old principle of art for art's sake, pushed to its furthest limits, where every truth sways over into falsehood. He tells us that 'the highest art rejects the burden of the human spirit, and gains more from a new medium or a fresh material than she does from any enthusiasm for art, or from any lofty passion, or from any fresh awakening of the human consciousness." But he forgets that he is only discussing technique, and that faultless technique, though art cannot exist without it, is not art.

And so with regard to life. Realising as he did that it is possible to be very watchfully cognisant of the 'quality of our moments as they pass," and to shape them after one's own ideal much more continuously and consciously than most people have ever thought of trying to do, he made for himself many souls, souls of intricate pattern and elaborate colour, webbed into infinite tiny cells, each the home of a strange perfume, perhaps a poison. Every soul had its own secret, and was secluded from the soul which had gone before it or was to come after it. And this show-man of souls was not always aware that he was juggling with real things, for to him they were no more than the coloured glass balls which the juggler keeps in the air, catching them one after another. For the most part the souls were content to be playthings; now and again they took a malicious revenge, and became so real that even the juggler was aware of it. But when they became too real he had to go on throwing them into the air and catching them, even though the skill of the game had lost its interest for him. But as he never lost his self-possession, his audience, the world, did not see the difference.

Among these souls there was one after the fashion of Flaubert, another after the fashion of Pater, others that had known Baudelaire, and Huysmans, and De Quincey, and Swinburne. Each was taken up, used, and dropped, as in a kind of persistent illustration of 'the truth of masks.' 'A truth in art is that whose contradictory is also true.' Well, it was with no sense of contradiction that the critic of beautiful things found himself appealing frankly to the public in a series of the wittiest plays that have been seen on the modern stage. It was another attitude, that was all; something external, done for its own sake, 'expressing nothing but itself,' and expressing, as it happened by accident, precisely what he himself was best able to express.

It may be, perhaps, now that the man is dead, that those who admired him too much or too little will do him a little justice. He was himself systematically unjust, and was never anxious to be understood too precisely, or to be weighed in very level balances. But he will be remembered, if not as an artist in English literature, at all events in the traditions of our time, as the supreme artist in intellectual attitudes.

1901.

Ernest Dowson

I

THE death of Ernest Dowson will mean very little to the world at large, but it will mean a great deal to the few people who care passionately for poetry. A little book of verses, the manuscript of another, a one-act play in verse, a few short stories, two novels written in collaboration, some translations from the French, done for money; that is all that was left by a man who was undoubtedly a man of genius, not a great poet, but a poet, one of the very few writers of our generation to whom that name can be applied in its most intimate sense. People will complain, probably, in his verses, of what will seem to them the factitious melancholy, the factitious idealism, and (peeping through at a few rare moments) the factitious suggestions of riot. They will see only a literary affectation, where in truth there is as genuine a note of personal sincerity as in the more explicit and arranged confessions of less admirable poets. Yes, in these few evasive, immaterial snatches of song, I find, implied for the most part, hidden away like a secret, all the fever and turmoil and the unattained dreams of a life which had itself so much of the swift, disastrous, and suicidal impetus of genius.

Ernest Christopher Dowson was born at The Grove, Belmont Hill, Lee, Kent, on August 2nd, 1867; he died at 26 Sandhurst Gardens, Catford, S.E., on Friday morning, February 23rd, 1900, and was buried in the Roman Catholic part of the Lewisham Cemetery on February 27th. His great-uncle was Alfred Domett, Browning's 'Waring,' at one time Prime Minister of New Zealand and author of 'Ranolf and Amohia,' and other poems. His father, who had himself a taste for literature, lived a good deal in France and on the Riviera, on account of the delicacy of his health, and Ernest had a somewhat irregular education, chiefly out of England, before he entered Queen's College, Oxford. He left in 1887 without taking a degree, and came to London, where he lived for several years, often revisiting France, which was always his favourite country. Latterly, until the last year of his life, he lived almost entirely in Paris, Brittany, and Normandy. Never robust, and always reckless with himself, his health had been steadily getting worse for some years, and when he came back to London he looked, as indeed he was, a dying man. Morbidly shy, with a sensitive independence which shrank from any sort of obligation, he would not communicate with his relatives, who would gladly have helped him, or with any of the really large number of attached friends whom he had in London; and, as his disease weakened him more and more, he hid himself away in his miserable lodgings, refused to see a doctor, let himself half starve, and was found one day in a Bodega with only a few shillings in his pocket, and so weak as to be hardly able to walk, by a friend, himself in some difficulties, who immediately took him back to the bricklayer's cottage in a muddy outskirt of Catford, where he was himself living, and there generously looked after him for the last six weeks of his life.

He did not realise that he was going to die, and was full of projects for the future, when the £600 which was to come to him from the sale of some property should have given him a fresh chance in the world; began to read Dickens, whom he had never read before, with singular zest; and, on the last day of his life, sat up talking eagerly till five in the morning. At the very moment of his death he did not know that he was dying. He tried to cough, could not cough, and the heart quietly stopped.

II

I cannot remember my first meeting with Ernest Dowson. It may have been in 1891, at one of the meetings of the Rhymers' Club, in an upper room at the Cheshire Cheese, where long clay pipes lay in slim heaps on the wooden tables, between tankards of ale; and young poets, then very young, recited their own verses to one another with a desperate and ineffectual attempt to get into key with the Latin Quarter. Though few of us were, as a matter of fact, Anglo-Saxon, we could not help feeling that we were in London, and the atmosphere of London is not the atmosphere of movements or of societies. In Paris it is the most natural thing in the world to meet and discuss literature, ideas, one's own and one another's work; and it can be done without pretentiousness or constraint, because, to the Latin mind, art, ideas, one's work and the work of one's friends, are definite and important things, which it would never occur to any one to take anything but seriously. In England art has to be protected, not only against the world, but against oneself and one's fellow-artist, by a kind of affected modesty which is the Englishman's natural pose, half pride and half self-distrust. So this brave venture of the Rhymers' Club, though it lasted for two or three years, and produced two little books of verse which will some day be literary curiosities, was not quite a satisfactory kind of *cénacle*. Dowson, who enjoyed the real thing so much in Paris, did not, I think, go very often; but his contributions to the first book of the club were at once the most delicate and the most distinguished poems which it contained. Was it, after all, at one of these meetings that I first saw him, or was it, perhaps, at another haunt of some of us at that time, a semi-literary tavern near Leicester Square, chosen for its convenient position between two stage-doors? It was at the time when one or two of us sincerely worshipped the ballet; Dowson, alas, never. I could never get him to see that charm in harmonious and coloured movement, like bright shadows seen through the floating gauze of the music, which held me night after night at the two theatres which alone seemed to me to give an amusing colour to one's dreams. Neither the stage nor the stage-door had any attraction for him; but he came to the tavern because it was a tavern, and because he could meet his friends there. Even before that time I have a vague impression of having met him, I forget where, certainly at night; and of having been struck, even then, by a look and manner of pathetic charm, a sort of Keats-like face, the face of a demoralised Keats, and by something curious in the contrast of a manner exquisitely refined, with an appearance generally somewhat dilapidated. That impression was only accentuated later on, when I came to know him, and the manner of his life, much more intimately.

I think I may date my first impression of what one calls 'the real man' (as if it were more real than the poet of the disembodied verses!) from an evening in which he first introduced me to those charming supper-houses, open all night through, the cabmen's shelters. I had been talking over another vagabond poet, Lord Rochester, with a charming and sympathetic descendant of that poet, and somewhat late at night we had come upon Dowson and another man wandering aimlessly and excitedly about the streets. He invited us to supper, we did not quite realise where, and the cabman came in with us, as we were welcomed, cordially and without comment, at a little place near the Langham; and, I recollect, very hospitably entertained. The cooking differs, as I found in time, in these supper houses, but there the rasher was excellent and the cups admirably clean. Dowson was known there, and I used to think he was always at his best in a cabmen's shelter. Without a certain sordidness in his surroundings he was never quite comfortable, never quite himself; and at those places you are obliged to drink nothing stronger than coffee or tea. I liked to see him occasionally, for a change, drinking nothing stronger than coffee or tea. At Oxford, I believe, his favourite form of intoxication had been haschisch; afterwards he gave up this somewhat elaborate experiment in visionary sensations for readier means of oblivion; but he returned to it, I remember, for at least one afternoon, in a company of which I had been the gatherer and of which I was the host. I remember him sitting, a little anxiously, with his chin on his breast, awaiting the magic, half-shy in the midst of a bright company of young people whom he had only seen across the footlights. The experience was not a very successful one; it ended in what should have been its first symptom, immoderate laughter.

Always, perhaps, a little consciously, but at least always sincerely, in search of new sensations, my friend found what was for him the supreme sensation in a very passionate and tender adoration of the most escaping of all ideals, the ideal of youth. Cherished, as I imagine, first only in the abstract, this search after the immature, the ripening graces which time can only spoil in the ripening, found itself at the journey's end, as some of his friends thought, a little prematurely. I was never of their opinion. I only saw twice, and for a few moments only, the young girl to whom most of his verses were to be written, and whose presence in his life may be held to account for much of that astonishing contrast between the broad outlines of his life and work. The situation seemed to me of the most exquisite and appropriate impossibility. The daughter of a refugee, I believe of good family, reduced to keeping a humble restaurant in a foreign quarter of London, she listened to his verses, smiled charmingly, under her mother's eyes, on his two years' courtship, and at the end of two years married the waiter instead. Did she ever realise more than the obvious part of what was being offered to her, in this shy and eager devotion? Did it ever mean very much to her to have made and to have killed a poet? She had, at all events, the gift of evoking, and, in its way, of retaining, all that was most delicate, sensitive, shy, typically poetic, in a nature which I can only compare to a weedy garden, its grass trodden down by many feet, but with one small, carefully tended flower-bed, luminous with lilies. I used to think, sometimes, of Verlaine and his 'girl-wife,' the one really profound passion, certainly, of that passionate career; the charming, child-like creature, to whom he looked back, at the end of his life, with an unchanged tenderness and disappointment: 'Vous n'avez rien compris à ma simplicité,' as he lamented. In the case of Dowson, however, there was a sort of virginal devotion, as to a Madonna; and I think had things gone happily, to a conventionally happy ending, he would have felt (dare I say?) that his ideal had been spoilt.

But, for the good fortune of poets, things rarely do go happily with them, or to conventionally happy endings. He used to dine every night at the little restaurant, and I can always see the picture, which I have so often seen through the window in passing: the narrow room with the rough tables, for the most part empty, except in the innermost corner, where Dowson would sit with that singularly sweet and singularly pathetic smile on his lips (a smile which seemed afraid of its right to be there, as if always dreading a rebuff), playing his invariable after-dinner game of cards. Friends would come in, during the hour before closing time; and the girl, her game of cards finished, would quietly disappear, leaving him with hardly more than the desire to kill another night as swiftly as possible.

Meanwhile she and the mother knew that the fragile young man who dined there so quietly every day was apt to be quite another sort of person after he had been three hours outside. It was only when his life seemed to have been irretrievably ruined that Dowson quite deliberately abandoned himself to that craving for drink, which was doubtless lying in wait for him in his blood, as consumption was also; it was only latterly, when he had no longer any interest in life, that he really wished to die. But I have never known him when he could resist either the desire or the consequences of drink. Sober, he was the most gentle, in manner the most gentlemanly, of men; unselfish to a fault, to the extent of weakness; a delightful companion, charm itself. Under the influence of drink, he became almost literally insane, certainly quite irresponsible. He fell into furious and unreasoning passions; a vocabulary unknown to him at other times sprang up like a whirlwind; he seemed always about to commit some act of absurd violence. Along with that forgetfulness came other memories. As long as he was conscious of himself, there was but one woman for him in the world, and for her he had an infinite tenderness and an infinite respect. When that face faded from him, he saw all the other faces, and he saw no more difference than between sheep and sheep. Indeed, that curious love of the sordid, so common an affectation of the modern decadent, and with him so genuine, grew upon him, and dragged him into more and more sorry corners of a life which was never exactly 'gay' to him. His father, when he died, left him in possession of an old dock, where for a time he lived in a mouldering house, in that squalid part of the East End which he came to know so well, and to feel so strangely at home in. He drank the poisonous liquors of those pot-houses which swarm about the docks; he drifted about in whatever company came in his way; he let heedlessness develop into a curious disregard of personal tidiness. In Paris, Les Halles took the place of the docks. At Dieppe, where I saw so much of him one summer, he discovered strange, squalid haunts about the harbour, where he made friends with amazing innkeepers, and got into rows with the fishermen who came in to drink after midnight. At Brussels, where I was with him at the time of the Kermesse, he flung himself into all that riotous Flemish life, with a zest for what was most sordidly riotous in it. It was his own way of escape from life.

To Dowson, as to all those who have not been 'content to ask unlikely gifts in vain,' nature, life, destiny, whatever one chooses to call it, that power which is strength to the strong, presented itself as a barrier against which all one's strength only served to dash one to more hopeless ruin. He was not a dreamer; destiny passes by the dreamer, sparing him because he clamours for nothing. He was a child, clamouring for so many things, all impossible. With a body too weak for ordinary existence, he desired all the enchantments of all the senses. With a soul too shy to tell its own secret, except in exquisite evasions, he desired the boundless confidence of love. He sang one tune, over and over, and no one listened to him. He had only to form the most simple wish, and it was denied him. He gave way to ill-luck, not knowing that he was giving way to his own weakness, and he tried to escape from the consciousness of things as they were at the best, by voluntarily choosing to accept them at their worst. For with him it was always voluntary. He was never quite without money; he had a little money of his own, and he had for many years a weekly allowance from a publisher, in return for translations from the French, or, if he chose to do it, original work. He was unhappy, and he dared not think. To unhappy men, thought, if it can be set at work on abstract questions, is the only substitute for happiness; if it has not strength to overleap the barrier which shuts one in upon oneself, it is the one unwearying torture. Dowson had exquisite sensibility, he vibrated in harmony with every delicate emotion; but he had no outlook, he had not the escape of intellect. His only escape, then, was to plunge into the crowd, to fancy that he lost sight of himself as he disappeared from the sight of others. The more he soiled himself at that gross contact, the further would he seem to be from what beckoned to him in one vain illusion after another vain illusion, in the delicate places of the world. Seeing himself moving to the sound of lutes, in some courtly disguise, down an alley of Watteau's Versailles, while he touched finger-tips with a divine creature in rose-leaf silks, what was there left for him, as the dream obstinately refused to realise itself, but a blind flight into some Teniers kitchen, where boors are making merry, without thought of yesterday or to-morrow? There, perhaps, in that ferment of animal life, he could forget life as he dreamed it, with too faint hold upon his dreams to make dreams come true.

For, there is not a dream which may not come true, if we have the energy which makes, or chooses, our own fate. We can always, in this world, get what we want, if we will it intensely and persistently enough. Whether we shall get it sooner or later is the concern of fate; but we shall get it. It may come when we have no longer any use for it, when we have gone on willing it out of habit, or so as not to confess that we have failed. But it will come. So few people succeed greatly because so few people can conceive a great end, and work towards that end without deviating and without tiring. But we all know that the man who works for money day and night gets rich; and the man who works day and night for no matter what kind of material power, gets the power. It is the same with the deeper, more spiritual, as it seems vaguer issues, which make for happiness and every intangible success. It is only the dreams of those light sleepers who dream faintly that do not come true.

We get out of life, all of us, what we bring to it; that, and that only, is what it can teach us. There are men whom Dowson's experiences would have made great men, or great writers; for him they did very little. Love and regret, with here and there the suggestion of an uncomforting pleasure snatched by the way, are all that he has to sing of; and he could have sung of them at much less 'expense of spirit,' and, one fancies, without the 'waste of shame' at all. Think what Villon got directly out of his own life, what Verlaine, what Musset, what Byron, got directly out of their own lives! It requires a strong man to 'sin strongly' and profit by it. To Dowson the tragedy of his own life could only have resulted in an elegy. 'I have flung roses, roses, riotously with the throng,' he confesses, in his most beautiful poem; but it was as one who flings roses in a dream, as he passes with shut eyes through an unsubstantial throng. The depths into which he plunged were always waters of oblivion, and he returned forgetting them. He is always a very ghostly lover, wandering in a land of perpetual twilight, as he holds a whispered *colloque sentimental* with the ghost of an old love:

> Dans le vieux parc solitaire et glacé
> Deux spectres ont évoqué le passé.

It was, indeed, almost a literal unconsciousness, as of one who leads two lives, severed from one another as completely as sleep is from waking. Thus we get in his work very little of the personal appeal of those to whom riotous living, misery, a cross destiny, have been of so real a value. And it is important to draw this distinction, if only for the benefit of those young men who are convinced that the first step towards genius is disorder. Dowson is precisely one of the people who are pointed out as confirming this theory. And yet Dowson was precisely one of those who owed least to circumstances; and, in succumbing to them, he did no more than succumb to the destructive forces which, shut up within him, pulled down the house of life upon his own head.

A soul 'unspotted from the world,' in a body which one sees visibly soiling under one's eyes; that improbability is what all who knew him saw in Dowson, as his youth fulphysical grace gave way year by year, and the personal charm underlying it remained unchanged. There never was a simpler or more attaching charm, because there never was a sweeter or more honest nature. It was not because he ever said anything particularly clever or particularly interesting, it was not because he gave you ideas, or impressed you by any strength or originality, that you liked to be with him; but because of a certain engaging quality, which seemed unconscious of itself, which was never anxious to be or to do anything, which simply existed, as perfume exists in a flower. Drink was like a heavy curtain, blotting out everything of a sudden; when the curtain lifted, nothing had changed. Living always that double life, he had his true and his false aspect, and the true life was the expression of that fresh, delicate, and uncontaminated nature which some of us knew in him, and which remains for us, untouched by the other, in every line that he wrote.

III

Dowson was the only poet I ever knew who cared more for his
prose than for his verse; but he was wrong, and it is not by his
prose that he will live, exquisite as that prose was at its best. He
wrote two novels in collaboration with Mr. Arthur Moore: 'A
Comedy of Masks,' in 1893, and 'Adrian Rome,' in 1899, both
done under the influence of Mr. Henry James, both interesting
because they were personal studies, and studies of known surroundings, rather than for their actual value as novels. A volume
of 'Stories and Studies in Sentiment,' called 'Dilemmas,' in
which the influence of Mr. Wedmore was felt in addition to the
influence of Mr. James, appeared in 1895. Several other short
stories, among his best work in prose, have not yet been reprinted
from the *Savoy*. Some translations from the French, done as
hack work, need not be mentioned here, though they were never
without some traces of his peculiar quality of charm in language.
The short stories were indeed rather 'studies in sentiment' than
stories; studies of singular delicacy, but with only a faint hold on
life, so that perhaps the best of them was not unnaturally a study
in the approaches of death: 'The Dying of Francis Donne.' For
the most part they dealt with the same motives as the poems,
hopeless and reverent love, the ethics of renunciation, the disappointment of those who are too weak or too unlucky to take
what they desire. They have a sad and quiet beauty of their own,
the beauty of second thoughts and subdued emotions, of choice
and scholarly English, moving in the more fluid and reticent
harmonies of prose almost as daintily as if it were moving to the
measure of verse. Dowson's care over English prose was like
that of a Frenchman writing his own language with the respect
which Frenchmen pay to French. Even English things had to
come to him through France, if he was to prize them very highly;
and there is a passage in 'Dilemmas' which I have always thought
very characteristic of his own tastes, as it refers to an 'infinitesimal
library, a few French novels, an Horace, and some well-thumbed
volumes of the modern English poets in the familiar edition of
Tauchnitz.' He was Latin by all his affinities, and that very
quality of slightness, of parsimony almost, in his dealings with
life and the substance of art, connects him with the artists of
Latin races, who have always been so fastidious in their rejection
of mere nature, when it comes too nakedly or too clamourously
into sight and hearing, and so gratefully content with a few choice
things faultlessly done.

And Dowson in his verse (the 'Verses' of 1896, 'The Pierrot
of the Minute, a dramatic phantasy in one act,' of 1897, the

posthumous volume, 'Decorations') was the same scrupulous artist as in his prose, and more felicitously at home there. He was quite Latin in his feeling for youth, and death, and 'the old age of roses,' and the pathos of our little hour in which to live and love; Latin in his elegance, reticence, and simple grace in the treatment of these motives; Latin, finally, in his sense of their sufficiency for the whole of one's mental attitude. He used the commonplaces of poetry frankly, making them his own by his belief in them: the Horatian Cynara or Neobule was still the natural symbol for him when he wished to be most personal. I remember his saying to me that his ideal of a line of verse was the line of Poe:

The viol, the violet, and the vine;

and the gracious, not remote or unreal beauty, which clings about such words and such images as these, was always to him the true poetical beauty. There never was a poet to whom verse came more naturally, for the song's sake; his theories were all aesthetic, almost technical ones, such as a theory, indicated by his preference for the line of Poe, that the letter 'v' was the most beautiful of the letters, and could never be brought into verse too often. For any more abstract theories he had neither tolerance nor need. Poetry as a philosophy did not exist for him; it existed solely as the loveliest of the arts. He loved the elegance of Horace, all that was most complex in the simplicity of Poe, most bird-like in the human melodies of Verlaine. He had the pure lyric gift, unweighted or unballasted by any other quality of mind or emotion; and a song, for him, was music first, and then whatever you please afterwards, so long as it suggested, never told, some delicate sentiment, a sigh or a caress; finding words, at times, as perfect as these words of a poem headed, 'O Mors! quam amara est memoria tua homini pacem habenti in substantiis suis':

> Exceeding sorrow
>   Consumeth my sad heart!
> Because tomorrow
>   We must depart,
> Now is exceeding sorrow
>   All my part!
>
> Give over playing,
>   Cast thy viol away:
> Merely laying
>   Thine head my way:
> Prithee, give over playing,
>   Grave or gay.

Be no word spoken;
   Weep nothing: let a pale
Silence, unbroken
   Silence prevail!
Prithee, be no word spoken,
   Lest I fail!

Forget to-morrow!
   Weep nothing: only lay
In silent sorrow
   Thine head my way:
Let us forget to-morrow,
   This one day!

There, surely, the music of silence speaks, if it has ever spoken. The words seem to tremble back into the silence which their whisper has interrupted, but not before they have created for us a mood, such a mood as the Venetian Pastoral of Giorgione renders in painting. Languid, half inarticulate, coming from the heart of a drowsy sorrow very conscious of itself, and not less sorrowful because it sees its own face looking mournfully back out of the water, the song seems to have been made by some fastidious amateur of grief, and it has all the sighs and tremors of the mood, wrought into a faultless strain of music. Stepping out of a paradise in which pain becomes so lovely, he can see the beauty which is the other side of madness, and, in a sonnet 'To One in Bedlam,' can create a more positive, a more poignant mood, with this fine subtlety:

With delicate, mad hands, behind his sordid bars,
Surely he hath his posies, which they tear and twine;
Those scentless wisps of straw, that miserably line
His straight, caged universe, whereat the dull world stares,

Pedant and pitiful. O, how his rapt gaze wars
With their stupidity! Know they what dreams divine
Lift his long, laughing reveries like enchaunted wine,
And make his melancholy germane to the stars'?

O lamentable brother! if those pity thee,
Am I not fain of all thy lone eyes promise me;
Half a fool's kingdom, far from men who sow and reap,
All their days, vanity? Better than mortal flowers,
Thy moon-kissed roses seem: better than love or sleep,
The star-crowned solitude of thine oblivious hours!

Here, in the moment's intensity of this comradeship with madness, observe how beautiful the whole thing becomes; how instinctively the imagination of the poet turns what is sordid into a radiance, all stars and flowers and the divine part of forgetfulness! It is a symbol of the two sides of his own life: the side open to the street, and the side turned away from it, where he could 'hush and bless himself with silence.' No one ever worshipped beauty more devoutly, and just as we see him here transfiguring a dreadful thing with beauty, so we shall see, everywhere in his work, that he never admitted an emotion which he could not so transfigure. He knew his limits only too well; he knew that the deeper and graver things of life were for the most part outside the circle of his magic; he passed them by, leaving much of himself unexpressed, because he would permit himself to express nothing imperfectly, or according to anything but his own conception of the dignity of poetry. In the lyric in which he has epitomised himself and his whole life, a lyric which is certainly one of the greatest lyrical poems of our time, 'Non sum qualis eram bonæ sub regno Cynaræ,' he has for once said everything, and he has said it to an intoxicating and perhaps immortal music:

> Last night, ah, yesternight, betwixt her lips and mine,
> There fell thy shadow, Cynara! thy breath was shed
> Upon my soul between the kisses and the wine;
> And I was desolate and sick of an old passion,
>   Yea, I was desolate and bowed my head:
> I have been faithful to thee, Cynara! in my fashion.

> All night upon mine heart I felt her warm heart beat,
> Night-long within mine arms in love and sleep she lay;
> Surely the kisses of her bought red mouth were sweet;
> But I was desolate and sick of an old passion,
>   When I awoke and found the dawn was grey:
> I have been faithful to thee, Cynara! in my fashion.

> I have forgot much, Cynara! gone with the wind,
> Flung roses, roses riotously with the throng,
> Dancing, to put thy pale, lost lilies out of mind;
> But I was desolate and sick of an old passion,
>   Yea, all the time, because the dance was long:
> I have been faithful to thee, Cynara! in my fashion.

> I cried for madder music and for stronger wine,
> But when the feast is finished and the lamps expire,
> Then falls thy shadow, Cynara! the night is thine;
> And I am desolate and sick of an old passion,
>   Yea, hungry for the lips of my desire:
> I have been faithful to thee, Cynara! in my fashion.

Here, perpetuated by some unique energy of a temperament rarely so much the master of itself, is the song of passion and the passions, at their eternal war in the soul which they quicken or deaden, and in the body which they break down between them. In the second book, the book of 'Decorations,' there are a few pieces which repeat, only more faintly, this very personal note. Dowson could never have developed; he had already said, in his first book of verse, all that he had to say. Had he lived, had he gone on writing, he could only have echoed himself; and probably it would have been the less essential part of himself; his obligation to Swinburne, always evident, increasing as his own inspiration failed him. He was always without ambition, writing to please his own fastidious taste, with a kind of proud humility in his attitude towards the public, not expecting or requiring recognition. He died obscure, having ceased to care even for the delightful labour of writing. He died young, worn out by what was never really life to him, leaving a little verse which has the pathos of things too young and too frail ever to grow old.

1900.

SIR MAX BEERBOHM
(1872 - 1959)

Max Beerbohm was born in London on 24 August 1872, and was the half-brother of the actor-manager Sir Herbert Beerbohm-Tree. He attested later to this theatrical connection by succeeding Bernard Shaw as dramatic critic of the *Saturday Review*.

He was educated at Charterhouse and Merton College, Oxford, where, as an undergraduate, he made a name for himself as a caricaturist, dandy and wit. He married an American actress in 1910, and made his home at Rapallo on the Italian Riviera. He was knighted in 1939.

'The incomparable Max', as Shaw called him, was famous both as a comic draughtsman and as a literary *petit maître* whose stylish and spritely essays and stories reflected 'the very deuce of a pose' ('Dandies and Dandies', *The Works of Max Beerbohm*, 1896). He was also a contributor to *The Yellow Book*, that famous periodical of the 'Nineties which ran for thirteen numbers between 1894 and 1897. It was published by John Lane, under the literary editorship of Henry Harland, and Beardsley acted as art editor to the first four issues.

Aubrey Beardsley

To ALL who knew him, and to all who did not know him but are lovers of lineal art, Aubrey Beardsley's death has been the occasion for much sorrow, an irreparable loss. But there is, I think, some consolation in the thought that he did not die suddenly. Though he died, a great artist, in his first youth, and at the very opening of life, as life is usually reckoned, Fate did not deal with him unfairly, did not take him, as she has taken others, with a kind of brutal treachery, before the fulfilment of all the work that was in him. From his quite early boyhood, Aubrey Beardsley had known quite well that his life would inevitably be a short one, and it was to this knowledge, partly, that we owe the great range of his achievement in art. Fate had given him a prematurity of power that was in accurate ratio to the appointed brevity of his life, and, in the exercise and the development of his genius, Aubrey Beardsley never rested. He worked on always, with a kind of desperate courage, and with a degree of force and enthusiasm that is given only to the doomed man. He knew that he had no time to lose. At the age when normal genius is still groping for its method, he was the unerring master of his method. He died, having achieved masterpieces, at an age when normal genius has as yet done little of which it will not be heartily ashamed hereafter. Normal genius is in no hurry. If it be struck down suddenly before its prime, it leaves no great legacy to us: we can only rail against Fate.

But Aubrey Beardsley was bound to die young. All his friends knew that as well as he did. The only wonder was that the fine thread of his life was not severed sooner. I remember that when I first saw him I thought I had never seen so utterly frail a creature—he looked more like a ghost than a living man. He was then, I believe, already in an advanced stage of pulmonary consumption. When I came to know him better, I realized that it was only by sheer force of nerves that he contrived to sustain himself. He was always, whenever one saw him, in the highest spirits, full of fun and of fresh theories about life and art. But one could not help feeling that as soon as he were alone he would sink down, fatigued and listless, with all the spirit gone out of him. One felt that his gaiety resulted from a kind of pride and was only assumed, as who should say, in company. Perhaps one underrated his strength. When he was alone, he must have worked at his drawings almost without intermission. It is a curious thing that none of his visitors ever found him at work, or saw any of his rough sketches, or even so much as his pen, ink, and paper. It was his pose to appear as a man of leisure, living among books. Certainly, he seemed to have read, and to have made his reading into culture, more than any man I have ever met; though how he, whose executive industry was so great, managed to read so much, is a question which I have never quite solved: I can only suppose that he read very rapidly. The literature of the Restoration and of the Eighteenth Century had always especially appealed to him. He delighted (oddly enough) in Voltaire. He was supposed to have read the whole of the *Comédie Humaine*, and he had all the modern schools of France at his finger-tips. He was a good Latin scholar, too, though ill-health had curtailed his schooldays, and he had practically had to teach himself all that he knew. His conversation had always the charm of scholarship. Though not less modest than are most young men, he had strong opinions on most subjects, and he expressed himself with clear precision, and with wit. But he had not the physical strength which is necessary to the really great or inspiring talker. With him, there was always the painful sense of effort. I remember an afternoon

I spent with him, at his house in Cambridge Street, soon after
The Yellow Book was started. He was in great form, and showed
even more than his usual wit and animation, as he paced up and
down the room, talking, with all his odd, abrupt gestures, about
one thing and another, about everything under the sun. I am a
very good listener, and I enjoyed myself very much. Next day I
heard that his mother and his sister and a doctor had been sitting
up with him till daybreak. He had been seized, soon after I had
left, with a terribly violent attack of haemorrhage, and it had been
thought, more than once, that he could not live through the
night. I remember, also, very clearly, a supper at which Beardsley
was present. After the supper we sat up rather late. He was the
life and soul of the party, till, quite suddenly, almost in the
middle of a sentence, he fell fast asleep in his chair. He had
overstrained his vitality, and it had all left him. I can see him now,
as he sat there with his head sunk on his breast: the thin face,
white as the gardenia in his coat, and the prominent, harshly-cut
features; the hair, that always covered his whole forehead in a
fringe and was of so curious a colour—a kind of tortoiseshell;
the narrow, angular figure, and the long hands that were so full of
power.

Last month, when Beardsley's death was announced in the
newspapers, the general public must have read the news with
some surprise. The 'Beardsley Boom,' as it was called, had begun
with *The Yellow Book*, and it had ceased with *The Savoy*, and
Beardsley had, to all intents and purposes, been forgotten by the
general public. For more than a year, he had been living in this
or that quiet place to which invalids are sent. There were no new
'Beardsley posters' on the London hoardings. The paragraphists
of the London Press gradually let him be. His book of fifty
collected drawings created no outcry, for even the book-reviewers
could no longer assert that he did not know how to draw, and
the tattlers at tea-parties had said all they had to say about him
long ago, and had found other subjects for their discussion. But,
while it lasted, how fierce the 'Beardsley Boom' had been! The
public, as I need hardly say, never admired Beardsley's drawings.
It thought them hideous. If the 'Beardsley woman' could have
been incarnated, she would have been singularly unattractive.
Then how could anyone admire her on paper? Besides, she was
all out of drawing. Look at her arm! Beardsley didn't know how
to draw. The public itself could draw better than that. Neverthe-
less, the public took great interest in all Beardsley's work, as it
does in the work of any new artist who either edifies or shocks it.
That Beardsley's really did shock the public, there can be no
doubt. There can be equally little doubt that the public like being

shocked, and sympathy would, therefore be superfluous. But, at the same time, there are, of course, people who do honestly dislike and deplore the morbid spirit that seemed to inspire Beardsley's work, and at such people I should not wish to sneer—on the contrary, I respect their feeling, which I know to be perfectly genuine. Nor would I seek to deny that in Beardsley's work—more especially in some of his early work—there is much that is morbid. But it must be remembered that, when he first began to publish his drawings, he had hardly emerged from that school-boy age when the mind is generally apt to brood on unpleasant subjects, and much of his work, which some people regarded as the sign of corrupt nature, was really the outcome of a perfectly normal phase of mind, finding an abnormal outlet through premature skill in art. I think, too, that he had a boyish delight in shocking people, and that it was often in mere mischief that he chose, as in many of his grotesques for the *Bon-Mots* series, to present such horribly ugly notions. Many of those who knew Beardsley only through his general work imagined that he must be a man of somewhat forbidding character. His powerful, morbid fancy really repelled them, and to them the very beauty of its expression may have seemed a kind of added poison. But I, or anyone else who ever saw him at his home, knew that whatever was morbid in his work reflected only one side of his nature. I knew him to be of a kindly, generous, and affectionate disposition; a devoted son and brother; a very loyal friend.

He lived, when I first saw him and till some two years later, in Cambridge Street, where he shared a house with his mother and sister. Here, every Thursday afternoon, was held a kind of little *salon*, which was always well attended. Aubrey himself was always present, very neatly dressed, handing round cake and bread-and-butter, and talking to each of his mother's guests in turn. There were always three or four new drawings of his passed from hand to hand, and he was always delighted with praise from any of his friends. I think it was at these little half-formal, half-intimate receptions that one saw him at his best. With all his affectations, he had that inborn kindliness which is the basis of all good manners. He was essentially a good host.

I have mentioned his grotesques for the volumes of *Bon-Mots*. These, if I am not mistaken, were among his very earliest published drawings, and simultaneously with them he was working at that great task, the illustration of the *Morte d'Arthur*, on which he spent such a wealth of skilful and appropriate fancy. In the drawings for the *Morte d'Arthur* he was still working, of course, under the influence of Sir Edward Burne-Jones—an influence which was oddly balanced by that of Japanese art in the drawings which he did, at this period, for his own pleasure, and of which *La Femme Incomprise* is a good example. The well-known drawings which, later, he made for *The Yellow Book* were, with their black masses, and very fine lines, arrived at through simplification of the method in *La Femme Incomprise*. These were the drawings that first excited the wrath of the general public and of the book-reviewers. Most of the qualified art-critics, also, were very angry. They did not know what to make of these drawings, which were referable to no established school or known method in art. Beardsley was not at all discouraged by the contempt with which his technique was treated. On the contrary, he revelled in his unfavourable press-cuttings, knowing how little they signified. I think it was in the third number of *The Yellow Book* that two pictures by hitherto-unkown artists were reproduced. One was a large head of Mantegna, by Philip Broughton; the other, a pastel-study of a Frenchwoman, by Albert Foschter. Both the drawings had rather a success with the reviewers, one of whom advised Beardsley 'to study and profit by the sound and scholarly draughtsmanship of which Mr. Philip Broughton furnishes another example in his familiar manner.' Beardsley, who had made both the drawings and invented both the signatures, was greatly amused and delighted.

Meanwhile, Beardsley's acknowledged drawings produced a large crop of imitators, both here and in America. Imitators are the plague to which every original artist is exposed. They inflict the wounds which, in other days, the critics were able to inflict. With the enormous increase of the Press and the wide employment of ignorant and stupid writers, bad criticism has become so general that criticism itself has lost its sting, and the time when an artist could be 'snuffed out by an article' is altogether bygone. Nowadays, it is only through his imitators that an artist can be made to suffer. He sees his power vulgarized and distorted by a hundred apes. Beardsley's *Yellow Book* manner was bound to allure incompetent draughtsmen. It *looked* so simple and so easy—a few blots and random curves, and there you were. Needless to say, the results were appalling. But Beardsley was always, in many ways, developing and modifying his method, and so was always ahead of his apish retinue. His imitators never got so far as to attempt his later manner, the manner of his *Rape of the Lock*, for to do that would have required more patience and more knowledge of sheer drawing than they could possibly afford. Such a design as the 'Coiffing' which came in a late number of *The Savoy*, and which has often seemed to me the most exquisite thing Beardsley ever did, offered them no possible short-cut to talent. To trace the sequence of technical phases through which Beardsley passed would be outside the scope of this brief essay. But I should like to remind my readers that, as he grew older, he became gradually more 'human', less curious of horrible things. Of this tendency the best example is perhaps his 'Ave atque Vale,' in *The Savoy*. Nothing could be more dramatic, more moving and simple, than the figure of that Roman who mourns his friend. The drawing was meant to illustrate one of Catullus' Odes, which Beardsley himself has thus rendered:

> By ways remote and distant waters sped,
> Brother, to thy sad grave-side am I come,
> That I may give the last gifts to the dead
> And vainly parley with thine ashes dumb;
> Since she who now bestows and now denies
> Hath ta'en thee, hapless brother, from mine eyes.

> But lo! these gifts, the heirlooms of past years,
> Are made sad things to grace thy coffin-shell,
> Take them, all drenchèd with a brother's tears,
> And, brother, for all time, hail and farewell!

These lines, which seem to me no less beautiful than the drawing itself, were written shortly before Beardsley left England for the last time. On the eve of his departure, he was received by Father Sebastian into the Catholic Church, to which he had long inclined. His conversion was no mere passing whim, as some people supposed it to be; it was made from true emotional and intellectual impulse. From that time to his death he was a pious and devout Catholic, whose religion consoled him for all the bodily sufferings he underwent. Almost to the very last he was full of fresh schemes for work. When at length, he knew that his life could but outlast a few more days, he awaited death with perfect resignation. He died last month, at Mentone, in the presence of his mother and his sister.

Thus ended this brief, tragic, brilliant life. It had been filled with a larger measure of sweet and bitter experience than is given to most men who die in their old age. Aubrey Beardsley was famous in his youth, and to be famous in one's youth has been called the most gracious gift that the gods can bestow. And, unless I am mistaken, he enjoyed his fame, and was proud of it, though, as a great artist who had a sense of humour, he was, perhaps, a little ashamed of it too, now and then. For the rest, was he happy in his life? I do not know. In a fashion, I think he was. He knew that his life must be short, and so he lived and loved every hour of it with a kind of jealous intensity. He had that absolute power of 'living in the moment' which is given only to the doomed man—that kind of self-conscious happiness, the delight in still clinging to the thing whose worth you have only realized through the knowledge that it will soon be taken from you. For him, as for the schoolboy whose holidays are near their close, every hour—every minute, even—had its value. His drawing, his compositions in prose and in verse, his reading—these things were not enough to satisfy his strenuous demands on life. He was himself an accomplished musician, he was a great frequenter of concerts, and seldom, when he was in London, did he miss a 'Wagner night' at Covent Garden. He loved dining out, and, in fact, gaiety of any kind. His restlessness was, I suppose, one of the symptoms of his malady. He was always most content where there was the greatest noise and bustle, the largest number of people, and the most brilliant light. The 'domino room' at the Café Royal had always a great fascination for him: he liked the mirrors and the florid gilding, the little parties of foreigners and the smoke and the clatter of the dominoes being shuffled on the marble tables. Yet, though he took such a keen delight in all the manifestations of life, he himself, despite his energy and his high spirits, his frankness and thoughtfulness, seemed always rather remote, rather detached from ordinary conditions, a kind of independent spectator. He enjoyed life, but he was never wholly of it.

This kind of aloofness has been noted in all great artists. Their power isolates them. It is because they stand at a little distance that they can see so much. No man ever *saw* more than Beardsley. He was infinitely sensitive to the aspect of all things around him. And that, I think, was the basis of his genius. All the greatest fantastic art postulates the power to see things, unerringly, as they are.

Diminuendo

IN THE year of grace 1890, and in the beautiful autumn of that year, I was a freshman at Oxford. I remember how my tutor asked me what lectures I wished to attend, and how he laughed when I said that I wished to attend the lectures of Mr. Walter Pater. Also I remember how, one morning soon after, I went into Ryman's to order some foolish engraving for my room, and there saw, peering into a portfolio, a small, thick, rock-faced man, whose top-hat and gloves of *bright* dog-skin struck one of the many discords in that little city of learning or laughter. The serried bristles of his moustachio made for him a false-military air. I think I nearly went down when they told me that this was Pater.

Not that even in those more decadent days of my childhood did I admire the man as a stylist. Even then I was angry that he should treat English as a dead language, bored by that sedulous ritual wherewith he laid out every sentence as in a shroud—hanging, like a widower, long over its marmoreal beauty or ever he could lay it at length in his book, its sepulchre. From that laden air, the so cadaverous murmur of that sanctuary, I would hook it at the beck of any jade. The writing of Pater had never, indeed, appealed to me, ἀλλ' αἰεί, having regard to the couth solemnity of his mind, to his philosophy, his rare erudition, τινα φῶτα μέγαν καὶ καλὸν ἐδέγμην. And I suppose it was when at length I saw him that I first knew him to be fallible.

At school I had read *Marius the Epicurean* in bed and with a dark lantern. Indeed, I regarded it mainly as a tale of adventure, quite as facinating as *Midshipman Easy*, and far less hard to understand, because there were no nautical terms in it. Marryat, moreover, never made me wish to run away to sea, whilst certainly Pater did make me wish for more 'colour' in the curriculum, for a renaissance of the Farrar period, when there was always 'a sullen spirit of revolt against the authorities'; when lockers were always being broken into and marks falsified, and small boys prevented from saying their prayers, insomuch that they vowed they would no longer buy brandy for their seniors. In some schools, I am told, the pretty old custom of roasting a fourth-form boy, whole, upon Founder's Day still survives. But in my school there was less sentiment. I ended by acquiescing in the slow revolution of its wheel of work and play. I felt that at Oxford, when I should be of age to matriculate, a 'variegated dramatic life' was waiting for me. I was not a little too sanguine, alas!

How sad was my coming to the university! Where were those sweet conditions I had pictured in my boyhood? Those antique contracts? Did I ride, one sunset, through fens on a palfrey, watching the gold reflections on Magdalen Tower? Did I ride over Magdalen Bridge and hear the consonance of evening-bells and cries from the river below? Did I rein in to wonder at the raised gates of Queen's, the twisted pillars of St. Mary's, the little shops, lighted with tapers? Did bull-pups snarl at me, or dons, with bent backs, acknowledge my salute? Anyone who knows the place as it is, must see that such questions are purely rhetorical. To him I need not explain the disappointment that beset me when, after being whirled in a cab from the station to a big hotel, I wandered out into the streets. *On aurait dit* a bit of Manchester through which Apollo had once passed; for here, among the hideous trams and the brand-new bricks—here, glared at by the electric-lights that hung from poles, screamed at by boys with the *Echo* and the *Star*—here, in a riot of vulgarity, were remnants of beauty, as I discerned. There were only remnants.

Soon also I found that the life of the place, like the place, had lost its charm and its tradition. Gone were the contrasts that made it wonderful. That feud between undergraduates and dons—latent, in the old days, only at times when it behoved the two academic grades to unite against the townspeople—was one of the absurdities of the past. The townspeople now looked just like undergraduates and the dons just like townspeople. So splendid was the train-service between Oxford and London that, with hundreds of passengers daily, the one had become little better than a suburb of the other. What more could extensionists demand? As for me, I was disheartened. Bitter were the comparisons I drew between my coming to Oxford and the coming of Marius to Rome. Could it be that there was at length no beautiful environment wherein a man might sound the harmonies of his soul? Had civilization made beauty, besides adventure, so rare? I wondered what counsel Pater, insistent always upon contact with comely things, would offer to one who could nowhere find them. I had been wondering that very day when I went into Ryman's and saw him there.

When the tumult of my disillusioning was past, my mind grew clearer. I discerned that the scope of my quest for emotion must be narrowed. That abandonment of one's self to life, that merging of one's soul in bright waters, so often suggested in Pater's writing, were a counsel impossible for to-day. The quest of emotions must be no less keen, certainly, but the manner of it must be changed forthwith. To unswitch myself from my surroundings, to guard my soul from contact with the unlovely things that compassed it about, therein lay my hope. I must approach the Benign Mother with great caution. And so, while most of the freshmen were doing her honour with wine and song and wreaths of smoke, I stood aside, pondered. In such seclusion I passed my first term—ah, how often did I wonder whether I was not wasting my days, and, wondering, abandon my meditations upon the right ordering of the future! Thanks be to Athene, who threw her shadow over me in those moments of weak folly!

At the end of term I came to London. Around me seethed

swirls, eddies, torrents, violent cross-currents of human activity.
What uproar! Surely I could have no part in modern life. Yet,
yet for a while it was fascinating to watch the ways of its children.
The prodigious life of the Prince of Wales fascinated me above
all; indeed, it still fascinates me. What experience has been
withheld from His Royal Highness? Was ever so supernal a
type, as he, of mere Pleasure? How often he has watched, at
Newmarket, the scud-a-run of quivering homuncules over the
vert on horses, or, from some night-boat, the holocaust of great
wharves by the side of the Thames; raced through the blue
Solent; threaded *les coulisses*! He has danced in every palace of
every capital, played in every club. He has hunted elephants
through the jungles of India, boar through the forests of Austria,
pigs over the plains of Massachusetts. From the Castle of Aber-
geldie he has led his Princess into the frosty night, Highlanders
lighting with torches the path to the deer-larder, where lay the
wild things that had fallen to him on the crags. He has marched
the Grenadiers to chapel through the white streets of Windsor.
He has ridden through Moscow, in strange apparel, to kiss the
catafalque of more than one Tzar. For him the Rajahs of India
have spoiled their temples, and Blondin has crossed Niagara
along the tight-rope, and the Giant Guard done drill beneath the
chandeliers of the Neue Schloss. Incline he to scandal, lawyers
are proud to whisper their secrets in his ear. Be he gallant, the
ladies are at his feet. *Ennuyé*, all the wits from Bernal Osborne
to Arthur Roberts have jested for him. He has been 'present
always at the focus where the greatest number of forces unite
in their purest energy,' for it is his presence that makes those
forces unite.

'*Ennuyé?*' I asked. Indeed he never is. How could he be when
Pleasure hangs constantly upon his arm! It is those others,
overtaking her only after arduous chase, breathless and footsore,
who quickly sicken of her company, and fall fainting at her feet.
And for me, shod neither with rank nor riches, what folly to join
the chase! I began to see how small a thing it were to sacrifice
those external 'experiences,' so dear to the heart of Pater, by a
rigid, complex civilization made so hard to gain. They gave
nothing but lassitude to those who had gained them through
suffering. Even to the kings and princes, who so easily gained
them, what did they yield besides themselves? I do not suppose
that, if we were invited to give authenticated instances of intelligence on the part of our royal pets, we could fill half a column
of the *Spectator*. In fact, their lives are so full they have no time
for thought, the highest energy of man. Now, it was to thought
that *my* life should be dedicated. Action, apart from its absorption

of time, would war otherwise against the pleasures of intellect, which, for me, meant mainly the pleasures of imagination. It is only (this is a platitude) the things one has not done, the faces or places one has not seen, or seen but darkly, that have charm. It is only mystery—such mystery as besets the eyes of children—that makes things superb. I thought of the voluptuaries I had known— they seemed so sad, so ascetic almost, like poor pilgrims, raising their eyes never or ever gazing at the moon of tarnished endeavour. I thought of the round, insouciant faces of the monks at whose monastery I once broke bread, and how their eyes sparkled when they asked me of the France that lay around their walls. I thought, *pardie*, of the lurid verses written by young men who, in real life, know no haunt more lurid than a literary public-house. It was, for me, merely a problem how I could best avoid 'sensations,' 'pulsations,' and 'exquisite moments' that were not purely intellectual. I would not attempt to combine both kinds, as Pater seemed to fancy a man might. I would make myself master of some small area of physical life, a life of quiet, monotonous simplicity, exempt from all outer disturbance. I would shield my body from the world that my mind might range over it, not hurt nor fettered. As yet, however, I was in my first year at Oxford. There were many reasons that I should stay there and take my degree, reasons that I did not combat. Indeed, I was content to wait for my life.

And now that I have made my adieux to the Benign Mother, I need wait no longer. I have been casting my eye over the suburbs of London. I have taken a most pleasant little villa in ——ham, and here I shall make my home. Here there is no traffic, no harvest. Those of the inhabitants who do anything go away each morning and do it elsewhere. Here no vital forces unite. Nothing happens here. The days and the months will pass by me, bringing their sure recurrence of quiet events. In the spring-time I shall look out from my window and see the laburnum flowering in the little front garden. In summer cool syrups will come for me from the grocer's shop. Autumn will make the boughs of my mountain-ash scarlet, and, later, the asbestos in my grate will put forth its blossoms of flame. The infrequent cart of Buszard or Mudie will pass my window at all seasons. Nor will this be all. I shall have friends. Next door, there is a retired military man who has offered, in a most neighbourly way, to lend me his copy of *The Times*. On the other side of my house lives a charming family, who perhaps will call on me, now and again. I have seen them sally forth, at sundown, to catch the theatre-train; among them walked a young lady, the charm of whose figure was ill concealed by the neat waterproof that overspread her evening-dress. Some day it may be ... but I anticipate. These things will be but the cosy accompaniment of my days. For I shall contemplate the world.

I shall look forth from my window, the laburnum and the mountain-ash becoming mere silhouettes in the foreground of my vision. I shall look forth and, in my remoteness, appreciate the distant pageant of the world. Humanity will range itself in the columns of my morning paper. No pulse of life will escape me. The strife of politics, the intriguing of courts, the wreck of great vessels, wars, dramas, earthquakes, national griefs or joys; the strange sequels to divorces, even, and the mysterious suicides of land-agents at Ipswich—in all such phenomena I shall steep my exhaurient mind. *Delicias quoque bibliothecae experiar.* Tragedy, comedy, chivalry, philosophy will be mine. I shall listen to their music perpetually and their colours will dance before my eyes. I shall soar from terraces of stone upon dragons with shining wings and make war upon Olympus. From the peaks of hills I shall swoop into recondite valleys and drive the pigmies, shrieking little curses, to their caverns. It may be my whim to wander through infinite parks where the deer lie under the clustering shadow of their antlers and flee lightly over the grass; to whisper with white prophets under the elms or bind a child with a daisy-chain or, with a lady, thread my way through the acacias. I shall swim down rivers into the sea and outstrip all ships. Unhindered I shall penetrate all sanctuaries and snatch the secrets of every dim confessional.

Yes! among books that charm, and give wings to the mind, will my days be spent. I shall be ever absorbing the things great men have written; with such experience I will charge my mind to the full. Nor will I try to give anything in return. Once, in the delusion that Art, loving the recluse, would make his life happy, I wrote a little for a yellow quarterly and had that *succès de fiasco* which is always given to a young writer of talent. But the stress of creation soon overwhelmed me. Only Art with a capital H gives any consolations to her henchmen. And I, who crave no knighthood, shall write no more. I shall write no more. Already I feel myself to be a trifle outmoded. I belong to the Beardsley period. Younger men, with months of activity before them, with fresher schemes and notions, with newer enthusiasm, have pressed forward since then. *Cedo junioribus.* Indeed, I stand aside with no regret. For to be outmoded is to be a classic, if one has written well. I have acceded to the hierarchy of good scribes and rather like my niche.

Chicago, 1895.

ARTHUR SYMONS

Introduction to the Symbolist Movement in Literature

> 'It is in and through Symbols that man, consciously or unconsciously, lives, works, and has his being: those ages, moreover, are accounted the noblest which can the best recognise symbolical worth, and prize it highest.'—CARLYLE.

WITHOUT symbolism there can be no literature; indeed, not even language. What are words themselves but symbols, almost as arbitrary as the letters which compose them, mere sounds of the voice to which we have agreed to give certain significations, as we have agreed to translate these sounds by those combinations of letters? Symbolism began with the first words uttered by the first man, as he named every living thing; or before them, in heaven, when God named the world into being. And we see, in these beginnings, precisely what Symbolism in literature really is: a form of expression, at the best but approximate, essentially but arbitrary, until it has obtained the force of a convention, for an unseen reality apprehended by the consciousness. It is sometimes permitted to us to hope that our convention is indeed the reflection rather than merely the sign of that unseen reality. We have done much if we have found a recognisable sign.

'A symbol,' says Comte Goblet d'Alviella, in his book on *The Migration of Symbols*, 'might be defined as a representation which does not aim at being a reproduction.' Originally, as he points out, used by the Greeks to denote 'the two halves of the tablet they divided between themselves as a pledge of hospitality,' it came to be used of every sign, formula, or rite by which those initiated in any mystery made themselves secretly known to one another. Gradually the word extended its meaning, until it came to denote every conventional representation of idea by form, of the unseen by the visible. 'In a Symbol,' says Carlyle, 'there is concealment and yet revelation: hence therefore, by Silence and by Speech acting together, comes a double significance.' And, in that fine chapter of *Sartor Resartus*, he goes further, vindicating

53

for the word its full value: 'In the Symbol proper, what we can call a Symbol, there is ever, more or less distinctly and directly, some embodiment and revelation of the Infinite; the Infinite is made to blend itself with the Finite, to stand visible, and as it were, attainable there.'

It is in such a sense as this that the word Symbolism has been used to describe a movement which, during the last generation, has profoundly influenced the course of French literature. All such words, used of anything so living, variable, and irresponsible as literature, are, as symbols themselves must so often be, mere compromises, mere indications. Symbolism, as seen in the writers of our day, would have no value if it were not seen also, under one disguise or another, in every great imaginative writer. What distinguishes the Symbolism of our day from the Symbolism of the past is that it has now become conscious of itself, in a sense in which it was unconscious even in Gérard de Nerval, to whom I trace the particular origin of the literature which I call Symbolist. The forces which mould the thought of men change, or men's resistance to them slackens; with the change of men's thought comes a change of literature, alike in its inmost essence and in its outward form: after the world has starved its soul long enough in the contemplation and the re-arrangement of material things, comes the turn of the soul; and with it comes the literature of which I write in this volume, a literature in which the visible world is no longer a reality, and the unseen world no longer a dream.

The great epoch in French literature which preceded this epoch was that of the offshoot of Romanticism which produced Baudelaire, Flaubert, the Goncourts, Taine, Zola, Leconte de Lisle. Taine was the philosopher both of what had gone before him and of what came immediately after; so that he seems to explain at once Flaubert and Zola. It was the age of Science, the age of material things; and words, with that facile elasticity which there is in them, did miracles in the exact representation of everything that visibly existed, exactly as it existed. Even Baudelaire, in whom the spirit is always an uneasy guest at the orgy of life, had a certain theory of Realism which tortures many of his poems into strange, metallic shapes, and fills them with imitative odours, and disturbs them with a too deliberate rhetoric of the flesh. Flaubert, the one impeccable novelist who has ever lived, was resolute to be the novelist of a world in which art, formal art, was the only escape from the burden of reality, and in which the soul was of use mainly as the agent of fine literature. The Goncourts caught at Impressionism to render the fugitive aspects of a world which existed only as a thing of flat spaces, and angles, and coloured movement, in which sun and shadow were the artists; as moods, no less flitting, were the artists of the merely receptive consciousness of men and women. Zola has tried to build in brick and mortar inside the covers of a book; he is quite sure that the soul is a nervous fluid, which he is quite sure some man of science is about to catch for us, as a man of science has bottled the air, a pretty, blue liquid. Leconte de Lisle turned the world to stone, but saw, beyond the world, only a pause from misery in a Nirvana never subtilised to the Eastern ecstasy. And, with all these writers, form aimed above all things at being precise, at saying rather than suggesting, at saying what they had to say so completely that nothing remained over, which it might be the business of the reader to divine. And so they have expressed, finally, a certain aspect of the world; and some of them have carried style to a point beyond which the style that says, rather than suggests, cannot go. The whole of that movement comes to a splendid funeral in Heredia's sonnets, in which the literature of form says its last word, and dies.

Meanwhile, something which is vaguely called Decadence had come into being. That name, rarely used with any precise meaning, was usually either hurled as a reproach or hurled back as a defiance. It pleased some young men in various countries to call themselves Decadents, with all the thrill of unsatisfied virtue masquerading as uncomprehended vice. As a matter of fact, the term is in its place only when applied to style; to that ingenious deformation of the language, in Mallarmé, for instance, which can be compared with what we are accustomed to call the Greek and Latin of the Decadence. No doubt perversity of form and perversity of matter are often found together, and, among the lesser men especially, experiment was carried far, not only in the direction of style. But a movement which in this sense might be called Decadent could but have been a straying aside from the main road of literature. Nothing, not even conventional virtue, is so provincial as conventional vice; and the desire to 'bewilder the middle-classes' is itself middle-class. The interlude, half a mock-interlude, of Decadence, diverted the attention of the critics while something more serious was in preparation. That something more serious has crystallised, for the time, under the form of Symbolism, in which art returns to the one pathway, leading through beautiful things to the eternal beauty.

In most of the writers whom I have dealt with as summing up in themselves all that is best in Symbolism, it will be noticed that the form is very carefully elaborated, and seems to count for at least as much as in those writers of whose over-possession by form I have complained. Here, however, all this elaboration comes from a very different motive, and leads to other ends. There is such a thing as perfecting form that form may be annihilated. All the art of Verlaine is in bringing verse to a bird's song, the art of Mallarmé in bringing verse to the song of an orchestra. In Villiers de l'Isle-Adam drama becomes an embodiment of spiritual forces, in Maeterlinck not even their embodiment, but the remote sound of their voices. It is all an attempt to spiritualise literature, to evade the old bondage of rhetoric, the old bondage of exteriority. Description is banished that beautiful things may be evoked, magically; the regular beat of verse is broken in order that words may fly, upon subtler wings. Mystery is no longer feared, as the great mystery in whose midst we are islanded was feared by those to whom that unknown sea was only a great void. We are coming closer to nature, as we seem to shrink from it with something of horror, disdaining to catalogue the trees of the forest. And as we brush aside the accidents of daily life, in which men and women imagine that they are alone touching reality, we come closer to humanity, to everything in humanity that may have begun before the world and may outlast it.

Here, then, in this revolt against exteriority, against rhetoric, against a materialistic tradition; in this endeavour to disengage the ultimate essence, the soul, of whatever exists and can be realised by the consciousness; in this dutiful waiting upon every symbol by which the soul of things can be made visible; literature, bowed down by so many burdens, may at last attain liberty, and its authentic speech. In attaining this liberty, it accepts a heavier burden; for in speaking to us so intimately, so solemnly, as only religion had hitherto spoken to us, it becomes itself a kind of religion, with all the duties and responsibilities of the sacred ritual.

STORIES

AUBREY VINCENT BEARDSLEY
(1872-1898)

Aubrey Beardsley was born on 21 August 1872 at Brighton, and was educated at the Grammar School there. In 1894 he was appointed art editor of *The Yellow Book* till the scandals attendant on the Wilde trial in 1895 led to his dismissal, after which he was associated with that magazine's rival *The Savoy*. Beardsley was consumptive all his life, and died at Mentone on 16 March 1898, having become a convert to Rome in March of the preceding year.

Famous for his black-and-white drawings, Beardsley liked also to think of himself as a man-of-letters, and his three poems and unfinished novel have a grace and felicity all their own.

Under the Hill

TO
THE MOST EMINENT AND REVERED PRINCE

GIULIO POLDO PEZZOLI

**CARDINAL OF THE HOLY ROMAN CHURCH
TITULAR BISHOP OF S. MARIA IN TRASTEVERE
ARCHBISHOP OF OSTIA AND VELLETRI
NUNCIO TO THE HOLY SEE
IN
NICARAGUA AND PATAGONIA
A FATHER TO THE POOR
A REFORMER OF ECCLESIASTICAL DISCIPLINE
A PATTERN OF LEARNING
WISDOM AND HOLINESS OF LIFE
THIS BOOK IS DEDICATED WITH DUE REVERENCE
BY HIS HUMBLE SERVITOR
A SCRIVENER AND LIMNER OF WORLDLY THINGS
WHO MADE THIS BOOK**

AUBREY BEARDSLEY

MOST EMINENT PRINCE,

I KNOW NOT BY WHAT MISCHANCE THE WRITING OF EPISTLES DEDICATORY HAS FALLEN INTO DISUSE, WHETHER THROUGH THE VANITY OF AUTHORS OR THE HUMILITY OF PATRONS. BUT THE PRACTICE SEEMS TO ME SO VERY BEAUTIFUL AND BECOMING THAT I HAVE VENTURED TO MAKE AN ESSAY IN THE MODEST ART, AND LAY WITH FORMALITIES MY FIRST BOOK AT YOUR FEET. I HAVE, IT MUST BE CONFESSED, MANY FEARS LEST I SHALL BE ARRAIGNED OF PRESUMPTION IN CHOOSING SO EXALTED A NAME AS YOUR OWN TO PLACE AT THE BEGINNING OF THIS HISTORY; BUT I HOPE THAT SUCH A CENSURE WILL NOT BE TOO LIGHTLY PASSED UPON ME, FOR IF I AM GUILTY IT IS BUT A MOST NATURAL PRIDE THAT THE ACCIDENTS OF MY LIFE SHOULD ALLOW ME TO SAIL THE LITTLE PINNACE OF MY WIT UNDER YOUR PROTECTION.

BUT THOUGH I CAN CLEAR MYSELF OF SUCH A CHARGE, I AM STILL MINDED TO USE THE TONGUE OF APOLOGY, FOR WITH WHAT FACE CAN I OFFER YOU A BOOK TREATING OF SO VAIN AND FANTASTICAL A THING AS LOVE? I KNOW THAT IN THE JUDGMENT OF MANY THE AMOROUS PASSION IS ACCOUNTED A SHAMEFUL THING AND RIDICULOUS; INDEED IT MUST BE CONFESSED THAT MORE BLUSHES HAVE RISEN FOR LOVE'S SAKE THAN FOR ANY OTHER CAUSE, AND THAT LOVERS ARE AN ETERNAL LAUGHING-STOCK. STILL, AS THE BOOK WILL BE FOUND TO CONTAIN MATTER OF DEEPER IMPORT THAN MERE VENERY, INASMUCH AS IT TREATS OF THE GREAT CONTRITION OF ITS CHIEFEST CHARACTER, AND OF CANONICAL THINGS IN CERTAIN PAGES, I AM NOT WITHOUT HOPES THAT YOUR EMINENCE WILL PARDON MY WRITING OF THE HILL OF VENUS, FOR WHICH EXTRAVAGANCE LET MY YOUTH EXCUSE ME.

THEN I MUST CRAVE YOUR FORGIVENESS FOR ADDRESSING YOU IN A LANGUAGE OTHER THAN THE ROMAN, BUT MY SMALL FREEDOM IN LATINITY FORBIDS ME TO WANDER BEYOND THE IDIOM OF MY VERNACULAR. I WOULD NOT FOR THE WORLD THAT YOUR DELICATE SOUTHERN EAR SHOULD BE OFFENDED BY A BARBAROUS ASSAULT OF RUDE AND GOTHIC WORDS; BUT METHINKS NO LANGUAGE IS RUDE THAT CAN BOAST POLITE WRITERS, AND NOT A FEW SUCH HAVE FLOURISHED IN THIS COUNTRY IN TIMES PAST, BRINGING OUR SPEECH TO VERY GREAT PERFECTION. IN THE PRESENT AGE, ALAS! OUR PENS ARE RAVISHED BY UNLETTERED AUTHORS AND UNMANNERED CRITICS, THAT MAKE A HAVOC RATHER THAN A BUILDING, A WILDERNESS RATHER THAN A GARDEN. BUT, ALACK! WHAT BOOTS IT TO DROP TEARS UPON THE PRETERIT?

IT IS NOT OF OUR OWN SHORTCOMINGS THOUGH, BUT OF YOUR NOW GREAT MERITS THAT I SHOULD SPEAK, ELSE I SHOULD BE FORGETFUL

OF THE DUTIES I HAVE DRAWN UPON MYSELF IN ELECTING TO ADDRESS YOU IN A DEDICATION. IT IS OF YOUR NOBLE VIRTUES (THOUGH ALL THE WORLD KNOW OF 'EM), YOUR TASTE AND WIT, YOUR CARE FOR LETTERS, AND VERY REAL REGARD FOR THE ARTS THAT I MUST BE THE PROCLAIMER.

THOUGH IT BE TRUE THAT ALL MEN HAVE SUFFICIENT WIT TO PASS A JUDGMENT ON THIS OR THAT, AND NOT A FEW SUFFICIENT IMPUDENCE TO PRINT THE SAME (THE LAST BEING COMMONLY ACCOUNTED CRITICS), I HAVE EVER HELD THAT THE CRITICAL FACULTY IS MORE RARE THAN THE INVENTIVE. IT IS A FACULTY YOUR EMINENCE POSSESSES IN SO GREAT A DEGREE THAT YOUR PRAISE OR BLAME IS SOMETHING ORACULAR, YOUR UTTERANCE INFALLIBLE AS GREAT GENIUS OR AS A BEAUTIFUL WOMAN. YOUR MIND, I KNOW, REJOICING IN FINE DISTINCTIONS AND SUBTLE PROCEDURES OF THOUGHT, BEAUTIFULLY DISCURSIVE RATHER THAN HASTILY CONTRIBUTED, HAS FOUND IN CRITICISM ITS HAPPIEST EXERCISE. IT IS A PITY THAT SO PERFECT A MÆCENAS SHOULD HAVE NO HORACE TO BEFRIEND, NO GEORGICS TO ACCEPT; FOR THE OFFICES AND FUNCTION OF PATRON OR CRITIC MUST OF NECESSITY BE LESSENED IN AN AGE OF LITTLE MEN AND LITTLE WORK. IN TIMES PAST IT WAS NOTHING DEROGATORY FOR GREAT PRINCES AND MEN OF STATE TO EXTEND THEIR LOVES AND FAVOUR TO POETS, FOR THEREBY THEY RECEIVED AS MUCH HONOUR AS THEY CONFERRED. DID NOT PRINCE FESTUS WITH PRIDE TAKE THE MASTERWORK OF JULIAN INTO HIS PROTECTION, AND WAS NOT THE ÆNEIS A PRETTY THING TO OFFER CÆSAR?

LEARNING WITHOUT APPRECIATION IS A THING OF NAUGHT, BUT I KNOW NOT WHICH IS GREATEST IN YOU—YOUR LOVE OF THE ARTS, OR YOUR KNOWLEDGE OF 'EM. WHAT WONDER THEN THAT I AM STUDIOUS TO PLEASE YOU, AND DESIROUS OF YOUR PROTECTION? HOW DEEPLY THANKFUL I AM FOR YOUR PAST AFFECTIONS YOU KNOW WELL, YOUR GREAT KINDNESS AND LIBERALITY HAVING FAR OUTGONE MY SLIGHT MERITS AND SMALL ACCOMPLISHMENTS THAT SEEMED SCARCE TO WARRANT ANY FAVOUR. ALAS! 'TIS A SLIGHT OFFERING I MAKE YOU NOW, BUT IF AFTER GLANCING INTO ITS PAGES (SAY OF AN EVENING UPON YOUR TERRACE) YOU SHOULD DEEM IT WORTHY OF THE REMOTEST PLACE IN YOUR PRINCELY LIBRARY, THE KNOWLEDGE THAT IT RESTED THERE WOULD BE REWARD SUFFICIENT FOR MY LABOURS, AND A CROWNING HAPPINESS TO MY PLEASURE IN THE WRITING OF THIS SLENDER BOOK.

THE HUMBLE AND OBEDIENT SERVANT OF YOUR EMINENCE,

AUBREY BEARDSLEY.

CHAPTER I

HOW THE CHEVALIER TANNHÄUSER ENTERED INTO THE HILL OF VENUS

The Chevalier Tannhäuser, having lighted off his horse, stood doubtfully for a moment beneath the ombre gateway of the mysterious Hill, troubled with an exquisite fear lest a day's travel should have too cruelly undone the laboured niceness of his dress. His hand, slim and gracious as La Marquise du Deffand's in the drawing by Carmontelle, played nervously about the gold hair that fell upon his shoulders like a finely-curled peruke, and from point to point of a precise toilet the fingers wandered, quelling the little mutinies of cravat and ruffle.

It was taper-time; when the tired earth puts on its cloak of mists and shadows, when the enchanted woods are stirred with light footfalls and slender voices of the fairies, when all the air is full of delicate influences, and even the beaux, seated at their dressing-tables, dream a little.

A delicious moment, thought Tannhäuser, to slip into exile.

The place where he stood waved drowsily with strange flowers, heavy with perfume, dripping with odours. Gloomy and nameless weeds not to be found in Mentzelius. Huge moths, so richly winged they must have banqueted upon tapestries and royal stuffs, slept on the pillars that flanked either side of the gateway, and the eyes of all the moths remained open and were burning and bursting with a mesh of veins. The pillars were fashioned in some pale stone and rose up like hymns in the praise of pleasure, for from cap to base, each one was carved with loving sculptures, showing such a cunning invention and such a curious knowledge, that Tannhäuser lingered not a little in reviewing them. They surpassed all that Japan has ever pictured from her maisons vertes, all that was ever painted in the cool bathrooms of Cardinal La Motte, and even outdid the astonishing illustrations to Jones's 'Nursery Numbers.'

'A pretty portal,' murmured the Chevalier, correcting his sash.

As he spoke, a faint sound of singing was breathed out from the mountain, faint music as strange and distant as sea-legends that are heard in shells.

'The Vespers of Venus, I take it,' said Tannhäuser, and struck a few chords of accompaniment, ever so lightly, upon his little lute. Softly across the spell-bound threshold the song floated and wreathed itself about the subtle columns, till the moths were touched with passion and moved quaintly in their sleep. One of them was awakened by the intenser notes of the Chevalier's lute-strings, and fluttered into the cave. Tannhäuser felt it was his cue for entry.

'Adieu,' he exclaimed with an inclusive gesture, 'and goodbye, Madonna,' as the cold circle of the moon began to show, beautiful and full of enchantments. There was a shadow of sentiment in his voice as he spoke the words.

'Would to heaven,' he sighed, 'I might receive the assurance of a looking-glass before I make my debut! However, as she is a goddess, I doubt not her eyes are a little sated with perfection, and may not be displeased to see it crowned with a tiny fault.'

A wild rose had caught upon the trimmings of his ruff, and in the first flush of displeasure he would have struck it brusquely away, and most severely punished the offending flower. But the ruffled mood lasted only a moment, for there was something so deliciously incongruous in the hardy petal's invasion of so delicate a thing, that Tannhäuser withheld the finger of resentment and vowed that the wild rose should stay where it had clung —a passport, as it were, from the upper to the lower world.

'The very excess and violence of the fault,' he said, 'will be its excuse,' and, undoing a tangle in the tassel of his stick, stepped into the shadowy corridor that ran into the bosom of the wan hill—stepped with the admirable aplomb and unwrinkled suavity of Don John.

CHAPTER II

OF THE MANNER IN WHICH VENUS WAS COIFFED AND PREPARED FOR SUPPER

Before a toilet that shone like the altar of Notre Dame des Victoires, Venus was seated in a little dressing-gown of black and heliotrope. The coiffeur Cosmé was caring for her scented chevelure, and with tiny silver tongs, warm from the caresses of the flame, made delicious intelligent curls that fell as lightly as a breath about her forehead and over her eyebrows, and clustered like tendrils round her neck. Her three favourite girls, Pappelarde, Blanchemains and Loreyne, waited immediately upon her with perfume and powder in delicate flacons and frail cassolettes, and held in porcelain jars the ravishing paints prepared by Châteline for those cheeks and lips that had grown a little pale with anguish of exile. Her three favourite boys, Claude, Clair and Sarrasine, stood amorously about with salver, fan and napkin. Millamant held a slight tray of slippers, Minette some tender gloves, La Popelinière—mistress of the robes—was ready with a frock of

yellow and white, La Zambinella bore the jewels, Florizel some
flowers, Amadour a box of various pins, and Vadius a box of
sweets. Her doves, ever in attendance, walked about the room that
was panelled with the gallant paintings of Jean Baptiste Dorat, and
some dwarfs and doubtful creatures sat here and there lolling out
their tongues, pinching each other, and behaving oddly enough.
Sometimes Venus gave them little smiles.

As the toilet was in progress, Mrs. Marsuple, the fat manicure
and fardeuse, strode in and seated herself by the side of the
dressing-table, greeting Venus with an intimate nod. She wore a
gown of white watered silk with gold lace trimmings, and a
velvet necklet of false vermilion. Her hair hung in bandeaux over
her ears, passing into a huge chignon at the back of her head,
and the hat, wide-brimmed and hung with a vallance of pink
muslin, was floral with red roses.

Mrs. Marsuple's voice was full of salacious unction; she had
terrible little gestures with the hands, strange movements with the
shoulders, a short respiration that made surprising wrinkles in
her bodice, a corrupt skin, large horny eyes, a parrot's nose, a
small loose mouth, great flaccid cheeks, and chin after chin. She
was a wise person, and Helen loved her more than any of her
servants, and had a hundred pet names for her, such as Dear
Toad, Pretty Poll, Cock Robin, Dearest Lip, Touchstone, Little
Cough Drop, Bijou, Buttons, Dear Heart, Dick-Dock, Mrs.
Manly, Little Nipper, Cochon-de-lait, Naughty-naughty, Blessed
Thing, and Trump. The talk that passed between Mrs. Marsuple
and her mistress was of that excellent kind that passes between
old friends, a perfect understanding giving to scraps of phrases
their full meaning, and to the merest reference a point. Naturally
Tannhäuser the newcomer was discussed a little. Venus had not
seen him yet, and asked a score of questions on his account that
were delightfully to the point. Mrs. Marsuple told the story of his
arrival, his curious wandering in the gardens, and calm satisfac-
tion with all he saw there, his impromptu affection for a slender
girl upon the first terrace, of the crowd of frocks that gathered
round and pelted him with roses, of the graceful way he defended
himself with his mask, and of the queer reverence he made to the
God of all gardens, kissing that deity with a pilgrim's devotion.
Just then Tannhäuser was at the baths, and was creating a
favourable impression.

The report and the coiffing were completed at the same
moment.

'Cosmé,' said Venus, 'you have been quite sweet and quite
brilliant, you have surpassed yourself tonight.'

'Madam flatters me,' replied the antique old thing, with a

girlish giggle under his black satin mask. 'Gad, Madam; sometimes I believe I have no talent in the world, but tonight I must confess to a touch of the vain mood.'

It would pain me horribly to tell you about the painting of her face; suffice it that the sorrowful work was accomplished; frankly, magnificently, and without a shadow of deception.

Venus slipped away the dressing-gown, and rose before the mirror in a flutter of frilled things. She was adorably tall and slender. Her neck and shoulders were wonderfully drawn, and the little malicious breasts were full of the irritation of loveliness that can never be entirely comprehended, or ever enjoyed to the utmost. Her arms and hands were loosely but delicately articulated, and her legs were divinely long. From the hip to the knee, twenty-two inches; from the knee to the heel, twenty-two inches, as befitted a goddess.

I should like to speak more particularly about her, for generalities are not of the slightest service in a description. But I am afraid that an enforced silence here and there would leave such numerous gaps in the picture that it had better not be begun at all than left unfinished. Those who have seen Venus only in the Vatican, in the Louvre, in the Uffizi, or in the British Museum, can have no idea of how very beautiful and sweet she looked. Not at all like the lady in 'Lemprière.'

Mrs. Marsuple grew quite lyrical over the dear little person, and pecked at her arms with kisses.

'Dear Tongue, you must really behave yourself,' said Venus, and called Millament to bring her the slippers.

The tray was freighted with the most exquisite and shapely pantoufles, sufficient to make Cluny a place of naught. There were shoes of grey and black and brown suède, of white silk and rose satin, and velvet and sarcenet; there were some of sea-green sewn with cherry blossoms, some of red with willow branches, and some of grey with bright-winged birds. There were heels of silver, of ivory, and of gilt; there were buckles of very precious stones set in most strange and esoteric devices; there were ribbons tied and twisted into cunning forms; there were buttons so beautiful that the buttonholes might have no pleasure till they closed upon them; there were soles of delicate leathers scented with maréchale, and linings of soft stuffs scented with the juice of July flowers. But Venus, finding none of them to her mind, called for a discarded pair of blood-red maroquin, diapered with pearls. They looked very distinguished over her white silk stockings. As the tray was being carried away, the capricious Florizel snatched as usual a slipper from it, and fitted the foot over his penis, and made the necessary movements. That was Florizel's little caprice. Meantime, La Popelinière stepped forward with the frock.

'I shan't wear one tonight,' said Venus. Then she slipped on her gloves.

When the toilet was at an end all her doves clustered round her feet loving to frôler her ankles with their plumes, and the dwarfs clapped their hands, and put their fingers between their lips and whistled. Never before had Venus been so radiant and compelling. Spiridion, in the corner, looked up from his game of Spellicans and trembled. Claude and Clair, pale with pleasure, stroked and touched her with their delicate hands, and wrinkled her stockings with their nervous lips, and smoothed them with their thin fingers; and Sarrasine undid her garters and kissed them inside and put them on again, pressing her thighs with his mouth. The dwarfs grew very daring, I can tell you. There was almost a mêlée. They illustrated pages 72 and 73 of Delvau's Dictionary.

In the middle of it all, Pranzmungel announced that supper was ready upon the fifth terrace. 'Ah!' cried Venus, 'I'm famished!'

ARTHUR SYMONS

An Autumn City

To DANIEL ROSERRA life was a matter of careful cultivation. He respected nature, for what might be cunningly extracted from nature; provided only that one's aim was a quite personal thing, willingly subject to surroundings on its way to the working out of itself. He tended his soul as one might tend some rare plant; careful above most things of the earth it was to take root in. And so he thought much of the influence of places, of the image a place makes for itself in the consciousness, of all that it might do in the formation of a beautiful or uncomely disposition. Places had virtues of their own for him; he supposed that he had the quality of divining their secrets; at all events, if they were places to which he could possibly be sensitive. Much of this time was spent in travelling, in a leisurely way, about Europe; not for the sake of seeing anything in particular, for he had no interest in historical associations or in the remains of ugly things that happened to be old, or in visiting the bric-à-brac museums of the fine arts which make some of the more tolerable countries tedious. He chose a city, a village, or a seashore for its charm, its appeal to him personally; nothing else mattered.

When Roserra was forty he fell in love, quite suddenly, though he had armed himself, as he imagined, against such disturbances of the aesthetic life, and was invulnerable. He had always said that a woman was like a liqueur: a delightful luxury, to be taken with discretion. He feared the influence of a companion in his delicate satisfactions: he realised that a woman might not even be a sympathetic companion. He had, it is true, often wished to try the experiment, a risky one, of introducing a woman to one of his friends among cities; it was a temptation, but he remembered how rarely such introductions work well among people. Would the cities be any more fortunate?

When, however, he fell in love, all hesitation was taken out of his hands by the mere force of things. Livia Dawlish was remarkably handsome, some people thought her beautiful; she was tall and dark, and had a sulky, enigmatical look that teased and attracted him. Some who knew her very well said that it meant nothing, and was merely an accident of colour and form, like the green eye of the cat or the golden eye of the buffalo. Roserra tried to study her, but he could get no point of view. He felt something that he had never felt before, and this something was like a magnetic current flowing subtly from her to him; perhaps, like the magnetic rocks in the 'Arabian Nights,' ready to draw out all the nails and bolts of his ship, and drown him among the wrecked splinters of his life.

He was rich, not too old, of a good Cornish family; he could be the most charming companion in the world; he knew so many things and so many places and was never tedious about them: Livia thought him on the whole the most suitable husband whom she was likely to meet. She was happy when he asked her to marry him, and she married him without a misgiving. She was not reflective.

After the marriage they went straight to Paris, and Roserra was surprised and delighted to find how childishly happy Livia could be among new surroundings. She had always wanted to see Paris, because of its gaiety, its bright wickedness, its names of pleasure and fashion. Everything delighted her; she seemed even to admire a little indiscriminatingly. She thought the Sainte-Chapelle the most beautiful thing in Paris.

They went back to London with more luggage than they had brought with them, and for six months Livia was quite happy. She wore her Paris hats and gowns, she was admired, she went to the theatre; she seemed to get on with Roserra even better than she had expected.

During all this time Roserra seemed to have found out very little about his wife. It gave him more pleasure to do what she wanted than it had ever given him to carry out his own wishes. So far, they had never had a dispute; he seemed to have put his own individuality aside as if it no longer meant anything to him. But he had not yet discovered her individuality from among her crowds of little likes and dislikes, which meant nothing. Nothing had come out yet from behind those enigmatical eyes; but he was waiting; they would open, and there would be treasure there.

Gradually, while he was waiting, his old self began to come back to him. He must do as he had always wanted to do: introduce the most intimate of his cities to a woman. Autumn was beginning; he thought of Arles, which was an autumn city, and the city which meant more to him than almost any other. He must share Arles with Livia.

Livia had heard of the Arlesiennes, she remembered Paris, and, though she was a little reluctant to leave the new London into

which she had come since her marriage, she consented without
apparent unwillingness.

They went by sea to Marseilles, and Livia wished they were not
going any further. Roserra smiled a little satisfied smile; she was
so pleased with even slight, superficial things, she could get
pleasure out of the empty sunlight and obvious sea of Marseilles.
When the deeper appeal of Arles came to her, that new world
in which one went clean through the exteriorities of modern life,
how she would respond to it!

They reached Arles in the afternoon, and drove to the little
old-fashioned house which Roserra had taken in the square
which goes uphill from the Amphitheatre, with the church of
Notre Dame la Major in the corner. Livia looked about her
vividly as the cab rattled round twenty sharp angles, in the midst
of narrow streets, on that perilous journey. Here were the
Arlesiennes, standing at doorways, walking along the pavements,
looking out of windows. She scarcely liked to admit to herself
that she had seen prettier faces elsewhere. The costume, certainly,
was as fine as its reputation; she would get one, she thought, to
wear, for amusement, in London. And the women were a noble
race; they walked nobly, they had beautiful black hair, sometimes
stately and impressive features. But she had expected so much
more than that; she had expected a race of goddesses, and she
found no more than a townful of fine-looking peasants.

'Do not judge too quickly,' said Roserra to her; 'you must
judge neither the place nor the people until you have lived yourself into their midst. The first time I came here I was disappointed.
Gradually I began to see why it was that even the guide-books
tell you to come to this quiet, out-of-the-way place, made up of
hovels that were once palaces.'

'I will wait,' said Livia contentedly. The queer little house,
with its homely furniture, the gentle, picturesque woman who
met her at the door, amused her. It was certainly an adventure.

Next day, and the days following, they walked about the town,
Roserra felt that his own luxuriating sensations could hardly fail
to be shared by Livia, though she said little and seemed at times
absent-minded. They strolled among the ruins of the theatre
begun under Augustus, and among the coulisses of the great
amphitheatre; they sat on the granite steps; they went up the
hundred steps of the western tower. From the cloisters of St.
Trophime they went across to the museum opposite, where a
kindly little dwarf showed them the altar to Leda, the statue of
Mithras, and the sarcophagi with the Good Shepherd. He sold
them some photographs of Arlesian women; one was very
beautiful. 'That is my sister,' he said shyly.

When the soul of Autumn made for itself a body, it made Arles. An autumn city, hinting of every gentle, resigned, reflective way of fading out of life, of effacing oneself in a world to which one no longer attaches any value; always remembering itself, always looking into a mournfully veiled mirror which reflects something at least of what it was, Arles sits in the midst of its rocky plains, by the side of its river, among the tombs. Everything there seems to grow out of death, and to be returning thither. The town rises above its ruins, does not seem to be even yet detached from them. The remains of the theatre look down on the public garden; one comes suddenly on a Roman obelisk and the fragments of Roman walls; a Roman column has been built into the wall of one of the two hotels which stand in the Forum, now the Place du Forum; and the modern, the comparatively modern houses, have an air which is neither new nor old, but entirely sympathetic with what is old. They are faded, just a little dilapidated, not caring to distinguish themselves from the faint colours, the aged slumber, of the very ancient things about them.

Livia tried to realise what it was that charmed Roserra in all this. To her there was no comfort in it; it depressed her; in the air itself there was something of decay. There was a smell of dead leaves everywhere, the moisture of stone, the sodden dampness of earth, water forming into little pools on the ground, creeping out of the earth and into the earth again. There was dust on everything; the trees that close in almost the whole city as with a leafy wall were dust-grey even in sunlight. The Aliscamps seemed to her drearier than even a modern cemetery, and she wondered what it was that drew Roserra to them, with a kind of fascination. On the way there, along the Avenue Victor Hugo, there were some few signs of life; the cafés, the Zouaves going in and out of their big barrack, the carts coming in from the country; and in the evening the people walked there. But she hated the little melancholy public garden at the side, with its paths curving upwards to the ruined walls and arches of the Roman theatre, its low balustrades of crumbling stone, its faint fountains, greenish grey. It was a place, she thought, in which no one could ever be young or happy; and the road which went past it did but lead to the tombs. Roserra told her that Dante, when he was in hell, and saw the 'modo più amaro' in which the people there are made into alleys of living tombs, remembered Arles:

Si com' ad ove 'l Rodano stagna.

She laughed uneasily, with a half shudder. The tombs are moved aside now from the Aliscamps, into the little secluded Allée des

Tombeaux, where they line both sides of the way, empty stone trough after empty stone trough, with here and there a more pompous sarcophagus. There is a quiet path between them, which she did not even like to walk in, leading to the canal and the bowling-green; and in the evening the old men creep out and sit among the tombs.

At first there was bright sunshine every day, but the sun scorched; and then it set in to rain. One night a storm wakened her, and it seemed to her that she had never heard such thunder, or seen such lightning, as that which shook the old roof under which she lay, and blazed and flickered at the window until it seemed to be licking up the earth with liquid fire. The storm faded out in a morning of faint sunshine; only the rain clung furtively about the streets all day.

Day after day it rained, and Livia sat in the house, listlessly reading the novels which she had brought with her, or staring with fierce impatience out of the window. The rain came down steadily, ceaselessly, drawing a wet grey curtain over the city. Roserra liked that softened aspect which came over things in this uncomfortable weather; he walked every day through the streets in which the water gathered in puddles between the paving-stones, and ran in little streams down the gutters; he found a kind of autumnal charm in the dripping trees and soaked paths of the Aliscamps; a peaceful, and to him pathetic and pleasant, odour of decay. Livia went out with him once, muffled in a long cloak, and keeping her whole face carefully under the umbrella. She wanted to know where he was taking her, and why; she shivered, sneezed, and gave one or two little coughs. When she saw the ground of the Aliscamps, and the first trees began to drip upon her umbrella with a faint tap-tapping on the strained silk, she turned resolutely, and hurried Roserra straight back to the house.

After that she stayed indoors day after day, getting more irritable every day. She took up one book after another, read a little, and then laid it down. She walked to and fro in the narrow room, with nothing, as she said, to think about, and nothing to see if she looked out of the window. There was the square, every stone polished by the rain; the other houses in the square, most of them shuttered; the little church in the corner, with its monotonous bell, its few worshippers. She knew them all; they were mostly women, plain, elderly women; not one of them had any interest, or indeed existence, for her. She wondered vaguely why they went backwards and forwards, between their houses and the church, in such a regular way. Could it really amuse them? Could they really believe certain things so firmly that it was worth while taking all that trouble in order to be on the right side at last? She supposed so, and ended her speculations.

When Roserra was with her, he annoyed her by not seeming to mind the weather. He would come in from a walk, and, if she seemed to be busy reading, would sit down cheerfully by the stove, and really read the book which he had in his hand. She looked at him over the pages of hers, hating to see him occupied when she could not fix her mind on anything. She felt imprisoned; not that she really wanted to go out: it was the not being able to that fretted her.

About the time when, if she had been in London, she would have had tea, the uneasiness came over her most actively. She would go upstairs to her room, and sit watching herself pityingly in the glass; or she would try on hat after hat, hats which had come from Paris, and were meant for Paris or London, hats which she could not possibly wear here, where her smallest and simplest ones seemed out of place. Sometimes she brought herself back into a good temper by the mere pleasurable feel of the things; and she would run downstairs forgetting that she was in Arles.

One afternoon, when she was in one of her easiest moods, Roserra persuaded her to attend Benediction with him at the church of Notre Dame la Major, in the corner of the square. The church was quite dark, and she could only dimly see the high-altar, draped in white, with something white rising up from its midst, like a figure mysteriously poised among the unlighted candles. Hooded figures passed, and knelt with bowed heads; presently a light passed across the church, and a lamp was let down by a chain, lighted, and drawn up again to its place. Then a few candles were lighted, and only then did she see the priest kneeling motionless before the altar. The chanting was very homely, like that in a village church; there was even the village church's harmonium; but the monotony of one air repeated over and over again brought even to Livia some sense of a harmony between this half-drowsy service and the slumbering city outside. They waited until the service was over, the priests went out, the lamps and the candles were extinguished, and the hooded figures, after a little silence, began to move again in the dimness of the church.

Sometimes she would go with Roserra to the cloisters of St. Trophime, where Arles, as he said, seemed to withdraw into its most intimate self. The oddness of the whole place amused her. Every side was built in a different century: the north in the ninth, the east in the thirteenth, the west in the fourteenth, and the south in the sixteenth; and the builders, century by century, have gathered into this sadly battered court a little of the curious piety of age after age, working here to perpetuate, not only the legends of the Church, but the legends that have their home about Arles. Again and again, among these naïve sculptures, one sees the local dragon, the man-eating Tarasque who has given its name to Tarascon. The place is full of monsters, and of figures tortured into strange dislocations. Adam swings ape-like among the branches of the apple-tree, biting at the leaves before he reaches the apple. Flames break out among companies of the damned, and the devil sits enthroned above his subjects. A gentle Doctor of the Church holding a book, and bending his head meditatively sideways, was shown to Livia as King Solomon; with, of course, in the slim saint on the other side of the pillar, the Queen of Sheba. Broken escutcheons, carved in stone, commemorate bishops on the walls. There is no order, or division of time; one seems shut off equally from the present and from any appreciable moment of the past; shut in with the same vague and timeless Autumn that has moulded Arles into its own image.

But it was just this, for which Roserra loved Arles above all other places, that made Livia more and more acutely miserable. Wandering about the streets which bring one back always to one's starting-point, or along the boulevards which suggest the beginning of the country, but set one no further into it, nothing seems to matter very much, for nothing seems very much to exist. In Livia, as Roserra was gradually finding out, there was none of that sympathetic submissiveness to things which meant for him so much of the charm of life. She wanted something definite to do, somewhere definite to go; her mind took no subtle colour from things, nor was there any active world within her which could transmute everything into its own image. She was dependent on an exterior world, cut to a narrow pattern, and, outside that, nothing had any meaning for her. He began to wonder if he had made the irremediable mistake, and, in his preoccupation with that uneasy idea, everything seemed changed; he, too, began to grow restless.

Meanwhile Livia was deciding that she certainly had made a mistake, unless she could, after all, succeed in getting her own way; and to do that she would have to take things into her own hands, much more positively than she had yet done. She would walk with him when it was fine, because there was nothing else to do. Once they walked out to the surprising remains of the abbey of Mont-Major, and it began to rain, and they lingered uncomfortably about the ruins and in the subterranean chapel. She walked back with him, nursing a fine hatred in silence. She turned it over in her heart, and it grew and gathered, like a snowball rolled over and over in the snow. It was comprehensive

and unreasoning, and it forgot the small grievance out of which
it rose, in a sense of the vast grievance into which it had swollen.
To Roserra such moods, which were now becoming frequent,
were unintelligible, and he suffered from them like one who has to
find his way through a camp of his enemies in the dark.

When they got back to the house, Livia would silently take up a
book and sit motionless for hours, turning over the pages without
raising her eyes, or showing a consciousness of his presence. He
pretended to do the same, but his eyes wandered continually, and
he had to read every page twice over. He wanted to speak, but
never knew what to say, when she was in this prickly state of
irritation. To her, his critical way of waiting, and doing nothing,
became an oppression. And his silence, and what she supposed
to be his indifference, grew upon her like a heavy weight, until
the silent woman, who sat there reading sullenly, felt the impulse
to rise and fling away the book, and shriek aloud.

Livia did not say that she wished to go away from Arles,
anywhere from Arles, but the desire spoke in all her silences.
She made no complaint, but Roserra saw an unfriendliness
growing up in her eyes which terrified him. She held him, as she
had held him since their first meeting, by a kind of magnetism
which he had come to realise was neither love nor sympathy.
He felt that he could hate her, and yet not free himself from that
influence. What was to be done? He would have to choose;
his life of the future could no longer be his life of the past. His
introduction of a woman to his best friend had been unfortunate,
as such introductions always are, in one way or another. He had
tended his soul for more than half a lifetime, waited upon it
delicately, served it with its favourite food; and now something
stronger had come forward and said: No more. What was it?
He had no wish to speculate; it mattered little whether it was
what people called his higher nature, or what they called his lower
nature, which had brought him to this result. At least he had
some recompense.

When he told Livia that he had decided to go back to Marseilles
('Arles does not suit you,' he said; 'you have not been well since
we came here') Livia flung herself into his arms with an uncontrollable delight. On the night before they left, he sat for a long
time, alone, under the Allée des Tombeaux. When he came back,
Livia was watching for him from the window. She ran to the door
and opened it.

It was midday when they reached Marseilles. The sun burned
on the blue water, which lay hot, motionless, and glittering. There
was not a breath of wind, and the dust shone on the roads like
a thick white layer of powder. The light beat downwards from

the blue sky, and upwards from the white dust of the roads. The heat was enveloping; it wrapped one from head to foot like the caress of a hot furnace. Roserra pressed his hands to his forehead, as he leaned with Livia over the terrace above the sea; his head throbbed, it was an effort even to breathe. He remembered the grey coolness of the Allée des Tombeaux, where the old men sat among the tombs. A nausea, a suffocating nausea, rose up within him as he felt the heat and glare of this vulgar, exuberant paradise of snobs and tourists. He sickened with revolt before this over-fed nature, sweating the fat of life. He looked at Livia; she stood there, perfectly cool under her sunshade, turning to watch a carriage that came towards them in a cloud of dust. She was once more in her element, she was quite happy; she had plunged back into the warmth of life out of that penitential chillness of Arles; and it was with real friendliness that she turned to Roserra, as she saw his eyes fixed upon her.

1905.

HUBERT MONTAGU CRACKANTHORPE
(1870-1896)

Son of a Queen's Counsel and Doctor of Civil Law, Crackanthorpe was born on 12 May 1870 at Newbiggin Hall in Westmorland. Both his parents were highly literate, and their concern with contemporary social problems was finely reflected in his own fiction. Crackanthorpe was tutored by George Gissing (another realist influence) and educated at Cambridge, but left without taking a degree.

He travelled in France and Spain, edited *The Albemarle* magazine, a monthly review which ran for nine numbers between January and September 1892, besides contributing to *The Yellow Book* and *The Savoy*. In his twenty-seventh year he threw himself into the Seine in Paris, following upon his wife's elopement with another man.

Just as Dowson is *the poet of the period*, and Beardsley its *illustrator*, so Crackanthorpe—through his short stories—has been justly described as 'the great imaginative prose-writer of the group' (Bernard Muddiman: *The Men of the Nineties*, 1920).

Profiles

I

IT WAS one of the first warm afternoons of the year; the vigorous rays of the sun lent the young leaves, whose delicate green suffused the wood, an exquisite transparency.

All was still; the rushes clustered immobile on the banks of the little stream; no breath of wind ruffled its surface.

Alone a water-rat splashed, and gently rippling the water, swam across.

On the bank a girl was sitting, her white cotton dress rucked about her knees, displaying a small pair of muddy boots, which dangled close to the water's surface. Her body was thrust forward in a cramped position, as with both hands she held a long, clumsy-looking fishing-rod. She was watching intently the movements of a fat, red float, which bobbed excitedly up and down.

She was bareheaded, and her crisp, auburn hair was riotously tumbling about her ears and neck.

Quite pale was her skin, but pale, transparent, soft; exquisite was the modelling of her fresh, firm lips.

There were great possibilities of beauty in the face; but now an all-absorbing look filled it, the forehead puckered over the eyebrows, the lips set tight together.

A little way off, on the grass, a young man, in a grey flannel suit, was lying on his back, his face shaded by her big-brimmed straw hat, inside the ribbon of which were tucked some bunches of primroses; one hand thrust in the armhole of his waistcoat, the other thrown back over his head—the limp abandon of his pose betrayed that he was asleep.

Down darted the fat, red float. Awkwardly the girl tugged at the rod; the line tightened, swaying about from side to side.

'Maurice!' she called; then louder, as he did not wake.

Maurice started, pushed the hat from off his eyes, murmuring sleepily—

'Hullo! what's up?'

'Make haste, do! I can't hold the rod any more.'

He jumped up, took it, and in a minute or two the fish was floundering on the grass, its sleek, silver sides gleaming in the sunlight.

'Why, Lilly, it's quite a big one,' he exclaimed.

Tall, with fine, broad shoulders, and a small, well-shaped head, evidently not a quite young man; but a trick of raising his eyebrows with an air of boyish surprise, made him appear some years younger.

'He pulled like anything. I should have had to let go the rod in another minute. My arms ache all over,' she added, ruefully.

'That rod's too heavy for you. I'll have to get another, if we're coming fishing again.'

'Oh, yes! Of course we are. I love it.'

Quite beautiful she looked, her face lit up in a delicate flush of excitement.

'Put on another worm, quick. There's sure to be some more, aren't there?'

Maurice pulled out his watch.

'Nearly four o'clock,' he said, shaking his head. 'I've got a guard at half-past five. We must pack up.'

At once her face clouded, the eyes half-closed, the mouth dropped, the chin pouted.

A pettish exclamation was on her lips, but, catching sight of an amused twinkle in Maurice's eyes, she checked herself, and her face cleared.

Together they unscrewed the rod, and when they had put the

joints into their canvas case, they started off through the wood, along the narrow path that led to the village.

Maurice, with the rod under his arm, and a long cigar in the corner of his mouth, Lilly bareheaded, her hair more unruly than ever, carrying her hat and her parasol in her hand.

II

They were engaged to be married, Lilly and Maurice. It had been so for nearly three months.

Lilly lived with her Aunt Lisbet in a semi-detached villa on the outskirts of Guildford, where Maurice's regiment was quartered.

She had never known her mother; when she ransacked the dim memories of her childhood, there was nobody further back than Aunt Lisbet. Her father she scarcely remembered at all, for he had died when she was a quite a little girl. He had been a bookmaker, and a coloured photograph of him—a burly, red-faced man, in a white top-hat, and a long, grey dust coat with a scarlet flower in the button-hole—hung over the fireplace in Aunt Lisbet's bedroom. Underneath the photograph was written, James Maguire—'Big Jock.'

During his lifetime 'Big Jock's' good luck had been almost proverbial, so that he was reputed to be worth a 'tidy pile.' But at his death, when all his debts had been paid, scarcely a hundred pounds remained. What had become of it all no one knew, and Aunt Lisbet had never forgiven her brother for this mystery. The disappearance of the money itself exasperated her; but the thought that for years he had been secretly making away with large sums without a word to her, his sister, who had kept house for him since his wife's death, and who had been a second mother to his child, made her especially furious.

This bitter feeling against her brother, instead of subsiding as time went on, only rankled the more in her mind, and now, except in terms of abuse, she never mentioned his name.

She was a thin, sharp-boned, little woman, with red lids to her greenish-coloured eyes, a long, aquiline nose and a pointed chin. When she spoke to Lilly of her father, there came into her voice a curious, rasping intonation.

Aunt Lisbet drank; chiefly brandy, and her drunkenness took the form of fits of ungovernable passion.

These outbursts were almost always directed against Lilly; not that Aunt Lisbet had any particular personal animosity towards her niece, but because Lilly was the handiest object on which to vent her feelings.

She would begin by recalling some evil trait in Jock's character. Lilly had no really tender affection for her father's memory, the little she knew of him was far from creditable. But this disparagement of him by Aunt Lisbet somehow made her blood boil, and at times the scenes between them were very violent.

And though, except for these occasions, they seldom quarrelled, Lilly loathed Aunt Lisbet with an instinctive, imperious loathing.

And this afternoon, as she drove home in the dog-cart by Maurice's side, her hatred for her aunt seemed fiercer than it had ever been before.

III

The horse's hoofs rang clear on the hard, white road, as they sped swiftly along, Lilly leaning against Maurice's shoulder, plunged in a brown study.

Presently she said, meditatively: 'What is the earliest date on which your father can arrive?'

'Well, he won't leave Bombay for another fortnight, then he'll not hurry himself on the journey, so it will be at least a month before he reaches England. It's a beastly long time, isn't it?'

'Oh, Maurice! What's the good of waiting? He will never consent, let's get married at once.'

Recklessly he dropped the reins and taking her face in his gloved hands, held it up to his. Their lips met, and putting both his arms round her, he strained her to him. The kiss was a long one; at last she gave a little moan; he let her go.

'You don't know the old gentleman, you see,' he continued. 'My infernal busybodies of relations have been writing all sorts of tales about you—at least, not about you, but about your aunt and your father, and about—well, a lot of damned rot. But directly he's seen you, I shall be able to make it all right with him. Of course, if you really wish it, we could get married next week, but I think it would be more prudent to wait. The very fact that I had not waited till his return might put his back up, and he might cut off my allowance on the spot.'

'Of course, Maurice, we'll wait. It was selfish of me to think of it. But—but——'

'Well?'

'I do hate Aunt Lisbet so.'

'I know; but it's not so very long now.'

They were entering the town.

'Shall I drive you to the door?'

'No, drop me at St. Luke's. I'll walk home from there.'

He pulled up and she got down.

'Be at Mrs. Newton's in good time tomorrow afternoon,' he called out, as, smartly flicking the horse, he rattled away down the street.

IV

The solitary candle flickering on the dressing-table made the shadows of the coming night creep back into the corners of the room, as Lilly, with swollen eyelids, and red patches on her cheeks, looked out through the window-pane.

All was still. The earth slept.

The moon poured her white light on the meadows opposite; a few fleecy clouds lazily chased one another across the sky. In the distance a dog barked, then all was again still.

Lilly threw herself on the bed, burying her face in the pillow.

And presently the cool linen began to soothe her burning forehead.

It had passed, the wild impulse to throw herself out of the window that people might know to what Aunt Lisbet had driven her. Now the resolve never to see her again ousted all else from her mind. Absolute, irrevocable was this resolve; any departure from it was a physical impossibility. Only she must wait till morning, and she turned to a cooler spot on the pillow.

And as she did so, a vivid vision of the scene in the kitchen below started before her eyes: Aunt Lisbet leaning against the dresser, her hair slipping down on one side, and in her voice a hissing sound.

It was the first time that she had said things about Maurice; that was what had made it worse than it had ever been before.

A blind desire to silence her, to stamp the life out of her, swept over Lilly. Seizing the parasol which lay on the kitchen-table, with all her strength she hit Aunt Lisbet across the side of the head.

And over the thought of that blow she lingered, recalling it again and again, repeating it in her mind with a strange, exquisite pleasure. For into it she had put the hatred of years.

Aunt Lisbet uttered a low, plaintive moan—the curious moan of sudden pain—and fell, dragging with her on to the floor a pile of plates.

The crash sent every nerve in Lilly's body tingling, but when, a moment later, Aunt Lisbet moved to get up, the blind, murderous desire returned. Another brutal blow of the parasol, and she knocked her back again.

With a dull thud her head bumped on the floor; and that thud was the point of reaction.

Its hideous sound seemed to pierce Lilly through and through; in a fit of hysterical sobbing she sank into an armchair.

Slowly Aunt Lisbet rose to her feet, and muttering incoherently under her breath, staggered out of the room.

Round and round all these incidents Lilly's thoughts revolved, dwelling on them, brooding over them, unable to escape from them.

And each time that she thought of the hissing sound in Aunt Lisbet's voice, the blind, murderous feeling swept over her, and each time that the thud of Aunt Lisbet's head on the floor sounded in her ears, the tears welled up in her eyes.

V

The Charing Cross platform was alive with people, some hurrying hither and thither, others standing together in groups or sauntering up and down.

Suddenly the fierce panting of an engine echoed through the building, and a cloud of dense smoke rose to melt away under the curved roof.

It was nearly a quarter to one, for when Lilly had awoken in her little bedroom at Aunt Lisbet's, weary and unrefreshed through having slept in her clothes, the morning was already half gone. Downstairs and out of the house she had crept, meeting only the servant-girl, who told her with a smirk that her aunt was still sleeping.

Her first impulse had been to go straight to the 'Barracks' to ask Maurice to take her away and marry her at once. It seemed the only alternative, for never again would she set foot in Aunt Lisbet's house.

But, as she hurried through the town, there came upon her, like a spasm of physical pain, a feeling of irresolution. She remembered what Maurice had said yesterday—'It's not for so very long.' She foresaw that he would advise her to go back and put up with it for a few weeks more, and that she would have to argue with him about it. The courage to face such a prospect was wanting.

No, there was only one thing, take the train for London, telegraph to Maurice to meet her there. Then he *must* understand how impossible it was for her to go back.

And this she had done.

Three hours and three quarters to wait till the next train from

Guildford, even if Maurice got the telegram in time. He might not be at the barracks when it arrived. At four, of course, he would go to Mrs. Newton's, as they had arranged yesterday. But would he go back home beforehand? And if not, would his servant send on the telegram or keep it till his return? These and many other possibilities whirled through Lilly's brain as anxiously she paced the platform.

Four hours had passed. The porters lined the platform edge as rapidly the train drew up. The doors flung open; out swarmed the crowd.

But Maurice was nowhere to be seen. Eagerly Lilly looked for him, up and down; once she fancied that she saw him talking to a porter at the other end of the train.

Desperately she pushed through the crowd, only to find herself face to face with a stranger.

There was not another train till five, and then not another till half-past seven.

With a numb feeling of hopelessness she wandered out into the Strand.

It had just stopped raining. Noisily the omnibuses splashed past, while the hansoms, one after another, crawled along the edge of the pavement.

Some hungry-looking boys were yelling the contents of an evening paper, two flower-girls and an old man selling bootlaces, stood in the gutter. Along the pavement, brown, and a-glimmer with the wet, poured a continual stream of men and women.

No one took any notice of Lilly, they only jostled roughly past her. And somehow the sight of all these strange faces and the movement of this seething turmoil made her feel sick and faint.

For the first time she realised her absolute loneliness.

The five-o'clock train and the seven-o'clock train had both come in, but still no signs of Maurice.

The last train was due at twenty minutes past nine.

Lilly sat staring lifelessly before her. She had scarcely eaten anything all day; exhausted, she was suffering much, but so great was her nervous tension, that she did not know that it was hunger.

What she would do if Maurice did not come she never considered. All her energy was occupied in counting the minutes till the train was due.

At last! That must be it! She had not the strength to move, but intently watched the passengers as they poured out through the barrier.

Yes! Maurice!—hastening towards her, yet somehow not looking as she had expected him to look.

VI

Maurice, rising abruptly from the breakfast-table, and throwing open the window, looked down on to the crowded street, for their rooms in the hotel faced the Strand.

Delicate, grey-blue streaks of smoke curled restlessly upwards; in streamed the morning sunlight, bathing Lilly in its full flood.

A newspaper lay before her on the sofa; but she was observing Maurice with stealthy glances from under her dark eyelashes.

Solemnly the clock ticked, while, with obvious constraint, he hummed discontentedly to himself.

An instant ago their voices were raised in angry dispute—not the first, though they had been but three days together. And Maurice, as he gazed out on to the sea of roof-tops, recalled the trivial incident from which their quarrel had sprung. The thought formed a central spot of pain amid the monotony of his gloom.

For the twentieth time he was aimlessly brooding on the change that had come over her.

Never for a moment had he treated her dislike for Aunt Lisbet seriously, though he had sympathised with it, vaguely, distantly. Lilly was to blame for this, he thought: beyond occasional references, she had told him nothing, and, in his blind contentedness, he had never troubled to question her. Besides, instinctively, even in thought, he had shrunk from that side of her life. It jarred upon him.

They had spent the night after his arrival together; it had seemed the more natural thing. Maurice only had hesitated for an instant with an indefinable shrinking. And when in the morning Lilly suddenly sat up in bed, and began the explanation of her flight, he listened impatiently to what seemed a series of clumsy an unnecessary exaggerations. He had imagined, with a subtle tickling of vanity, that somehow she had been driven to it out of love for him, and he felt an annoyance, vague but real, at learning that it was not so.

But in a minute or two this had passed; in bewilderment he lay watching her.

Tremulously, with a look of passionate fierceness, her face was working as if some strange light were playing on it.

She had done. He knew that every word was true.

And afterwards, if, at odd moments, the improbability of it all flashed upon him, the recollection of that look would at once drive all doubt from his mind.

No longer could he love her lazily as before. The half-girl, half-child, simple and heedless, with occasional moods of confiding, dreamy gravity, and fits of charming pettishness, the easy dispelling of which he had enjoyed, was gone.

The events of the past few days had broken down the barrier, behind which the strong passions of her nature had laid dormant, and now, let loose for the first time, they mastered her; she was their slave.

Capricious and irritable, with outbursts of nervous exasperation, followed by hot tears of remorse and a desperate sensuality that disturbed and almost frightened him.

And strangest of all, when he had proposed yesterday that they should be married at the end of the week, with an evasive reply she had at once started another topic.

As he turned to throw away his cigarette, he saw that she was by his side. How silently she had crossed the room! Putting both hands on his shoulders, she murmured:

'Maurice, dear Maurice, kiss me; don't be angry with me.'

VII

'We must go back to Guildford, tomorrow,' he said, after a pause. 'I can't get any more leave, and there are all kinds of arrangements to be made down there—fresh quarters, servants, and heaps of things. You can stay at Mrs. Newton's till everything is ready,' he went on hurriedly, 'it will only take a few days and then we will come back here and get married. I will keep on the room, so that there will be no difficulty about a licence.'

'I don't want to go back. I hate the place,' she muttered sullenly.

'But, Lilly, dear, do be reasonable. There's nothing else to be done.'

'You can go alone. I shall stay here till you come back.'

Angrily he was on the point of replying, but the words died away on his lips. Expostulation, he saw, would be worse than useless.

He went on to tell her about a red-tiled house just outside the town, on which he had had his eye for months, but catching sight of her face, he stopped short, and burst out despairingly:

'Why, Lilly, doesn't it interest you?'

'I don't think I could ever go back,' she answered slowly.

'But we can't live anywhere else, unless I exchange, and that would take time.'

A pause, during which she was nervously tearing strips off the edge of the newspaper.

'How long will you be away?' she asked at length.

'Let's see, today's Wednesday. If I go tomorrow morning, I ought to be back by Friday night or Saturday morning. But what on earth will you do with yourself?'

'I don't know, but I can't go back there. You don't know how impossible it is."

'But after we are married?'

'Perhaps it will be different then,' she answered musingly.

He drew her to the sofa, and putting both arms round her, began with infinite tenderness:

'Lilly, darling, what is it? Tell me. Is it that you don't care for me as you did? What is it? Tell me, little woman. Oh! I can't bear the thought of leaving you here all alone by yourself.'

'Maurice, I don't know what it is. Only I feel very miserable. Everything seems in such a tangle. I feel as if something strange were going to happen to me. I want to think about lots of things. That's why I want to be alone, quite alone.'

VIII

Eight o'clock had just struck; a continuous hum resounded through the restaurant, a Babel of voices and a clatter of knives and forks.

'I do love the crowd, the bustle, and all that,' exclaimed Lilly, excitedly.

Then,

'Oh! Maurice, who's that? I'm sure he knows you; look!'

Against the pillar in the centre of the room a powerfully built, dark-faced man was leaning. His face, in contrast to the whiteness of his shirt-front, seemed copper-coloured, and there was a singular massiveness about it; bushy eyebrows, heavy, black moustache and vermilion lips.

Dominating the whole room, he stood leisurely casting his eyes over the crowd of diners.

'That man by the pillar?' answered Maurice. 'Yes, I know him a little. His name is Adrian Safford. Some more soup?' And he went on with his dinner.

Safford's eyes were on them now, travelling from one to the other with a deliberateness that was almost insolent.

Lilly's eyelids dropped; she hurriedly crumbled a piece of bread.

But the temptation was irresistible; nervously she glanced up. Quite close now, his back towards her, both hands in his pockets, and a crush hat tucked under one arm.

'Maurice, he can't find a seat.'

'Can't find a seat—who can't?'

'That big man—Mr. Safford. Tell him that there's room next you.'

In the glass opposite she could see the reflection of his face. As she spoke he made a sudden, half-arrested movement of his head. He had overheard.

Maurice touched him on the shoulder. And, as shaking hands they exchanged greetings, Lilly noticed the prickliness of his eyebrows, and the strong muscles on each side of the bull-like throat.

And Maurice introduced him to her; under the stare from his lustrous black eyes she flushed hotly.

He was speaking, his voice sounded slow, drawling almost.

But she scarcely heard what he was saying, she was watching his hands, as they smoothed the cloth in front of him—white and fat, tipped with pink finger-nails, carefully trimmed to a point.

IX

All the morning and during luncheon Maurice had been gloomily taciturn; this had induced in Lilly a strained, nervous gaiety.

The moment of parting drew near and the tension became more more painful.

Yet it did not snap till they were slowly pacing the platform before the departure of the train. Then, of a sudden, he turned his face, contorted as in acute physical pain, and with a dryness in his voice, passionately implored her to return.

But he did not touch her. Strange that she was observing him, curiously, for the first time conscious of distinct antipathy towards him. He looked—yes, ridiculous, as if ashamed of having betrayed his emotion. The sight of this emotion sent a spasm of irritation through her. Next she felt an almost uncontrollable inclination to laugh.

But he did not press her any longer, for he dimly saw how it was. The porters began to slam the doors; in silence he entered the train.

After it had gone she sauntered about the streets, staring at the people, reading the posters on the hoardings, gazing into the shop windows, now and then buying with the money he had given her little objects that took her fancy.

At last, hot and dusty, she found herself back at the hotel. Tired out, she stretched herself on the sofa, and, closing her eyes, let thoughts float aimlessly across her brain.

There passed visions of a woman with yellow hair indolently reclining against the cushions of a victoria; of the red-bearded policeman who had told her the way to the hotel; of the stare of a thin man in frock coat pinched at the waist; of the gold-spotted veil, and of the brooch set in imitation pearls, which she had carried home with her.

Then the bronzed countenance of Safford, his bright, red lips, and fat, white hands appeared as he leant against the central pillar of the restaurant.

And now Maurice was there too. Side by side they disputed for her. Maurice troubled, with tears in his eyes; Safford still, massive as a statue.

'Which loves her best?' cried the crowd.

'I do,' answered his low tones. He encircled her cheeks with his hands, which were soft and warm, and his bright, red lips kissed her softly on the eyes.

X

Abruptly, without effort, her eyes opened. And immediately their gaze fell upon Safford. For an instant, the impression of her dream remained vivid; to see him there seemed natural. But before the returning sense of reality, it faded quickly; bewilderment sweeping in, arrested all thought.

Astride of a chair, the broad expanse of his back blocking the light, he sat, looking out of the window, apparently absorbed in the street below. This unconcernedness alarmed her.

How did he come there?

A minute or two slipped by, then he shifted his chair, as if to rise. Her eyes shut hastily, involuntarily; she pretended to be asleep. He came to her, so close that his breath played on her cheek, but in spite of the loud throbbing of her heart, she never stirred. He moved away: his heavy tread sounded about the room. Then silence.

Had he gone? No, she would have heard the click of the doorhandle. The darkness, the suspense became intolerable, yet it was a full minute before she could summon courage to reopen her eyes.

Her gaze met his.

'I say, if I couldn't sham better than that, I wouldn't try at all,' and his broad teeth gleamed.

Somehow his voice calmed her. His self-possession communicated itself to her, giving her confidence.

'I wasn't shamming.'

'I could see it.'

'How?'

'Your eyes were trembling.'

She smiled, almost frankly.

'Weren't you surprised to see me?'

'Yes, no—I mean yes.'

'Where's Radford?'

'Maurice? He's gone.'

'Gone? Where?'

'To Guildford.'

'And you're here all alone?'

She nodded.

A moment's pause—he thoughtfully jingling some money in his trouser-pocket; she, wondering that he looked so much darker than he had done in evening dress.

'When is he coming back?'

'I'm not sure, either tomorrow night or Saturday morning.'

Another pause.

'What did you do last night—after I went away?'

'We went to the theatre.'

'Did you like it?'

'Yes, awfully.'

'You're fond of the theatre?'

'I've only been twice—in London at least.'

'Would you like to go again tonight?'

'I couldn't.'

'Why not?'

'Maurice—I promised him.'

'What a pity! You'd have liked it.'

'Yes, I should.'

'Look here, it will be all right; he won't mind, he knows me well enough.' And again the broad teeth gleamed.

'I don't know—perhaps——'

But as she spoke, his soft, warm hands encircled her face, his bright, red lips kissed her on the eyes, just as in her dream.

The blood rushed to her face, in hot gasps her breath came and went, everything but Safford swam in a mist and was gone; impulsively she lifted her burning face to his and murmured:

'Tell me that you love me. Then I'll come.'

XI

Adrian Safford's chambers were sombre; even on this summer morning shadows lurked in the corners of the lofty spacious room. There was no window; the light struggled in as best it could, through a ground glass skylight. On the walls, maroon-coloured hangings; from the fireplace to the ceiling reached a huge overmantel of black, carved oak. The rich scent of a burning pastille struck a note of sensuous mystery. It was all curiously characteristic of the man.

Amid the dark tints, a single patch of colour—the white table-cloth on which an exquisitely fresh breakfast was laid. Safford had just seated himself before it, a scowl deepening the bronze of his face. Yet he ate in a vigorous, business-like way. His appetite was always splendidly regular.

The girl asleep in the next room was the cause of his scowl.

Something about the crispness of her hair; something about the modelling of her chin; something in the questioning look that darted out from the liquidness of her big eyes; something—he knew not what—had haunted him, ever since their first meeting. A spark of caprice fanned into fitful flame of the offensiveness of Radford's ill-concealed pride of possession.

And so the day before yesterday he had gone to the hotel. To find her alone was more than he had hoped for, but directly he saw her lying asleep on the sofa, he knew instinctively that she was his. Women were so easy.

The rest had been the old story, only this time more commonplace than ever—a dinner at the Café Royal, a box at the Empire, and back to his chambers afterwards. And yet she was different from the others; she remained; he kept her for her mutinous freshness.

He had asked nothing about her relations with Radford. He had made a rule never to question them about themselves; the tedious monotony of their stories bored him immensely.

It was she who, in her wilfulness, had blurted it all out. He saw it coming and did his best to stop her. But it was not to be. And when he heard that she and Radford were to have been married in a day or two, his feeling was one of pure disgust—not disgust at her treachery, but disgust at the blunder he had committed—blunder ahead of which he foresaw a whole series of unpleasant complications.

And in that instant he tired of her—her passion, from being a thing to be toyed with complacently, suddenly filled him with active dislike. The very searching gaze which had amused him before now seemed merely stupid. With the exasperation of a trapped animal, he realised that she was one of the clinging sort, whose dismissal was generally difficult, always disagreeable.

'Damn,' he muttered, savagely biting the end of a cigar.

XII

Safford, his huge frame stretched on two chairs, from time to time carefully inserted the cigar between his teeth. He smoked thoughtfully, deliberately, yet the cigar had nearly burnt to an end before Lilly ran in, with the fresh morning bloom upon her.

'Why, how late! Ten o'clock,' she cried. 'And you've eaten nearly all the breakfast. For shame! I believe that's why you got up without waking me.'

'There's some left under the cover. Ring for more if it's cold,' he answered, without removing the cigar from his mouth.

But she, in her radiant unconsciousness, did not notice his gloom.

'Do come and cut this bread for me,' she called out presently, 'it hurts my fingers, it's so awfully hard.' He did as she asked; then flicking the ash from his cigar, stood looking down at her as she ate.

'Sugar, please. I say, what shall we do today? It's so splendid out. I can't stop inside. Besides, it's so stuffy in here.' Safford shifted his feet uneasily. 'I tell you what—I know. We'll go down to Kingston and go on the river. It's awfully jolly down there. I went once last summer.'

'With Radford, I suppose?'

'Why, I believe you're jealous of him—yes, you are, else you wouldn't look so solemn. Come, aren't you?'

No answer.

She rose, and both hands toying with the lapels of his coat, said hurriedly:

'But I don't care for him—not a bit. He seems like a stranger now. It seems months since I saw him. I love you—oh! I can never tell you how I love you. I want to be with you always—you know I do. Come kiss, kiss me again like the first time.' Her voice, though rapid, had great earnestness in it.

With an impatient movement he repulsed her.

'You must go back this morning,' he said, more brutally than he had intended, but his exasperation had got the better of him. 'When I sent for your things yesterday, they said he would return this morning.'

She stepped back, as if he had struck her; the light went out of her face; her eyes blinked quickly as she tried to grasp his meaning, her under-lip began to twitch.

'You're joking! Oh! don't! Say it's a joke! You don't know how it hurts!'

'No, I'm quite serious. Now be sensible and listen. I should never have brought you here if I'd known about you and him. You must go back—at once.'

'You really mean it?'

'Yes, I mean it.'

'Then you don't love me any more,' she burst out. 'I don't believe you ever did. It was only just to amuse yourself that you brought me here. You made me love you, and now that you've had enough of me you want to send me back to him. You——'

Unheeding, he went on slowly:

'Besides, I'm going away.'

'It's a lie! You only want to get rid of me.'

'Do as I tell you, and don't make a fuss.' There was an imperiousness in his voice that cowed her. The passionate fierceness left her. 'And if you are careful,' he went on, 'it will be all right; not a soul knows where you've been. Very likely he won't find out that you've been away. And even if he does, he's quite fool enough'—and with a grim smile at the words that were rising to his lips, he checked himself.

But she did not hear what he was saying. Like some nightmare procession, the incidents in her life since her departure from Guildford were passing before her.

'I sha'n't tell any lies. I shall tell him straight out,' she said half to herself.

Impatiently he shrugged his shoulders.

'And then, when I've told him, I may come back, mayn't I?'

'Come back? Here?'

'Yes, when it's all over with him. I mean when he's gone away again.'

'It's quite impossible. Just understand that.'

'But what am I to do, then?' It was the cry of concentrated despair.

'You've got to do what I've told you. It will be all right. I know what I'm talking about. If you don't choose to—well, then, it's your lookout. You can't come back here, that's certain. I'm going away.'

She was not looking at him; her big eyes, wide-open, were staring vacantly at something beyond.

'Where are you going?' she said faintly, after a pause.

'Never mind. Nowhere where you can come.'

'Oh! for God's sake, don't send me away.' The vacant expression had given way to the feverish pleading of her childish passion. 'You will kill me if you do. Can't you see how I love you? There seems to be nothing else in the world for me but you. Perhaps you think that I shall be in the way. But I promise you that I will do whatever you tell me; I will be no trouble; I will not speak to you if you do not want me to—I will do anything.' And down streamed the tears.

'Poor little devil,' he muttered under his breath.

He drew her towards him and her frail body shook convulsively on his chest.

'Lilly, dear, you must go, you really must. It's for your own good. There are lots of reasons why you must, that you don't understand—you will soon forget all about this. Now come, kiss me, and say you will go quietly.'

Her sobbing had ceased. His slow tones had mastered her.

She looked up through her tears and nodded. 'I will go,' she said through her teeth, 'because I can't help doing what you tell me. But I shall come back.'

So absorbing was his sense of relief that he did not hear her last words.

'Make haste and get your hat. I'll see you into a hansom. I'll get your things packed and sent after you at once. And remember all that I told you. You've only got to play your cards well, and it will be all right.'

So fearful was he lest she should resent her submission, that the unnatural calm which had come over her passed unnoticed.

XIII

'Lieutenant Radford has just come back; he was asking for you just now ma'am,' said a waiter as she mounted the staircase.

Pushing past him, she laid her hand on the door of the room. As she did so, it opened suddenly from within, and a man, whom she recognised as the manager of the hotel, held it open for her to pass.

Maurice was seated at the table, writing.

'Lilly,' he cried as she entered. 'Thank God!'

Wildly he poured kisses on her hair and face. She submitted passively, quite white, her teeth set, in her eyes a stony stare.

The first rush of emotion passed, he let her go.

'But where have you been?'

She made no answer, only a dangerous light—a light that boded mischief—suddenly animated her face. He was so different from him whom she had just left. And, as she recalled Safford's massive frame and bronzed countenance, she found herself looking at Maurice, critically, as at some stranger, each detail of whose person was acutely repulsive. But for him Safford would never have sent her away. She hated him for it.

'Lilly, they tell me that you've been away since Thursday. What have you been doing?'

She had expected anger; but there was none in his voice, only a tone of tender entreaty that made her wince. An irresistible, evil desire to wound him came to her.

'I've been with Adrian.'

'Adrian? Who? Safford?'

'Good God!' and as the truth dawned on him, with a gradual, ugly contraction, his face turned a greyish colour.

Sinking into a chair, he buried his head in his hands.

Some minutes passed, but he did not stir. The silence soon became intolerable to Lilly; fiercely she fidgeted with her glove, pulling at a button, trying to wrench it off.

At last she could bear it no longer. She spoke, and as she did so, the sound of her own voice startled her.

'Have you anything more to say to me?'

He looked up, tears were in his eyes.

'What do you mean?'

'I'm going if you haven't anything more to say.'

'Going? Where?'

'Back. I only came to tell you.'

In supreme unconsciousness of his suffering, she spoke quite naturally, as if the matter was of no consequence.

His lips moved, but he uttered no words, only a choking, gurgling sound.

Again dropping his head in his hands, he sobbed audibly.

The sobs rose, and fell regularly, harshly. It was the first time that she had seen a man cry. And an element of contempt entered into her bitterness.

Then for one short moment she pitied him. Vaguely, as one pities an animal in pain.

She stepped forward, as if to say something, but almost immediately the impulse died away. She went quickly out through the door, closing it softly behind her.

And Maurice, blinded by his grief, did not know that she was gone.

XIV

Lilly was now alone. Maurice and she had parted—probably for ever. And Safford had disappeared. They had told her at his chambers that he was gone. At first she believed that they were lying, and obstinately waited for him during long hours. But it was in vain. Then she searched for him in the streets, wandering hither and thither in the hope of meeting him. But amid the crowd there were no signs of his massive frame.

So for several days. And then the seething turmoil of the great city, ruthless in its never-flagging lust, caught up the frailty of her helpless beauty, and playing with it, marred it, mutilated it. Like a flower, frost-bitten in the hour of its budding, she drooped and withered.

Against the inevitable she made no continuous resistance. How could she? Only for a while; with the feeble struggles of a drowning creature she clung to the memory of her great love for Safford, and to every little thing that reminded her of it.

First, it was a dark-faced foreigner about Safford's build and height. He was kind to her—at least he treated her with no selfish brutality—and listened indulgently when she opened her heart to him. As he listened he would feverishly strive to delude herself into believing that he was the lover she had lost. But even this consolation of self-deception was denied her.

After a while, she somehow lost sight of him, and then it was any one who by some detail of his person recalled Safford to her— a drawling voice heard one night in a restaurant; two prickly eyebrows caught sight of one night under a lamp-post in Piccadilly; a red and black necktie like the one he wore the afternoon that he had come to the hotel.

Fierce, fitful loves, prompted by curious twistings of caprice, born to die within an hour or two.

She grew careless of her dress and of her person, and at last callous to all around her. She sunk into the irretrievable morass of impersonal prostitution. She ceased to live; mechanically she trudged on across the swamp-level of existence.

One evening, before starting out, as she dragged through the ceremony of her toilet, wearily staring in her glass, there flashed across her murky brain a resemblance between her own wasted, discoloured face, and the hard angularity of Aunt Lisbet's features.

After that the recollections of her girlhood—Aunt Lisbet, Maurice and even Safford faded into the twilight of the past. With no common speed, the end was drawing near.

XV

Pain beyond a certain degree of intensity ceases to be pain. Thus it was with Maurice. In a state of mental numbness he went back to Guildford. His mind, stunned as it was, could only feebly revolve about these words of Lilly's: 'I'm going back to him. I only came to tell you.' All else was blurred; this alone, and the vision of her white, set face, and stony glare stood out distinct and sharp.

It was many days before consciousness began to return, before his thoughts, emerging from their torpor, started to explore the extent of his pain.

But when the awakening came, with a morbid craving for self-inflicted torture, he lingered over every detail; starting from the very beginning, he lived once again through the events of the last three months.

Now and then, the memory of some happy day they had spent together would come back so vividly as to drive away the dull pain, but it was only for an instant. With a quiver like that caused by the turning of a knife in an old wound, he heard the words ringing once more in his ears: 'I'm going back to him. I only came to tell you.'

And yet, realising the grim hideousness of it, he felt no resentment against her.

Of a sudden, an infinite pity for her filled him. From that moment all was changed. His love for her, which had lived on in spite of it all, and the new-born pity, each nourishing the other, lessened the sense of his pain, lifting him above it.

For the first time the mechanism of her nature was laid bare before him. He saw many things that he had never heeded before, passing them over as of no significance, things that now, with curious intuition, he understood.

And the exaltation of his love and of his pity rose.

The tragedy was no longer his, but hers. It was not his life that was spoilt, but hers. Pitilessly he upbraided himself—to have left her in the hands of a brute like Safford (the very thought of the man's swarthy skin made his blood boil)—Lilly—his Lilly—who was to have been his wife. How had he ever done it? How contemptible, what a weak creature he was! Poor little child!

And the exaltation of his love and his pity rose still higher.

Yes, he must save her. It was not too late. All the fine elements in his nature forced their way to the front in support of this resolve.

This resolve was the outcome of no blind impulse; he knew to the full the extent of the sacrifice he was about to make. His eyes were opened; he had counted the cost, but he never wavered.

On the contrary, the very sense of her unfitness to be his wife only strengthened his determination to do what was right.

XVI

A small servant-girl, slatternly in her dress, led the way up some narrow stairs, and Maurice stumbled once or twice, catching his feet in the torn stair-carpet, which was colourless with dirt.

'This is the room,' she said, and he followed her in.

The first thing that struck him was its shameless disorder— on the table, in the centre, a great litter of old newspapers; some tattered, yellow-backed novels; a half-finished cup of tea, stale and greasy; the remains of a cake, with crumbs scattered on the floor; a packet of cigarettes, two almost empty glasses. There were only three chairs, and on each some article of clothing had been thrown, a bonnet, a petticoat, or a pair of stockings. On the mantelpiece lay a bunch of withered roses, and opposite the mantelpiece stretched a curtain which evidently divided off the bedroom.

Presently a voice—her voice, just the same as in the old days— called out from behind the curtain.

'Who's there?'

'It's some one to see you,' answered the servant-girl.

'All right. I'll be out in a minute.'

A sound of splashing water, and the strained humming of a music-hall song.

'I say, who are you?' she called out.

He did not answer.

'Speak up, don't be shy. You're Dick? Ned Chalmers, then? Eh? Well, I give it up. Just wait till I've brushed my hair a bit, and I'll come and see for myself.'

At each fresh word revealing the extent of her downfall, he winced.

But his resolve was as strong as ever.

The curtain moved. In a gaudy, pink dressing-gown, stained and torn, she stood before him. Lilly, and yet not Lilly—like, but different with a difference that chilled him.

At the sight of him, her whole body stiffened in astonishment. 'Maurice!' she gasped.

Face to face they stood, looking into each other's eyes, 'Lilly,' he heard himself saying at last, 'come away.' He could find no other words, so imperious was the desire to remove her immediately out of these loathsome surroundings.

'Come away,' he repeated, 'away from all this.'

'Yes, it is rather messy,' she assented, looking round the room with a forced smile. 'But I'll get the girl to tidy up a bit. Sit down, chuck those things on to the floor. How it took me aback seeing you all of a sudden like that! Fancy your finding me out. I never expected to see you again. I thought you had forgotten all about me.' (She spoke hurriedly to conceal her agitation.) 'Just look at this table, did you ever see such a beastly mess? The people here never think of cleaning out the room.'

'Lilly,' he heard saying again, 'you must come away with me at once. You shall make a fresh start with me. I will marry you, and together we will forget all this awful time.'

'You're quite serious?' she asked slowly. 'You want to marry me now—after all that has happened?'

'Yes,' he answered steadily, yet with the absolute futility of it quite clear before him.

'Well, you're more curious than I thought you were,' was all her reply.

'What have you been doing all this time?' she added presently.

'I've been back at Guildford. But you must come away from here first. I can't talk things over with you in this horrible place.'

'All right, I'll come if you like. But it's no good.'

'What do you mean?'

'I mean about your marrying me. I could never marry a man I didn't care for.'

He took a full minute to grasp her meaning. The possibility of this had never crossed his mind.

'But you can't go on like this.' He was so staggered that words failed him. 'Do you know what the life you're leading means? Don't you see how it must all end?'

'Oh! I know all that as well as you do. You don't suppose I find it so extra pleasant, do you?' she burst out bitterly. 'But they say it won't last long; that's one comfort. I'm done for, and the sooner it's over the better.'

Her voice was hard and reckless.

'For heaven's sake don't talk like that.'

'Look here,' she interrupted almost fiercely. 'It's no good your going on about it. I could never marry a man I didn't love. And I don't love you. I thought I did once. But it was all different then.'

'Is there any one else then?'

'Any one else,' and there was a savageness in her voice as she caught up his words. 'They're just a lot of beasts, the whole lot of them. And if you go on talking about it you'll make me just mad —yes, they're all beasts—I hate them—every one of them, and the sooner it's all over the better. Have a cigarette, there's some on the table. For God's sake do something, say something; don't stand staring at me like that—you've seen me often enough. I'm a precious fright, I know. But how's a girl to keep her looks in this hell of a life?'

'But it's not too late to mend it all.'

'Oh! don't go on saying that over and over again. Just get the idea out of your head, once and for all. That's my last word.'

And he saw that she meant it. Somehow an immense relief that it was not to be came to him and struggled with his pity for her.

'At least give up this life. Here's some money. Go away somewhere, where you can make a fresh start.'

She took the sovereigns from his hand, quickly, with an angry movement as if to fling them on the floor. But, instead, she poured them into a china box on the mantelpiece.

'I'll see about it,' she answered.

But he saw the deceit written on her face, and he could bear the strain no longer. An irresistible longing to escape from the stifling atmosphere of the room, to be once more in the street, swept over him.

And as he groped his way down the dirty staircase he felt physically sick.

XVII

The next day Maurice went back to her lodgings.

She was gone, leaving no address behind. He set to work to trace her, and found her at last, late one rainy night, in the Charing Cross Road, but she passed by without recognising him.

And when he entreated her, she was sullenly obdurate.

In despair he went back to his regiment.

For some time more she was seen at intervals in a little public-house at the back of Regent Street. Then she disappeared. What had become of her, no one knew and no one cared.

Maurice alone remembered her, but he never saw her again.

GEORGE SLYTHE STREET
(1867-1936)

G. S. Street was born in Wimbledon on 17 July 1867, and educated at Charterhouse and Exeter College, Oxford.

Essayist, wit and short-storyist, he succeeded H. G. Wells as the dramatic critic on the *Pall Mall* magazine, eventually becoming His Majesty's Examiner of Plays; but that book which 'assures him of a perpetual niche in the corridors of the nineties' (Katherine Lyon Mix: *A Study in Yellow*, 1960) was his *Autobiography of a Boy*, 1894—issued in pale grey-green cloth that shone like watered silk—a work which gently parodies the Aesthetic Type. Tubby, the hero of *Autobiography of a Boy*, ranks with Esmé Amarinth of Robert Hichens' novel *The Green Carnation* and Reginald Bunthorne (of Gilbert and Sullivan's comic opera *Patience*) as memorable literary caricatures of Wilde and the Aesthetic Ideal.

Autobiography of a Boy

THE EDITOR'S APOLOGY

IN fulfilling a promise made to my friend, whom by your leave I will call simply Tubby, I have been conscious of a somewhat difficult dilemma. When he went to Canada, he placed the manuscript of his autobiography in my hands, with power to select and abridge. I perceived that if I published it in all its length nobody would read it: his life in England was not various, his orbit was circumscribed, the people he met and the situations he faced had a certain sameness, the comments he made on them dealt in repetitions. On the other hand, having made my selections on the principle of giving you none but typical incidents, and these but once, I find the result is meagre, and fear you may be angry at being troubled with it at all. Tubby himself was for publishing the whole. But craving your pardon, if you be angry, I think it is better to be amused (if amused you be) for an hour to so than to be bored for a day. I do assure you, you could have borne no more.

The autobiography covers only the period from his leaving

Oxford to the other day, and it may therefore be well to give you a few facts of his earlier life, and perhaps a word or two concerning the period mentioned above, since I may be deceived by my intimate acquaintance with him in thinking that his mode of life, his point of view, and his peculiar qualities are indicated sufficiently by himself.

He was expelled from two private and one public school; but his private tutor gave him an excellent character, proving that the rough and ready methods of schoolmasters' appreciation were unsuited to the fineness of his nature. As a young boy he was not remarkable for distinction of the ordinary sort—at his prescribed studies and at games involving muscular strength and activity. But in very early life the infinite indulgence of his smile was famous, and as in after years was often misunderstood; it was even thought by his schoolfellows that its effect at a crisis in his career was largely responsible for the rigour with which he was treated by the authorities: 'they were not men of the world,' was the harshest comment he himself was ever known to make on them. He spoke with invariable kindness also of the dons at Oxford (who sent him down in his third year), complaining only that they had not absorbed the true atmosphere of the place, which he loved. He was thought eccentric there, and was well known only in a small and very exclusive set. But a certain amount of general popularity was secured to him by the disfavour of the powers, his reputation for wickedness, and the supposed magnificence of his debts. His theory of life also compelled him to be sometimes drunk. In his first year he was a severe ritualist, in his second an anarchist and an atheist, in his third wearily indifferent to all things, in which attitude he remained in the two years since he left the University until now when he is gone from us. His humour of being carried in a sedan chair, swathed in blankets and reading a Latin poet, from his rooms to the Turkish bath, is still remembered in his college.

When he came to live in town, he used to quote 'Ambition was my idol, which was broken'; but I think he never really thought of it, certainly not in its common forms, but lived his artistic life naturally, as a bird sings. One or two ambitions he did, however, confide to his intimates. He desired to be regarded as a man to whom no chaste woman should be allowed to speak, an aim he would mention wistfully, in a manner inexpressibly touching, for he never achieved it. I did indeed persuade a friend of his and mine to cut him in the park one crowded afternoon; but his joy, which was as unrestrained as his proud nature permitted, was short-lived, for she was cruelly forgetful, and asked him to dinner the next day.

He confessed to me once that he regretted he had played ill his part in the drama of domestic life. It is true that no member of his family, except his mother, will allow you to mention his name now. There are a few women who look perplexed when they hear it, and many who laugh. Some men there are who disliked the smiling tolerance I have mentioned above; but those who took advantage of his real humility to swear at and romp with him— perhaps it was a higher pride that made him allow it—were fond of his society. People with a common reputation of being artistic regarded him, I believe, with suspicion, since his own devotion to art went far deeper than theirs. Children bullied him, and he was charming with old ladies.

The end was dramatic in its swiftness. A little speech he made to a bishop who was dining with his people was taken in ill part by his father. He said it was the last straw, and under cover of the metaphor sent Tubby away from home, giving him but five pounds a week on which to live his life. The cruel injustice of his proceeding but served to invigorate the spirits of my friend. He made a noble effort to take the vulgar burden of toil on to his shoulders. I procured him that beginning of a literary career, a parcel of books to review. But his devotion to art prevented his success. He ranged the books on his table, forming a charming harmony of colour, and spoke of them wittily and well. His review was merely a quotation from Shelley—

'I looked on them nine several days,
    And then I saw that they were bad.'

It was all his self-respect allowed him to say; but they sent him no more books. On leaving home he went into a delightful little flat in Jermyn Street, which the friend whom he calls Bobby had just left, and gave Thursday supper-parties, at which he was an ideal host. But troubles came thick upon him. His man refused to wear a dress which Tubby had spent many hours in designing. Nobody would print his poems. His expenditure exceeded his income.

Finally, he accepted his father's proposal he should go to Canada. It is supposed that the capital he has taken with him will serve him for at least six months, at the end of which we look to see him in our midst again.

G. S. S.

ALAS!

I SHALL never forget the horror of the moment when I knew that Juliet loved me. Our intercourse had been so pleasant; it was hard that this barrier should be raised between us. Not, of course, that I realised its effect at once; I confess to a thrill of common humanity; I believe I even kissed her; I know I am only a man. But the rush of despondency was upon me soon: my mind, before my sense, had grasped the inevitable conclusion.

I had worshipped this woman. That subtle delight which (I dare to say) most strong natures feel in yielding them captive to a weaker had been mine for several months. I had gloried in fetching and carrying, and smiled at my contentment with her little words of thanks. As I turn the pages of my diary I find noted down all her rudenesses and rebuffs, and my musings—not cynical, but large-hearted—on the perversity of her sex. I had grown quite accustomed to her being unmarried, and was unreservedly happy. And now it was all over!

It was but last Thursday that, when I put my customary question, 'Can you not love me a little?' instead of her delightful 'I'm sorry, but I'm afraid I can't,' she hung her head and stammered, 'I don't know.' As I have confessed, I was gratified at first and went through the interview in an orthodox sort of way. It was as I sat in the smoking-room at my club—nobody seemed inclined to talk that night—that the ghastliness of the situation flashed upon me. If she had been married, one might have found a temporary solution; there would have been an experience, at least, in the sordid notoriety of the Divorce Court. (Ah, why did I abandon my caution, and venture off the track?) Even then, however, I knew that my nature could never have supported a mutual passion for long. To have my every movement followed by loving eyes, to be adored, and to meet with constant gratitude—it would have bored me to death. Still, I could have risked that and gone through with the matter. But an unmarried girl! She would expect a proposal of marriage. Me, engaged to be married! Even in my misery I smiled at the idea. The inevitable suggestion of the 'young man' and the 'Sunday out,' the horrible stereotyped vulgarities, the foolish engagement ring, the dreadful sense of being imprisoned, the constant necessity of leaving charming strangers to talk to somebody you know by heart (I thought of this view impersonally, for I really loved Juliet)—the utter impossibility of the whole business simply confounded me, and I could not allow myself to think of it. I have never affected a superiority over other men in the common things of life, nor studied to seem different from them, but this thing I could not face; it would make even me ridiculous. To marry in secret and to go to some remote place until the time for congratulation was over was conceivable. . . . But I knew she would not; no, no, some worthy, common man was her proper mate; I was not made for constancy. If I pained her now, it was that she might escape a greater pain when her love increased as mine diminished. So I wrote a letter to Juliet. I will copy down her answer, for it seems an indication of a curiously frequent phase in women. 'Dear Harry,' she wrote, 'you are delightful! I hoped that Thursday would lead to some agreeable variety in the monotonous course of your foolishness, but I never expected anything quite so delicious as your letter. Of course I knew before it arrived that your protestations meant nothing, or I should not have acted as I did. Your idea of "sparing me future pain" is most amusing, and I cannot be angry with you. You can hardly think I need apologise for humbugging you on Thursday; your vanity made it so absurdly easy. If you would do some honest work, and acquire an elementary sense of humour, you would be quite a nice boy. You see I am very indulgently yours, J. C.'

Ah, the vanity of women, and the pains they are at to save it! I fear she must have suffered keenly to deceive herself (or to try to deceive me) so grossly. Poor child, poor child!

THE OLD GENERATION

It seems worth the pains to make a note of my experience of today; for though it is trivial as regards my history, there is some instruction in this contact of a worthy, middle-aged pedagogue, with his curious narrowness of outlook and mediocre intelligence, and one like myself.

Even all those years ago, at school, I think that I differed from the others in seeing the excellent creature as he was. To some few he was of course the Doctor, a subject for abuse, but not for detailed criticism; to others he was a kindly superior or a great scholar; to me he was simply John Herbert Baxter, a poor human engine, striving with imperfect powers to do what an uninstructed habit of mind told him was his duty, a man of some reading doubtless, and a distinct ability for organisation, as impartial as his prejudices—those queer unlovely prejudices! —allowed; one who, Heaven help the poor fellow, had never lived. As for his scholarship, such a stamp as University honours might put on a man was his, but even then I was more exigent in that matter and saw no trace in him of a comprehension of the Greek spirit; it is true I was never in the sixth, and so had no close observation of the result of his reading, but I often listened to his sermons in the chapel. I used to try to cultivate him in those days, and took an interest, a weary interest, perhaps, in his wife: poor dear, she was a sweet person in many ways. When the rupture came, and his ridiculous, natural prejudices and absurd reverence for his silly rules inflicted an agreeable but undoubted injury upon me, and we parted, as I thought, for ever, my judgment of him was unaltered; I felt as some Charles the First towards his executioner, and could find it in my heart to praise while I pitied him. So when we met today there was no malice in my mind, and I was ready to observe kindly this specimen of a class that I have passed, as it were, in the race of development.

I recognised him at once when he came into my railway carriage (we were alone in it), and I smiled at him as he sat down opposite to me. As I expected, after greeting me, his first question was: 'What are you doing now?' To explain the folly of it would have been to explain a philosophy quite unknown to him; so I merely waved my hands, and inquired about his wife, calling her dear lady, as indeed she was. He answered stiffly, and I saw he remembered our ridiculous quarrel. But I wished to have some profit from this encounter, and even hoped he might go from it a fresher and more clearly thinking man, and therefore I tried, with gently searching questions, to draw him out about his work and its effects upon his mind. His answers told me more than he (with that bluff defensiveness which marks the national character in the rough, and is so sad a comment on our egotism) intended that they should, and the gulf between us seemed indeed impassable. I felt myself half angry at this imprisonment of an intellect I knew to be fairly capable, but also sorrowful—sorrowful almost to tears. At length our conversation came to this. He said to me: 'You spoke just now of "the elect." May I ask if you are one of them, and if so, who elected you and for what purpose?' I have a habit, when rude or sarcastic questions are addressed to me, of looking at the questioner with half-closed lids. It seemed to irritate the poor Doctor, and he asked me angrily if I were going to sleep. This gave me animation to speak plainly, and risking his affection for me I determined to throw a rope to this poor ignorant swimmer. 'I am elected,' I said smiling, 'to try to show you how inadequate are the ideas implied by your remarks; to restore to you what might have been. We have been talking for some time with a wall between us; I want you to scale it. I may seem to presume on too slight an acquaintance, but from boyhood you have interested me. Baxter,' I said, leaning forward and tapping him on the knee, and speaking familiarly, as to an equal, 'Baxter, do you never feel that your life is wasted? It is wholly spent in fulfilling a mechanical function that hundreds of others would fulfil as well as you. Doctrinal prejudices shut you off from the joy of untrammelled thinking, moral prejudices from the joy of untrammelled living. Believe me both sorts are foolish, and they are so dull. You munch the dry bones of life; the taste and the colour of it might not exist for you. Be one of us; perform, if you must, the vulgar duties of your calling, but perform them with your mind set on what is fine and rare. Rouse yourself....' Alas! He interrupted me. 'I suppose,' he said, 'there are people who think this sort of thing amusing, but I think it grossly impertinent. But I won't resent it, as I might. You used to be a fool, and now you are a mass of conceit as well, and seem to be fast losing your manners. Probably, what little brains you have will go with them. It's a waste of words, but I may as well tell you, you are preparing for yourself a discontented manhood and a friendless old age.'

I put down his *ipsissima verba*, to be a standing warning to me that I never again try to fight against the perversity of his generation. It is all very sad and terribly disappointing. But the lesson is useful: we must live our lives and beware of altruism. I wished to be of service to this foolish brother, but after all I was not his keeper.

POEMS

OSCAR WILDE

The Harlot's House

WE CAUGHT the tread of dancing feet,
We loitered down the moonlit street,
And stopped beneath the harlot's house.

Inside, above the din and fray,
We heard the loud musicians play
The 'Treues Liebes Herz' of Strauss.

Like strange mechanical grotesques,
Making fantastic arabesques,
The shadows raced across the blind.

We watched the ghostly dancers spin
To sound of horn and violin,
Like black leaves wheeling in the wind.

Like wire-pulled automatons,
Slim-silhouetted skeletons
Went sidling through the slow quadrille.

They took each other by the hand,
And danced a stately saraband;
Their laughter echoed thin and shrill.

Sometimes a clockwork puppet pressed
A phantom lover to her breast,
Sometimes they seemed to try to sing.

Sometimes a horrible marionette
Came out, and smoked its cigarette
Upon the steps like a live thing.

Then, turning to my love, I said,
'The dead are dancing with the dead,
The dust is whirling with the dust.'

But she—she heard the violin,
And left my side, and entered in:
Love passed into the house of lust.

Then suddenly the tune went false,
The dancers wearied of the waltz,
The shadows ceased to wheel and whirl.

And down the long and silent street,
The dawn, with silver-sandalled feet,
Crept like a frightened girl.

Le Jardin: Impressions I

The lily's withered chalice falls
    Around its rod of dusty gold
    And from the beech trees in the wold
The last wood-pigeon coos and calls.

The gaudy leonine sunflower
    Hangs black and barren on its stalk,
    And down the windy garden walk
The dead leaves scatter—hour by hour.

Pale privet-petals white as milk
Are blown into a snowy mass:
    The roses lie upon the grass
Like little shreds of crimson silk.

Les Ballons

FANTAISIES DECORATIVES II

Against these turbid turquoise skies
    The light and luminous balloons
    Dip and drift like satin moons
Drift like silken butterflies;

Reel with every windy gust,
    Rise and reel like dancing girls,
    Float like strange transparent pearls,
Fall and float like silver dust.

Now to the low leaves they cling,
 Each with coy fantastic pose,
 Each a petal of a rose
Straining at a gossamer string.

Then to the tall trees they climb,
 Like thin globes of amethyst,
 Wandering opals keeping tryst
With the rubies of the lime.

Theocritus

A Villanelle

O singer of Persephone!
 In the dim meadows desolate
Dost thou remember Sicily?

Still through the ivy flits the bee
 Where Amaryllis lies in state;
O Singer of Persephone!

Simætha calls on Hecate
 And hears the wild dogs at the gate;
Dost thou remember Sicily?

Still by the light and laughing sea
 Poor Polypheme bemoans his fate;
O Singer of Persephone!

And still in boyish rivalry
 Young Daphnis challenges his mate;
Dost thou remember Sicily?

Slim Lacon keeps a goat for thee,
 For thee the jocund shepherds wait;
O Singer of Persephone!
Dost thou remember Sicily?

JOHN DAVIDSON
(1857-1909)

John Davidson was born on 11 April 1857 at Barrhead, Renfrewshire, and was the son of a minister of the Evangelical Union.

Between 1870 and 1889 he was mostly employed as a teacher, though he managed to secure for himself a year as arts student at Edinburgh University. In 1889 he came to London, where his poetry initially enjoyed a boom, but shortly after 1894 he was reporting to Yeats: 'The fires are out . . . and I must hammer the cold iron.'

A proud man disheartened by lack of recognition, by failing health and too small a Civil List Pension, he committed suicide by drowning on, or about, 23 March 1909 at, or near, Penzance while holidaying.

Lionel Johnson has described him as 'a Scotch metaphysician turned into a romantic and realistic poet' (Lionel Johnson, *Literary Essays of Ezra Pound*, 1954).

In a prologue to the volume in which the following poem appears, the poet tells us that in 1884, when he was a young clerk in Glasgow, he spent his evenings in a music-hall, 'rancid and hot.' This poem was one of six sketches in verse which he made of six 'artistes' performing. Davidson, Symons and Wratislaw all wrote poems on the music-hall.

Selene Eden

MY DEAREST lovers know me not;
I hide my life and soul from sight;
I conquer all whose blood is hot;
    My mystery is my mail of might.

I had a troupe who danced with me;
    I veiled myself from head to foot;
My girls were nude as they dared be;
    They sang a chorus, I was mute.

But now I fill the widest stage
    Alone, unveiled, without a song;
And still with mystery I engage
    The aching senses of the throng.

A dark-blue vest with stars of gold,
    My only diamond in my hair,
An Indian scarf about me rolled;
    That is the dress I always wear.

At first the sensuous music whets
   The lustful crowd; the dim-lit room
Recalls delights, recalls regrets;
   And then I enter in the gloom.

I glide, I trip, I run, I spin,
   Lapped in the lime-light's aureole,
Hushed are the voices, hushed the din,
   I see men's eyes like glowing coal.

My loosened scarf in odours drenched
   Showers keener hints of sensual bliss;
The music swoons, the light is quenched,
   Into the dark I throw a kiss.

Then, like a long wave rolling home,
   The music gathers speed and sound;
I, dancing, am the music's foam,
   And wilder, fleeter, higher bound,

And fling my feet above my head;
   The light grows; none aside may glance;
Crimson and amber, green and red,
   In blinding baths of these I dance.

And soft, and sweet, and calm, my face
   Looks pure as unsunned chastity,
Even in the whirling triple pace:
   That is my conquering mystery.

Thirty Bob a Week

I couldn't touch a stop and turn a screw,
   And set the blooming world a-work for me,
Like such as cut their teeth—I hope, like you—
   On the handle of a skeleton gold key;
I cut mine on a leek, which I eat it every week:
   I'm a clerk at thirty bob as you can see.

But I don't allow it's luck and all a toss;
   There's no such thing as being starred and crossed;
It's just the power of some to be a boss,
   And the bally power of others to be bossed:
I face the music, sir; you bet I ain't a cur;
   Strike me lucky if I don't believe I'm lost!

For like a mole I journey in the dark,
　　A-travelling along the underground
From my Pillar'd Halls and broad Suburbean Park,
　　To come the daily dull official round;
And home again at night with my pipe all alight,
　　A-scheming how to count ten bob a pound.

And it's often very cold and very wet,
　　And my missis stitches towels for a hunks;
And the Pillar'd Halls is half of it to let—
　　Three rooms about the size of travelling trunks.
And we cough, my wife and I, to dislocate a sigh,
　　When the noisy little kids are in their bunks.

But you never hear her do a growl or whine,
　　For she's made of flint and roses, very odd;
And I've got to cut my meaning rather fine,
　　Or I'd blubber, for I'm made of greens and sod:
So p'r'aps we are in Hell for all that I can tell,
　　And lost and damn'd and served up hot to God.

I ain't blaspheming, Mr Silver-tongue;
　　I'm saying things a bit beyond your art:
Of all the rummy starts you ever sprung,
　　Thirty bob a week's the rummiest start!
With your science and your books and your the'ries
　　　　about spooks,
　　Did you ever hear of looking in your heart?

I didn't mean your pocket, Mr, no:
　　I mean that having children and a wife,
With thirty bob on which to come and go,
　　Isn't dancing to the tabor and the fife:
When it doesn't make you drink, by Heaven! it makes
　　　　you think,
　　And notice curious items about life.

I step into my heart and there I meet
　　A god-almighty devil singing small,
Who would like to shout and whistle in the street,
　　And squelch the passers flat against the wall;
If the whole world was a cake he had the power to take,
　　He would take it, ask for more, and eat it all.

And I meet a sort of simpleton beside,
　　The kind that life is always giving beans;

With thirty bob a week to keep a bride
    He fell in love and married in his teens:
At thirty bob he stuck; but he knows it isn't luck:
    He knows the seas are deeper than tureens.

And the god-almighty devil and the fool
    That meet me in the High Street on the strike,
When I walk about my heart a-gathering wool,
    Are my good and evil angels if you like.
And both of them together in every kind of weather
    Ride me like a double-seated bike.

That's rough a bit and needs its meaning curled.
    But I have a high old hot un in my mind—
A most engrugious notion of the world,
    That leaves your lightning 'rithmetic behind:
I give it at a glance when I say 'There ain't no chance,
    Nor nothing of the lucky-lottery kind.'

And it's this way that I make it out to be:
    No fathers, mothers, countries, climates—none;
Not Adam was responsible for me,
    Nor society, nor systems, nary one:
A sleeping seed, I woke—I did, indeed—
    A million years before the blooming sun.

I woke because I thought the time had come;
    Beyond my will there was no other cause;
And everywhere I found myself at home,
    Because I chose to be the thing I was;
And in whatever shape of mollusc or of ape
    I always went according to the laws.

I was the love that chose my mother out;
    I joined two lives and from the union burst;
My weakness and my strength without a doubt
    Are mine alone for ever from the first:
It's just the very same with a difference in the name
    As 'Thy will be done.' You say it if you durst!

They say it daily up and down the land
    As easy as you take a drink, it's true;
But the difficulties go to understand,
    And the difficultest job a man can do,
Is to come it brave and meek with thirty bob a week,
    And feel that that's the proper thing for you.

It's a naked child against a hungry wolf;
　　It's playing bowls upon a splitting wreck;
It's walking on a string across a gulf
　　With millstones fore-and-aft about your neck;
But the thing is daily done by many and many a one;
　　And we fall, face forward, fighting, on the deck.

A New Ballad of Tannhäuser

'What hardy, tattered wretch is that
　　Who on our Synod dares intrude?'
Pope Urban with his council sat,
　　And near the door Tannhäuser stood.

His eye with light unearthly gleamed;
　　His yellow hair hung round his head
In elf locks lustreless: he seemed
　　Like one new-risen from the dead.

'Hear me, most Holy Father, tell
　　The tale that burns my soul within.
I stagger on the brink of hell;
　　No voice but yours can shrive my sin.'

'Speak, sinner.' 'From my father's house
　　Lightly I stepped in haste for fame;
And hoped by deeds adventurous
　　High on the world to carve my name.

'At early dawn I took my way,
　　My heart with peals of gladness rang;
Nor could I leave the woods all day,
　　Because the birds so sweetly sang.

'But when the happy birds had gone
　　To rest, and night with panic fears
And blushes deep came stealing on,
　　Another music thrilled my ears.

'I heard the evening wind serene,
　　And all the wandering waters sing
The deep delight the day had been,
　　The deep delight the night would bring.

'I heard the wayward earth express
  In one long-drawn melodious sigh
The rapture of the sun's caress,
  The passion of the brooding sky.

'The air, a harp of myriad chords,
  Intently murmured overhead;
My heart grew great with unsung words:
  I followed where the music led.

'It led me to a mountain-chain,
  Wherein athwart the deepening gloom,
High-hung above the wooded plain,
  Appeared a summit like a tomb.

'Aloft a giddy pathway wound
  That brought me to a darksome cave:
I heard, undaunted, underground
  Wild winds and wilder voices rave,

'And plunged into that stormy world.
  Cold hands assailed me impotent
In the gross darkness; serpents curled
  About my limbs; but on I went.

'The wild winds buffeted my face;
  The wilder voices shrieked despair;
A stealthy step with mine kept pace,
  And subtle terror steeped the air.

'But the sweet sound that throbbed on high
  Had left the upper world; and still
A cry rang in my heart—a cry!
  For lo, far in the hollow hill,

'The dulcet melody withdrawn
  Kept welling through the fierce uproar.
As I have seen the molten dawn
  Across a swarthy tempest pour,

'So suddenly the magic note,
  Transformed to light, a glittering brand,
Out of the storm and darkness smote
  A peaceful sky, a dewy land.

'I scarce could breathe, I might not stir,
  The while there came across the lea,
With singing maidens after her,
  A woman wonderful to see.

'Her face—her face was strong and sweet;
  Her looks were loving prophecies;
She kissed my brow: I kissed her feet—
  A woman wonderful to kiss.

'She took me to a place apart
  Where eglantine and roses wove
A bower, and gave me all her heart—
  A woman wonderful to love.

'As I lay worshipping my bride,
  While rose-leaves in her bosom fell,
And dreams came sailing on a tide
  Of sleep, I heard a matin bell.

'It beat my soul as with a rod
  Tingling with horror of my sin;
I thought of Christ, I thought of God,
  And of the fame I meant to win.

'I rose; I ran; nor looked behind;
  The doleful voices shrieked despair
In tones that pierced the crashing wind;
  And subtle terror warped the air.

'About my limbs the serpents curled;
  The stealthy step with mine kept pace;
But soon I reached the upper world:
  I sought a priest; I prayed for grace.

'He said, "Sad sinner, do you know
  What fiend this is, the baleful cause
Of your dismay?" I loved her so
  I never asked her what she was.

'He said, "Perhaps not God above
  Can pardon such unheard-of ill:
It was the pagan Queen of Love
  Who lured you to her haunted hill!

"'Each hour you spent with her was more
   Than a full year! Only the Pope
Can tell what heaven may have in store
   For one who seems past help and hope."

'Forthwith I took the way to Rome:
   I scarcely slept; I scarely ate:
And hither quaking am I come,
   But resolute to know my fate.

'Most Holy Father, save my soul!...
   Ah God! again I hear the chime,
Sweeter than liquid bells that toll
   Across a lake at vesper time...

'Her eyelids drop... I hear her sigh...
   The rose-leaves fall.... She falls asleep...
The cry rings in my blood—the cry
   That surges from the deepest deep.

'No man was ever tempted so!—
   I say not this in my defence....
Help, Father, help! or I must go!
   The dulcet music draws me hence!'

He knelt—he fell upon his face.
   Pope Urban said, 'The eternal cost
Of guilt like yours eternal grace
   Dare not remit: your soul is lost.

'When this dead staff I carry grows
   Again and blossoms, heavenly light
May shine on you.' Tannhäuser rose;
   And all at once his face grew bright.

He saw the emerald leaves unfold,
   The emerald blossoms break and glance;
They watched him, wondering to behold
   The rapture of his countenance.

The undivined, eternal God
   Looked on him from the highest heaven,
And showed him by the budding rod
   There was no need to be forgiven.

He heard melodious voices call
   Across the world, an elfin shout;
And when he left the council-hall,
   It seemed a great light had gone out.

With anxious heart, with troubled brow,
   The Synod turned upon the Pope.
They saw; they cried, 'A living bough,
   A miracle, a pledge of hope!'

And Urban trembling saw: 'God's way
   Is not as man's,' he said. 'Alack!
Forgive me, gracious heaven, this day
   My sin of pride. Go, bring him back.'

But swift as thought Tannhäuser fled,
   And was not found. He scarcely slept;
He scarcely ate; for overhead
   The ceaseless, dulcet music kept

Wafting him on. And evermore
   The foliate staff he saw at Rome
Pointed the way; and the winds bore
   Sweet voices whispering him to come.

The air, a world-enfolding flood
   Of liquid music poured along;
And the wild cry within his blood
   Became at last a golden song.

'All day,' he sang—'I feel all day
   The earth dilate beneath my feet;
I hear in fancy far away
   The tidal heart of ocean beat.

'My heart amasses as I run
   The depth of heaven's sapphire flower;
The resolute, enduring sun
   Fulfils my soul with splendid power.

'I quiver with divine desire;
   I clasp the stars; my thoughts immerse
Themselves in space; like fire in fire
   I melt into the universe.

'For I am running to my love:
  The eager roses burn below;
Orion wheels his sword above,
  To guard the way God bids me go.'

At dusk he reached the mountain chain,
  Wherein athwart the deepening gloom,
High hung above the wooded plain
  Hörselberg rose like a tomb.

He plunged into the under-world;
  Cold hands assailed him impotent
In the gross darkness; serpents curled
  About his limbs; but on he went.

The wild winds buffeted his face;
  The wilder voices shrieked despair;
A stealthy step with his kept pace;
  And subtle terror steeped the air.

But once again the magic note,
  Transformed to light, a glittering brand,
Out of the storm and darkness smote
  A peaceful sky, a dewy land.

And once again he might not stir,
  The while there came across the lea
With singing maidens after her
  The Queen of Love so fair to see.

Her happy face was strong and sweet;
  Her looks were loving prophecies;
She kissed his brow; he kissed her feet—
  He kissed the ground her feet did kiss.

She took him to a place apart
  Where eglantine and roses wove
A bower, and gave him all her heart—
  The Queen of Love, the Queen of Love.

As he lay worshipping his bride
  While rose-leaves in her bosom fell,
And dreams came sailing on a tide
  Of sleep, he heard a matin-bell.

'Hark! Let us leave the magic hill,'
   He said, 'And live on earth with men.'
'No; here,' she said, 'we stay, until
   The Golden Age shall come again.'

And so they wait, while empires sprung
   Of hatred thunder past above,
Deep in the earth for ever young
   Tannhäuser and the Queen of Love.

The Merchantman. The Markethaunters

ECLOGUES I

The Markethaunters

Now, while our money is piping hot
   From the mint of our toil that coins the sheaves,
Merchantman, merchantman, what have you got
   In your tabernacle hung with leaves?
      What have you got?
        The sun rides high;
      Our money is hot;
        We must buy, buy, buy!

The Merchantman

I come from the elfin king's demesne
   With chrysolite, hyacinth, tourmaline;
I have emeralds here of living green;
   I have rubies, each like a cup of wine;
And diamonds, diamonds that never have been
   Outshone by eyes the most divine!

The Markethaunters

Jewellery?—Baubles; bad for the soul;
   Desire of the heart and lust of the eye!
Diamonds, indeed! We wanted coal.
   What else do you sell? Come, sound your cry!
      Our money is hot;
        The night draws nigh;
      What have you got
        That we want to buy?

The Merchantman

I have here enshrined the soul of the rose
    Exhaled in the land of the daystar's birth;
I have casks whose golden staves enclose
    Eternal youth, eternal mirth;
And cordials that bring repose,
    And the tranquil night, and the end of the earth.

The Markethaunters

Rapture of wine? But it never pays:
    We must keep our common-sense alert.
Raisins are healthier, medicine says—
    Raisins and almonds for dessert.
        But we want to buy;
           For our money is hot,
        And age draws nigh:
           What else have you got?

The Merchantman

I have lamps that gild the lustre of noon;
    Shadowy arrows that pierce the brain;
Dulcimers strung with beams of the moon;
    Psalteries fashioned of pleasure and pain;
A song and a sword and a haunting tune
    That may never be offered the world again.

The Markethaunters

Dulcimers! psalteries! Whom do you mock?
    Arrows and songs? We have axes to grind!
Shut up your booth and your mouldering stock,
    For we never shall deal.—Come away; let us find
        What the others have got
          We must buy, buy, buy;
        For our money is hot,
           And death draws nigh.

FRANCIS JOSEPH THOMPSON
(1859-1907)

Son of a homeopathic physician, Thompson was born at Preston, Lancashire, on 18 December 1859. He was brought up as a Catholic and educated at Ushaw College, where he was intended for the priesthood but was considered to be temperamentally unfitted.

For the next six years he studied medicine at Owen's College, Manchester, but after failing his examination three times, he disappeared to London where he lived till 1888 sunk in poverty and laudanum addiction. Thompson was rescued from his plight by the Meynells; Wilfrid Meynell found him work to do for his magazine *Merrie England* and Alice his wife offered him the family comfort of her home and the social amenities of her salon at 47 Palace Court, Kensington. He then went on to write his two greatest works—his poem *The Hound of Heaven* and his iridescent essay *Shelley* (first published 1908)—at a monastery in Storrington, Sussex.

Wilfrid Scawen Blunt called him 'Crashaw born again, but born greater' and R. L. Mégroz described him as 'the greatest poet of Catholicism since Dante'. The best contemporary evaluation of Thompson as a poet is the balanced and discriminating essay on him in Arthur Symons's *Dramatis Personae*, 1925.

The Singer Saith of His Song

THE touches of man's modern speech
    Perplex her unacquainted tongue;
There seems through all her songs a sound
    Of falling tears. She is not young.
Within her eyes' profound arcane
    Resides the glory of her dreams;
Behind her secret cloud of hair
    She sees the Is beyond the Seems.
Her heart sole-towered in her steep spirit,
    Somewhat sweet is she, somewhat wan;
And she sings the songs of Sion
    By the streams of Babylon.

At Lord's

It is little I repair to the matches of the Southron folk,
    Though my own red roses there may blow;
It is little I repair to the matches of the Southron folk,
    Though the red roses crest the caps, I know.
For the field is full of shades as I near the shadowy coast,
And a ghostly batsman plays to the bowling of a ghost,
And I look through my tears on a soundless-clapping host
    As the run-stealers flicker to and fro,
        To and fro:—
O my Hornby and my Barlow long ago!

To a Snowflake

What heart could have thought you?—
Past our devisal
(O filigree petal!)
Fashioned so purely
Fragilely, surely,
From what Paradisal
Imagineless metal,
Too costly for cost?
Who hammered you, wrought you,
From argentine vapour?—
'God was my shaper.
Passing surmisal,
He hammered, He wrought me,
From curled silver vapour,
To lust of His mind:—
Thou could'st not have thought me!
So purely, so palely,
Tinily, surely,
Mightily, fraily,
Insculped and embossed,
With His hammer of wind,
And His graver of frost.'

A Dead Astronomer

STEPHEN PERRY, S.J.

Starry amorist, starward gone,
Thou art—what thou didst gaze upon!
Passed through thy golden garden's bars,
Thou seest the Gardener of the Stars.
She, about whose moonèd brows
Seven stars make seven glows,
Seven lights for seven woes;
She, like thine own Galaxy,
All lustres in one purity:—
What said'st thou, Astronomer,
When thou did'st discover *her*?
When thy hand its tube let fall,
Thou found'st the fairest Star of all!

Memorat Memoria

Come you living or dead to me, out of the silt of the Past,
With the sweet of the piteous first, and the shame of the shameful
    last?
Come with your dear and dreadful face through the passes of Sleep,
The terrible mask, and the face it masked—the face you did not keep?
You are neither two nor one—I would you were one or two,
For your awful self is embalmed in the fragrant self I knew:
And Above may ken, and Beneath may ken, what I mean by these
    words of whirl,
But by my sleep that sleepeth not,—O Shadow of a Girl!—
Naught here but I and my dreams shall know the secret of this
    thing:—
For ever the songs I sing are sad with the songs I never sing,
Sad are sung songs, but how more sad the songs we dare not sing!
Ah, the ill that we do in tenderness, and the hateful horror of love!
It has sent more souls to the unslaked Pit than it ever will draw above.

I damned you, girl, with my pity, who had better by far been
    thwart,
And drave you hard on the track to hell, because I was gentle of
    heart.
I shall have no comfort now in scent, no ease in dew, for this;
I shall be afraid of daffodils, and rose-buds are amiss;
You have made a thing of innocence as shameful as a sin,
I shall never feel a girl's soft arms without horror of the skin.
My child! what was it that I sowed, that I so ill should reap?
You have done this to me. And I, what I to you?—It lies with Sleep.

Envoy

Go, songs, for ended is our brief, sweet play;
    Go, children of swift joy and tardy sorrow:
And some are sung, and that was yesterday,
    And some unsung, and that may be tomorrow.

Go forth; and if it be o'er stony way,
    Old joy can lend what newer grief must borrow:
And it was sweet, and that was yesterday,
    And sweet is sweet, though purchasèd with sorrow.

Go, songs, and come not back from your far way:
    And if men ask you why ye smile and sorrow,
Tell them ye grieve, for your hearts know Today,
    Tell them ye smile, for your eyes know Tomorrow.

ERNEST RHYS
(1859-1946)

Ernest Rhys was born of a Welsh father and English mother on 17 July 1859 at Islington. He spent much of his youth in his father's county of Carmarthenshire. He then became a mining engineer in the North but left it to follow a literary career in London.

Co-founder with Yeats and others of the Rhymers' Club, he wrote his charming toast for that body. Known better as an editor than a poet, he supervised the Camelot Series (published by Walter Scott) between 1886 and 1890 and the first 967 titles of Dent's Everyman's Library between 1906 and 1940. Three books by Rhys of autobiography and reminiscence throw light on certain of the Rhymer poets and other figures of the 'nineties: *Everyman Remembers*, 1931, *Letters from Limbo*, 1936 and *Wales England Wed*, 1941.

At the Rhymers' Club

I. THE TOAST

SET fools untó their folly!
　Our folly is pure wit,
As 'twere the Muse turned jolly:
For poets' melancholy,—
　We will not think of it.

As once Rare Ben and Herrick
　Set older Fleet Street mad,
With wit, not esoteric,
And laughter that was lyric,
　And roystering rhymes and glad

As they, we drink defiance
　Tonight to all but Rhyme,
And most of all to Science,
And all such skins of lions
　That hide the ass of time.

Tonight, to rhyme as they did
　　Were well,—ah, were it ours,
Who find the Muse degraded,
And changed, I fear, and faded,
　　Her laurel crown and flowers.

Ah, rhymers, for that sorrow
　　The more o'ertakes delight,
The more this madness borrow:
If care be king tomorrow,
　　We toast Queen Rhyme tonight.

An Autobiography

Wales England wed; so I was bred. 'Twas merry
　　London gave me breath.
I dreamt of love, and fame: I strove. But Ireland
　　taught me love was best:
And Irish eyes, and London cries, and streams of
　　Wales, may tell the rest.
What more than these I asked of Life, I am
　　content to have from Death.

WILLIAM BUTLER YEATS
(1865-1939)

W. B. Yeats was the son of an agnostic attorney of Protestant stock, and was born on 13 June 1865 at Sandymount, near Dublin. His father became a painter and Yeats received an art school education in Ireland and attended the Godolphin School at Hammersmith.

During the 1890s he lived with his family at Bedford Park, W.4, and then with Arthur Symons in the Temple, later removing to Woburn Place, Holborn. Wherever he found himself dwelling, however, it was the vision of his own country which inspired him both as a poet and as a critic. His theory of literature and the arts (as held by him in the 'nineties) is seen best in the essays collected in his book *Ideas of Good and Evil*, 1903. Yeats also painted a vivid personal picture of his friends of the 'nineties in the second of his autobiographies, entitled *The Trembling of the Veil*, 1922, particularly Books II and IV.

Down by the Salley Gardens[1]

DOWN by the salley gardens my love and I did meet;
She passed the salley gardens with little snow-white feet.
She bid me take love easy, as the leaves grow on the tree;
But I, being young and foolish, with her would not agree.

In a field by the river my love and I did stand,
And on my leaning shoulder she laid her snow-white hand.
She bid me take life easy, as the grass grows on the weirs;
But I was young and foolish, and now am full of tears.

---

[1] The text of this poem in *Poems* (1899)—the last edition of the poet's poems written in the decade of the 'nineties which carries many revisions of earlier versions—in no wise differs from the version which appears in *Collected Poems* (1933). The term 'salley' signifies 'willows.'

The Man Who Dreamed of Faeryland[1]

He stood among a crowd at Drumahair;
His heart hung all upon a silken dress,
And he had known at last some tenderness,
Before earth made of him her sleepy care;
But when a man poured fish into a pile,
It seemed they raised their little silver heads,
And sang how day a Druid twilight sheds
Upon a dim, green, well-beloved isle,
Where people love beside star-laden seas;
How Time may never mar their faery vows
Under the woven roofs of quicken boughs:
The singing shook him out of his new ease.

He wandered by the sands of Lisadill;
His mind ran all on money cares and fears,
And he had known at last some prudent years
Before they heaped his grave under the hill;
But while he passed before a plashy place,
A lug-worm with its gray and muddy mouth
Sang how somewhere to north or west or south
There dwelt a gay, exulting, gentle race;
And how beneath those three times blessed skies
A Danaan fruitage makes a shower of moons,
And as it falls awakens leafy tunes:
And at that singing he was no more wise.

Stanza I Line 4   Before earth took him to her stony care;
          Lines 7–11 And sang what gold morning or evening sheds
                      Upon a woven world-forgotten isle
                      Where people love beside the ravelled seas;
                      That time can never mar a lover's vows
                      Under that woven changeless roof of boughs:

Stanza II Line 1   He wandered by the sands of Lissadell;
           Line 7   Sang that somewhere to north or west or south
           Lines 9–11 Under the golden or the silver skies,
                       That if a dancer stayed his hungry foot
                       It seemed the sun and moon were in the fruit:

[1] The version of the poem given here is that as printed in *Poems* (1899), which differs considerably from the text of *Collected Poems* (1933). The changes made by Yeats in this final version of the 1933 edition are given above and on page 132:

131

He mused beside the well of Scanavin,
He mused upon his mockers: without fail
His sudden vengeance were a country tale,
Now that deep earth has drunk his body in;
But one small knot-grass growing by the pool
Told where, ah, little, all-unneeded voice!
Old Silence bids a lonely folk rejoice,
And chaplet their calm brows with leafage cool;
And how, when fades the sea-strewn rose of day,
A gentle feeling wraps them like a fleece,
And all their trouble dies into its peace:
The tale drove his fine angry mood away.

He slept under the hill of Lugnagall;
And might have known at last unhaunted sleep
Under that cold and vapour-turbaned steep,
Now that old earth had taken man and all:
Were not the worms that spired about his bones
A-telling with their low and reedy cry,
Of how God leans His hands out of the sky,
To bless that isle with honey in His tones;
That none may feel the power of squall and wave,
And no one any leaf-crowned dancer miss
Until He burn up Nature with a kiss:
The man has found no comfort in the grave.

Stanza III Line 4   When earthy night had drunk his body in

Lines 6–11 Sang where—unnecessary cruel voice—
Old silence bids its chosen race rejoice,
Whatever ravelled waters rise and fall
Or stormy silver fret the gold of day,
And midnight there enfold them like a fleece
And lover there by lover be at peace.

Stanza IV Lines 4–11 Now that the earth had taken man and all:
Did not the worms that spread about his bones
Proclaim with that unwearied, reedy cry
That God has laid His fingers on the sky,
That from these fingers glittering summer runs
Upon the dancer by the dreamless cave.
Why should those lovers that no lovers miss
Dream, until God burns Nature with a kiss?

NORMAN ROWLAND GALE
(1862-1936)

Norman Gale was born at Kew in 1862, and was educated at Exeter College, Oxford. For a while he taught at Rugby, from which town he published two small volumes, *Meadowsweets* and *Violets*, limited to eighty copies apiece and done up in cardboard boxes like valentines.

He made his name when a first selection of these poems was published as *A Country Muse* in London in 1892.

Richard Le Gallienne described him as 'a six-foot-three nightingale,' praising Gale for his 'union of warmth and chasteness,' writing of his poems that they possessed 'the fragrance, the spontaneity, and the strength of all earth-born things' *(Retrospective Reviews: A Literary Log*, 1895). Victor Plarr, more soberly, wrote of him as 'the pastoral poet among young English writers' *(Men and Women of the Time*, fifteenth revised edition, 1899).

The Shaded Pool

A LAUGHING knot of village maids
Goes gaily tripping to the brook,
For water-nymphs they mean to be,
And seek some still, secluded nook.
Here Laura goes, my own delight,
And Colin's love, the madcap Jane,
And half a score of goddesses
Trip over daisies in the plain:
Already now they loose their hair
And peep from out the tangled gold,
Or speed the flying foot to reach
The brook that's only summer-cold;
The lovely locks stream out behind
The shepherdesses on the wing,
And Laura's is the wealth I love,
And Laura's is the gold I sing.

A-row upon the bank they pant,
And all unlace the country shoe;
Their fingers tug the garter-knots
To loose the hose of varied hue.
The flashing knee at last appears,
The lower curves of youth and grace,
Whereat the girls intently scan
The mazy thickets of the place.
But who's to see except the thrush
Upon the wild crab-apple tree?
Within his branchy haunt he sits—
A very Peeping Tom is he!
Now music bubbles in his throat,
And now he pipes the scene in song—
The virgins slipping from their robes,
The cheated stockings lean and long,
The swift-descending petticoat,
The breasts that heave because they ran,
The rounded arms, the brilliant limbs,
The pretty necklaces of tan.
Did ever amorous God in Greece,
In search of some young mouth to kiss,
By any river chance upon
A sylvan scene as bright as this?
But though each maid is pure and fair,
For one alone my heart I bring,
And Laura's is the shape I love,
And Laura's is the snow I sing.

And now upon the brook's green brink,
A milk-white bevy, lo, they stand,
Half shy, half frightened, reaching back
The beauty of a poising hand!
How musical their little screams
When ripples kiss their shrinking feet!
And then the brook embraces all
Till gold and white and water meet!
Within the streamlet's soft cool arms
Delight and love and gracefulness
Sport till a flock of tiny waves
Swamps all the beds of floating cress;
And on his shining face are seen
Great yellow lilies drifting down
Beyond the ringing apple-tree,
Beyond the empty homespun gown.

Did ever Orpheus with his lute,
When making melody of old,
E'er find a stream in Attica
So ripely full of pink and gold?

At last they climb the sloping bank
And shake upon the thirsty soil
A treasury of diamond-drops
Not gained by aught of grimy toil.
Again the garters clasp the hose,
Again the velvet knee is hid,
Again the breathless babble tells
What Colin said, what Colin did.
In grace upon the grass they lie
And spread their tresses to the sun,
And rival, musical as they,
The blackbird's alto shake and run.
Did ever Love, on hunting bent,
Come idly humming through the hay,
And, to his sudden joyfulness,
Find fairer game at close of day?
Though every maid's a lily-rose,
And meet to sway a sceptred king,
Yet Laura's is the face I love,
And Laura's are the lips I sing.

VICTOR GUSTAVE PLARR
(1863-1929)

Son of a Doctor of Science from Alsace and a British mother whose father was a Lombard Street banker, Plarr was born on 21 June 1863 near Strassburg. He was educated at Tonbridge School and Worcester College, Oxford, where he met the poet Ernest Dowson, of whom he later wrote an account, *Ernest Dowson: Reminiscences 1887–1897*, 1914, a book of great charm in the annals of literary friendship. Plarr's daughter Marion presented a portrait of her father's friend in her novel *Cynara, the Story of Ernest and Adelaide*, 1933. Librarian first to King's College, London, and then to the Royal College of Surgeons, he died at Wimbledon on 28 January 1929.

'Plarr is delightful,' wrote Lionel Johnson of his conservative-minded fellow-Rhymer (both were members of the Rhymers' Club), 'a kind of half-French, half-Celtic Dobson' (a reference to the poet Austin Dobson who elegantly revived many old French forms of verse).

Epitaphium Citharistriæ

STAND not uttering sedately
   Trite oblivious praise above her!
Rather say you saw her lately
   Lightly kissing her last lover.

Whisper not, 'There is a reason
   Why we bring her no white blossom'!
Since the snowy bloom's in season
   Strow it on her sleeping bosom:

Oh, for it would be a pity
   To o'erpraise her or to flout her:
She was wild, and sweet, and witty—
   Let's not say dull things about her.

Ad Cinerarium

Who in this small urn reposes,
   Celt or Roman, man or woman,
Steel of steel, or rose of roses?

Whose is the dust set rustling slightly,
   In its hiding-place abiding,
When this urn is lifted lightly?

Sure some mourner deemed immortal
   What thou holdest and enfoldest,
Little house without a portal!

When the artificers had slowly
   Formed thee, turned thee, sealed thee, burned thee,
Freighted with thy freightage holy,

Surely he thought there's no forgetting
   All the sweetness and completeness
Of his rising, of her setting,

And so bade them grave no token,
   Generation, age, or nation,
On thy round side still unbroken;—

Let them score no cypress verses,
   Funeral glories, prayers, or stories,
Mourner's tears, or mourner's curses,

Ah, 'twas well! It scarcely matters
   What is sleeping in the keeping
Of this house of human tatters,—

Steel of steel, or rose of roses,
   Man, or woman, Celt or Roman,
If but soundly he reposes!

STEPHEN PHILLIPS
(1864-1915)

Son of a father who later became a Canon of Peterborough Cathedral, and a mother related to the Wordsworth family, Phillips was born on 28 July 1864 at Somertown near Oxford.

He was educated at Kings School, Peterborough and Oundle, and although intended for the Civil Service, he worked instead as an actor for six years in the travelling company of his cousin Frank Benson.

His *Poems* (published by John Lane) won the £100 First Prize offered by the *Academy* in 1898, and for something like a decade (1897–1906) he received much acclamation for his poetic dramas and verse, before sinking into drunkenness and neglect. There is a severe but just essay on Phillips's work in Arthur Symons's *Studies in Prose and Verse*, 1904, and a kind and generous impression of the poet and the man in Richard Le Gallienne's *The Romantic '90s*, 1926.

The Apparition

I

MY DEAD Love came to me, and said:
  'God gives me one hour's rest,
To spend upon the earth with thee:
  How shall we spend it best?

'Why as of old,' I said, and so
  We quarrelled as of old.
But when I turned to make my peace,
  That one short hour was told.

II

Nine nights she did not come to me:
  The heaven was filled with rain;
And as it fell, and fell, I said,
  'She will not come again.'

Last night she came, not as before,
　But in a strange attire;
Weary she seemed, and very faint,
　As though she came from fire.

III

She is not happy! It was noon;
　The sun fell on my head:
And it was not an hour in which
　We think upon the dead.

She is not happy! I should know
　Her voice, much more her cry;
And close beside me a great rose
　Had just begun to die.

She is not happy! As I walked,
　Of her I was aware:
She cried out, like a creature hurt,
　Close by me in the air.

IV

Under the trembling summer stars,
　I turned from side to side;
When she came in and sat with me,
　As though she had not died.

And she was kind to me and sweet,
　She had her ancient way;
Remembered how I liked her hand
　Amid my hair to stray.

She had forgotten nothing, yet
　Older she seemed, and still:
All quietly she took my kiss,
　Even as a mother will.

She rose, and in the streak of dawn
　She turned as if to go:
But then again came back to me;
　My eyes implored her so!

She pushed the hair from off my brow,
　And looked into my eyes.
'I live in calm,' she said, 'and there
　Am learning to be wise.'

'Why grievest thou? I pity thee
   Still turning on this bed.'
'And art thou happy?' I exclaimed.
   'Alas!' she sighed, and fled.

V

I woke: she had been standing by,
   With wonder on her face.
She came toward me, very bright,
   As from a blessed place.

She touched me not, but smiling spoke,
   And softly as before.
'They gave me drink from some slow stream;
   I love thee now no more.'

VI

The other night she hurried in,
   Her face was wild with fear:
'Old friend,' she said, 'I am pursued,
   May I take refuge here?'

HERBERT PERCY HORNE
(1864-1916)

Herbert Horne was born in Chelsea in 1864, and was a member of the Century Guild founded in 1882 ' to render all branches of art the sphere no longer of the tradesman but the artist.' Along with Selwyn Image, he edited its magazine *The Hobby Horse* from 1886 to 1892, becoming in 1893 its sole editor. In 1900 he retired to Florence, leaving his art collection (now known as the Museo Horne) to that city on his death in 1916.

Art historian, architect, typographer, textile designer and poet, his verse is 'much influenced by Caroline models, in particular by the carols of Herrick, Cartwright and Lluelyn' (*The Complete Poems of Lionel Johnson*, edited by Ian Fletcher, 1953).

Paradise Walk

She is living in Paradise Walk,
With the dirt and the noise of the street;
And heaven flies up, if she talk,
With Paradise down at her feet.

She laughs through a summer of curls;
She moves in a garden of grace:
Her glance is a treasure of pearls,
How saved from the deeps of her face!

And the magical reach of her thigh
Is the measure, with which God began
To build up the peace of the sky,
And fashion the pleasures of man.

With Paradise down at her feet,
While heaven flies up if she talk;
With the dirt and the noise of the street,
She is living in Paradise Walk.

Cease, Cease Reproachful Eyes!

Cease, cease reproachful eyes! I have not done
  Aught, that should bring me ever this unrest.
Tell me my fault! Have end! Search, one by one,
  All possible errors, which have Time possessed;
I swear you, naught upon me shall you prove;
Unless it be a fault in me to love.

Oh! were you here with me, that I might speak
  No matter what unheeded words, and vain;
I would persuade me, that the look I seek
  Was given: but for me there must remain,
Beneath the one, unalterable guise,
This torture. Nay! Cease, cease; relentless eyes!

A Carol for Christmas Eve

We are but of such mortal mould,
  Nos exaudi, Domine!
That the night can scarce withhold
  In its shroud our sins from Thee.

That night comes, when Thou shalt come
  Nos exaudi, Domine!
From Thy home to this sad home,
  And die for us upon the tree.

If then the stars shine out so bright,
  Nos exaudi, Domine!
That Thou seest by their light,
  How great our sins and many be;

Thou wilt come, as they were not,
  Nos exaudi, Domine!
Or as they were all forgot,
  Or forgiven, Lord, by Thee.

A Question and an Answer

The Question What is Love? Is Love in this,
That flies between us, in a kiss?
Nay, what is Love? Is Love the zest,
That wakes, when I unloose my breast?
But what is Love? Say now: who knows,
Or where he lurks, or how he shows?

The Answer Dearest, Truth is stern, I fear:
Love, as yet, can scarce be here.

Love is poor; nay, Love is sorry;
   Tears, not kisses, chiefly stay him;
His sad weeds best tell his story;
   Vain delights befool, bewray him.

Truth, alas! is hard to bear:
Know, as yet, Love is not here.

But, when the evil days are come,
   If those same lips, which kiss you now,
Still make your tearful eyes their home,
   And chide the sorrow from your brow;

Then say to your own heart, my Dear;
Abide, poor heart, for Love is here.

Love is a light, in darkened ways;
   Love is a path, in pathless lands;
Love is a fire, in winter days;
   A staff, in chill, unsteady hands.

Speak to your heart, my own, my Dear;
Say: this is Love, and Love is here.

The Measure

'CORINA CORINNAE: III'

Between the pansies and the rye,
Flutters my purple butterfly;

Between her white brow and her chin,
Does Love his fairy wake begin:

By poppy-cups and drifts of heather,
Dances the sun and she together;

But o'er the scarlet of her mouth,
Whence those entreated words come forth,
Love hovers all the live-long day,
And cannot, through its spell, away;
But there, where he was born, must die,
Between the pansies and the rye.

'Bella immagine d'un fior'

Lilia with the magic hair,
Unto you an holy hour
Love himself, constrained, hath granted;
Lilia with the magic hair,
Beautiful likeness of a flower.

Too happy, whom that time ordains,
By these high spells, to lie enchanted;
Red lips, white limbs with sapphire veins;
Lilia with the magic hair,
Beautiful likeness of a flower!

O Rare concent of all delight,
Put forth, and use, your utmost power;
Keep and entangle him to-night,
Lilia with the magic hair,
Beautiful likeness of a flower.

ARTHUR SYMONS

The Opium-Smoker

I am engulfed, and drown deliciously.
Soft music like a perfume, and sweet light
Golden with audible odours exquisite,
Swathe me with cerements for eternity.
Time is no more. I pause and yet I flee.
A million ages wrap me round with night.
I drain a million ages of delight.
I hold the future in my memory.

Also I have this garret which I rent,
This bed of straw, and this that was a chair,
This worn-out body like a tattered tent,
This crust, of which the rats have eaten part,
This pipe of opium; rage, remorse, despair;
This soul at pawn and this delirious heart.

Episode of a Night of May

SCÈNES DE LA VIE DE BOHÈME: I

The coloured lanterns lit the trees, the grass,
The little tables underneath the trees,
And the rays dappled like a delicate breeze
Each wine-illumined glass.

The pink light flickered, and a shadow ran
Along the ground as couples came and went;
The waltzing fiddles sounded from the tent,
And *Giroflée* began.

They sauntered arm in arm, these two; the smiles
Grew chilly, as the best spring evenings do.
The words were warmer, but the words came few,
And pauses fell at whiles.

But she yawned prettily. 'Come then,' said he.
He found a chair, Veuve Clicquot, some cigars.
They emptied glasses and admired the stars,
The lanterns, night, the sea.

Nature, the newest opera, the dog
(So clever) who could shoulder arms and dance;
He mentioned Alphonse Daudet's last romance,
Last Sunday's river-fog.

Love, Immortality; the talk ran down
To these mere lees: they wearied each of each,
And tortured ennui into hollow speech,
And yawned, to hide a frown.

She jarred his nerves; he bored her—and so soon.
Both were polite, and neither cared to say
The word that mars a perfect night of May.
They watched the waning moon.

May 21, 1888.

In Kensington Gardens

Under the almond tree,
Room for my love and me!
Over our heads the April blossom;
April-hearted are we.

Under the pink and white,
Love in her eyes alight;
Love and the Spring and Kensington Gardens:
Hey for the heart's delight!

At Dieppe: Grey and Green

INTERMEZZO AND PASTORALE: III

To Walter Sickert

The grey-green stretch of sandy grass,
Indefinitely desolate;
A sea of lead, a sky of slate;
Already autumn in the air, alas!

One stark monotony of stone,
The long hotel, acutely white,
Against the after-sunset light
Withers grey-green, and takes the grass's tone.

Listless and endless it outlies,
And means, to you and me, no more
Than any pebble on the shore,
Or this indifferent moment as it dies.

Liber Amoris

BIANCA: X

What's virtue, Bianca? Have we not
Agreed the word should be forgot,
That ours be every dear device
And all the subtleties of vice,
And, in diverse imaginings,
The savour of forbidden things,
So only that the obvious be
Too obvious for you and me,
And the one vulgar final act,
Remain an unadmitted fact?

And, surely, we were wise to waive
A gift we do not lose, but save.
What moments' reeling blaze of sense
Were rationally recompense
For all the ecstasies and all
The ardours demi-virginal?
Bianca, I tell you, no delights
Of long, free, unforbidden nights,
Have richlier filled and satisfied
The eager moments as they died,
Than your voluptuous pretence
Of unacquainted innocence,
Your clinging hands and closing lips
And eyes slow sinking to eclipse
And cool throat flushing to my kiss;
That sterile and mysterious bliss,
Mysterious, and yet to me
Deeper for that dubiety.

Once, but that time was long ago,
I loved good women, and to know
That lips my lips dared never touch
Could speak, in one warm smile, so much.
And it seemed infinitely sweet
To worship at a woman's feet,
And live on heavenly thoughts of her
Till earth itself grew heavenlier.
But that rapt mood, being fed on air,
Turned at the last to a despair,
And, for a body and soul like mine,
I found the angel's food too fine.
So the mood changed, and I began
To find that man is merely man,
Though women might be angels; so,
I let the aspirations go,
And for a space I held it wise
To follow after certainties.
My heart forgot the ways of love,
No longer now my fancy wove
Into admitted ornament
Its spider's web of sentiment.
What my hands seized, that my hands held,
I followed as the blood compelled,
And finding that my brain found rest
On some unanalytic breast,
I was contented to discover
How easy 'tis to be a lover.

No sophistries to ravel out,
No devious martyrdoms of doubt,
Only the good firm flesh to hold,
The love well worth its weight in gold,
Love, sinking from the infinite,
Now just enough to last one night.
So the simplicity of flesh
Held me a moment in its mesh,
Till that too palled, and I began
To find that man was mostly man
In that, his will being sated, he
Will ever new variety.
And then I found you, Bianca! Then
I found in you, I found again
That chance or will or fate had brought
The curiosity I sought.

Ambiguous child, whose life retires
Into the pulse of those desires
Of whose endured possessions speaks
The passionate pallor of your cheeks;
Child, in whom neither good nor ill
Can sway your sick and swaying will,
Only the aching sense of sex
Wholly controls, and does perplex,
With dubious drifts scarce understood,
The shaken currents of your blood;
It is your ambiguity
That speaks to me and conquers me,
Your swooning heats of sensual bliss,
Under my hands, under my kiss,
And your strange reticences, strange
Concessions, your illusive change,
The strangeness of your smile, the faint
Corruption of your gaze, a saint
Such as Luini loved to paint.
What's virtue, Bianca? nay, indeed,
What's vice? for I at last am freed,
With you, of virtue and of vice:
I have discovered Paradise.
And Paradise is neither heaven,
Where the spirits of God are seven,
And the spirits of men burn pure,
Nor is it hell, where souls endure
An equal ecstasy of fire,
In like repletion of desire;
Nay, but a subtlier intense
Unsatisfied appeal of sense,
Ever desiring, ever near
The goal of all its hope and fear,
Ever a hair's-breadth from the goal.

So Bianca satisfies my soul.

December 10, 1894.

Chopin

O passionate music beating the troubled beat
I have heard in my heart, in the wind, in the passing of feet,
In the passing of dreams when on heart-throbbing wings
   they move;

O passionate music pallid with ghostly fears,
Chill with the coming of rain, the beginning of tears,
I come to you, fleeing you, finding you, fever of love!

When I am sleepless at night and I play through the night,
Lest I hear a voice, lest I see, appealing and white,
The face that never, in dreams or at dawn, departs,
Then it is, shuddering music my hands have played,
I find you, fleeing you, finding you, music, made
Of all passionate, wounded, capricious, consuming hearts.

Arques: 1. Noon

The shadows of the rooks fly up the hill,
Up the green grass, and over the white wall;
The trees drowse in the sunlight; all is still;
Only the black rooks cry and call.

Out of the ruined castle, a slow crowd,
Their sultry wings against the sunlight beat;
They float across the valley like a cloud
Across the blue sky's cloudless heat.

Idly I watch them indolently fly,
And idly, like their wings, across my brain,
Drunken with sunlight, black-winged thoughts float by,
Pass, and return, and pass, and turn again.

Arques La Bataille,
September 27, 1896.

Why?

AMOR TRIUMPHANS: II

Why is it, since I know you now
As light as any wanton is,
And, knowing, need not wonder how
You work that wonder of your kiss,
Why is it, since I know you now,

Still, in some corner of my brain,
There clings a lost, last, lingering
Doubt of my doubts of you again,
A foolish, unforgetting thing,
Still, in some corner of my brain?

Is it because your lips are soft,
And warm your hands, and strange your eyes,
That I believe again the oft
Repeated, oft permitted lies,
Because your lips are warm and soft?

For what you are I know you now,
For what it means I know your kiss;
Yet, knowing, need one wonder how,
Beneath your kisses, how it is,
Knowing you, I believe you now?

On Inishmaan: Isles of Aran

IN IRELAND: I

In the twilight of the year,
Here, about these twilight ways,
When the grey moth night drew near
Fluttering on a faint flying,
I would linger out the day's
Delicate and moth-grey dying.

Grey, and faint with sleep, the sea
Should enfold me, and release,
Some old peace to dwell with me,
I would quiet the long crying
Of my heart with mournful peace,
The grey sea's, in its low sighing.

Wanderer's Song

I have had enough of women, and enough of love,
But the land waits, and the sea waits, and day and night is enough;
Give me a long white road, and the grey wide path of the sea,
And the wind's will and the bird's will, and the heart-ache still in me.

Why should I seek out sorrow, and give gold for strife?
I have loved much and wept much, but tears and love are not life;
The grass calls to my heart, and foam to my blood cries up,
And the sun shines and the road shines, and the wine's in the cup.

I have had enough of wisdom, and enough of mirth,
For the way's one and the end's one, and it's soon to the ends of
   the earth;
And it's then good-night and to bed, and if heels or heart ache,
Well, it's sound sleep and long sleep, and sleep too deep to wake.

The Sick Heart

O sick heart, be at rest!
Is there nothing that I can do
To quiet your crying in my breast?
Will nothing comfort you?

'I am sick of a malady
There is but one thing can assuage:
Cure me of youth, and, see,
I will be wise in age!'

Epilogue

O little waking hour of life out of sleep!
When I consider the many million years
I was not yet, and the many million years
I shall not be, it is easy to think of the sleep
I shall sleep for the second time without hopes or fears.
Surely my sleep for the million years was deep?
I remember no dreams from the million years, and it seems
I may sleep for as many million years without dreams.

Pantomime

FROM PAUL VERLAINE: FÊTES GALANTES: VI

Pierrot, no sentimental swain,
Washes a pâté down again
With furtive flagons, white and red.

Cassandre, to chasten his content,
Greets with a tear of sentiment
His nephew disinherited.

That blackguard of a Harlequin
Pirouettes, and plots to win
His Columbine that flits and flies.

Columbine dreams, and starts to find
A sad heart sighing in the wind,
And in her heart a voice that sighs.

From Romances sans Paroles

FROM PAUL VERLAINE: FÊTES GALANTES: IX

Tears in my heart that weeps,
Like the rain upon the town.
What drowsy languor steeps
In tears my heart that weeps?

O sweet sound of the rain
On earth and on the roofs!
For a heart's weary pain
O the song of the rain!

Vain tears, vain tears, my heart!
What, none hath done thee wrong?
Tears without reason start
From my disheartened heart.

This is the weariest woe,
O heart, of love and hate
Too weary, not to know
Why thou hast all this woe.

O Flame of Living Love

FROM SAN JUAN DE LA CRUZ: II

O flame of living love,
That dost eternally
Pierce through my soul with so consuming heat,
Since there's no help above,
Make thou an end of me,
And break the bond of this encounter sweet.

O burn that burns to heal!
O more than pleasant wound!
And O soft hand, O touch most delicate,
That dost new life reveal,
That dost in grace abound,
And, slaying, dost from death to life translate!

O lamps of fire that shined
With so intense a light,
That those deep caverns where the senses live,
Which were obscure and blind,
Now with strange glories bright,
Both heat and light to his beloved give!

With how benign intent
Rememberest thou my breast,
Where thou alone abidest secretly;
And in thy sweet ascent,
With glory and good possessed,
How delicately thou teachest love to me!

From Saint Teresa: II

Let mine eyes see thee,
Sweet Jesus of Nazareth
Let mine eyes see thee,
And then see death.

Let them see that care
Roses and jessamine;
Seeing thy face most fair
All blossoms are therein.
Flower of seraphin,
Sweet Jesus of Nazareth,
Let mine eyes see thee,
And then see death.

Nothing I require
Where my Jesus is;
Anguish all desire,
Saving only this;
All my help is his,
He only succoureth.
Let mine eyes see thee,
Sweet Jesus of Nazareth,
Let mine eyes see thee,
And then see death.

JOHN HENRY GRAY
(1866-1934)

John Gray, the eldest child of a family of nine, was born on 10 March 1866 at Woolwich. His father, a Nonconformist Scot, was a carpenter and wheelwright, but through his diligence and charm the boy rose to be a librarian at the Foreign Office.

Converted to Catholicism in 1889, he was ordained a priest in 1901. He moved to Edinburgh with his friend André Raffalovich, who built a church for him there, and died in that city on 14 June 1934. The fascinating story of Gray and Raffalovich has been chronicled by Fr. Brocard Sewell (v. Bibliography).

Gray's odd and studied poems were much prized by Wilde and Beardsley.

The Barber

I DREAMED I was a barber; and there went
Beneath my hand, oh! manes extravagant.
Beneath my trembling fingers, many a mask
Of many a pleasant girl. It was my task
To gild their hair, carefully, strand by strand;
To paint their eyebrows with a timid hand;
To draw a bodkin, from a vase of kohl,
Through the closed lashes; pencils from a bowl
Of sepia to paint them underneath;
To blow upon their eyes with a soft breath.
Then lay them back and watch the leaping bands.

The dream grew vague. I moulded with my hands
The mobile breasts, the valleys; and the waist
I touched; and pigments reverently placed
Upon their thighs in sapient spots and stains,
Beryls and crysolites and diaphanes,
And gems whose hot harsh names are never said.
I was a masseur; and my fingers bled
With wonder as I touched their awful limbs.

Suddenly, in the marble trough, there seems
O, last of my pale mistresses, Sweetness!
A twy-lipped scarlet pansy. My caress
Tinges thy steel-gray eyes to violet.
Adown thy body skips the pit-a-pat
Of treatment once heard in a hospital
For plagues that fascinate, but half appal.

So, at the sound, the blood of one stood cold.
The chaste hair ripened into sudden gold.
The throat, the shoulders, swelled and were uncouth;
The breasts rose up and offered each a mouth.
And on the belly pallid blushes crept.
That maddened me, until I laughed and wept.

Complaint

Men, women, call thee so or so;
    I do not know.
    Thou hast no name
For me, but in my heart a flame

Burns tireless, 'neath a silver vine.
    And round entwine
    Its purple girth
All things of fragrance and of worth.

Thou shout! thou burst of light! thou throb
    Of pain! thou sob!
    Thou like a bar
Of some sonata, heard from far

Through blue-hue'd veils! When in these wise,
    To my soul's eyes,
    Thy shape appears,
My aching hands are full of tears.

Les Demoiselles de Sauve

Beautiful ladies through the orchard pass;
Bend under crutched-up branches, forked and low;
Trailing their samet palls o'er dew-drenched grass.

Pale blossoms, looking on proud Jacqueline,
Blush to the colour of her finger tips,
And rosy knuckles, laced with yellow lace.

High-crested Berthe discerns, with slant, clinched eyes,
Amid the leaves pink faces of the skies;
She locks her plaintive hands Sainte-Margot-wise.

Ysabeau follows last, with languorous pace;
Presses, voluptuous, to her bursting lips,
With backward stoop, a branch of eglantine.

Courtly ladies through the orchard pass;
Bow low, as in lords' halls; and springtime grass
Tangles a snare to catch the tapering toe.

ERNEST CHRISTOPHER DOWSON
(1867-1900)

Ernest Dowson was born on 2 August 1867 at Belmont Hill, Lee, in Kent, and was the son of an East End dry-dock owner, a fascinating picture of whose property appears in the novel *A Comedy of Masks*, 1893, which Dowson wrote with his friend Arthur Moore.

Educated in France and at Queen's College, Oxford, Dowson, with his frail constitution, stood up very indifferently to a regimen of late nights and 'the verdant liquid' (absinthe) as well as a deep disappointment in love. His last years were spent mostly in Brittany, but he died, a Roman convert since 1891, at a friend's cottage in Catford. There is a vivid account of his death by his friend R. H. Sherard in his books *Twenty-five Years in Paris*, 1905, and *The Real Oscar Wilde*, 1915.

Poet, short-storyist and translator, Dowson preferred his prose to his verse, but posterity's judgment has gone against his choice. His most famous poem, *Non sum qualis eram . . .*, 'Cynara', is printed in Arthur Symons's essay 'Ernest Dowson' (p. 39). 'Extreme Unction' is a skilful paraphrase, précis and adaptation into verse of a scene from Flaubert's famous novel in which Madame Bovary receives the Last Sacrament.

Spleen

For Arthur Symons

I was not sorrowful, I could not weep,
And all my memories were put to sleep.

I watched the river grow more white and strange,
All day till evening I watched it change.

All day till evening I watched the rain
Beat wearily upon the window pane.

I was not sorrowful, but only tired
Of everything that ever I desired.

Her lips, her eyes, all day became to me
The shadow of a shadow utterly.

All day mine hunger for her heart became
Oblivion, until the evening came,

And left me sorrowful, inclined to weep,
With all my memories that could not sleep.

Vitae summa brevis spem nos vetat incohare longam

They are not long, the weeping and the laughter,
    Love and desire and hate:
I think they have no portion in us after
    We pass the gate.

They are not long, the days of wine and roses:
    Out of a misty dream
Our path emerges for a while, then closes
    Within a dream.

A Coronal

*With His songs and Her days to His Lady
and to Love*

Violets and leaves of vine,
    Into a frail, fair wreath
We gather and entwine:
    A wreath for Love to wear,
    Fragrant as his own breath,
To crown his brow divine,
    All day till night is near.
Violets and leaves of vine
We gather and entwine.

Violets and leaves of vine
    For Love that lives a day,
We gather and entwine.
    All day till Love is dead,
    Till eve falls, cold and gray,
These blossoms, yours and mine,
    Love wears upon his head.
Violets and leaves of vine
We gather and entwine.

Violets and leaves of vine,
  For Love when poor Love dies
We gather and entwine.
  This wreath that lives a day
  Over his pale, cold eyes,
Kissed shut by Proserpine,
  At set of sun we lay:
Violets and leaves of vine
We gather and entwine.

Villanelle of His Lady's Treasures

I took her dainty eyes, as well
  As silken tendrils of her hair:
And so I made a Villanelle!

I took her voice, a silver bell,
  As clear as song, as soft as prayer;
I took her dainty eyes as well.

It may be, said I, who can tell,
  These things shall be my less despair?
And so I made a Villanelle!

I took her whiteness virginal
  And from her cheek two roses rare:
I took her dainty eyes as well.

I said: 'It may be possible
  Her image from my heart to tear!'
And so I made a Villanelle.

I stole her laugh, most musical:
  I wrought it in with artful care;
I took her dainty eyes as well;
And so I made a Villanelle.

To One in Bedlam

For HENRY DAVRAY

With delicate, mad hands, behind his sordid bars,
Surely he hath his posies, which they tear and twine;
Those scentless wisps of straw, that miserably line
His strait, caged universe, whereat the dull world stares,

Pedant and pitiful. O, how his rapt gaze wars
With their stupidity! Know they what dreams divine
Lift his long, laughing reveries like enchaunted wine,
And make his melancholy germane to the stars'?

O lamentable brother! if those pity thee,
Am I not fain of all thy lone eyes promise me;
Half a fool's kingdom, far from men who sow and reap,
All their days, vanity? Better than mortal flowers,
Thy moon-kissed roses seem: better than love or sleep,
The star-crowned solitude of thine oblivious hours!

Chanson sans Paroles

In the deep violet air,
    Not a leaf is stirred;
    There is no sound heard,
But afar, the rare
    Trilled voice of a bird.

Is the wood's dim heart,
    And the fragrant pine,
    Incense, and a shrine
Of her coming? Apart,
    I wait for a sign.

What the sudden hush said,
    She will hear, and forsake,
    Swift, for my sake,
Her green, grassy bed:
    She will hear and awake!

She will hearken and glide,
   From her place of deep rest,
   Dove-eyed, with the breast
Of a dove, to my side:
   The pines bow their crest.

I wait for a sign:
   The leaves to be waved,
   The tall tree-tops laved
In a flood of sunshine,
   This world to be saved!

In the deep violet air,
   Not a leaf is stirred;
   There is no sound heard,
But afar, the rare
   Trilled voice of a bird.

Nuns of the Perpetual Adoration

For The Countess Sobieska von Platt

Calm, sad, secure; behind high convent walls,
   These watch the sacred lamp, these watch and pray:
And it is one with them when evening falls,
   And one with them the cold return of day.

These heed not time; their nights and days they make
   Into a long, returning rosary,
Whereon their lives are threaded for Christ's sake:
   Meekness and vigilance and chastity.

A vowed patrol, in silent companies,
   Life-long they keep before the living Christ:
In the dim church, their prayers and penances
   Are fragrant incense to the Sacrificed.

Outside, the world is wild and passionate;
   Man's weary laughter and his sick despair
Entreat at their impenetrable gate:
   They heed no voices in their dream of prayer.

They saw the glory of the world displayed;
   They saw the bitter of it, and the sweet;
They knew the roses of the world should fade,
   And be trod under by the hurrying feet.

Therefore they rather put away desire,
  And crossed their hands and came to sanctuary;
And veiled their heads and put on coarse attire:
  Because their comeliness was vanity.

And there they rest; they have serene insight
  Of the illuminating dawn to be:
Mary's sweet Star dispels for them the night,
  The proper darkness of humanity.

Calm, sad, secure; with faces worn and mild:
  Surely their choice of vigil is the best?
Yea! for our roses fade, the world is wild;
  But there, beside the altar, there, is rest.

Flos Lunae

For Yvanhoé Rambosson

I would not alter thy cold eyes,
  Nor trouble the calm fount of speech
With aught of passion or surprise.
  The heart of thee I cannot reach:
I would not alter thy cold eyes!

I would not alter thy cold eyes;
  Nor have thee smile, nor make thee weep:
Though all my life droops down and dies,
  Desiring thee, desiring sleep,
I would not alter thy cold eyes.

I would not alter thy cold eyes;
  I would not change thee if I might,
To whom my prayers for incense rise,
  Daughter of dreams! my moon of night!
I would not alter thy cold eyes.

I would not alter thy cold eyes,
  With trouble of the human heart:
Within their glance my spirit lies,
  A frozen thing, alone, apart;
I would not alter thy cold eyes.

'You would have understood me, had you waited'

Ah, dans ces mornes séjours
Les jamais sont les toujours.

PAUL VERLAINE

You would have understood me, had you waited;
    I could have loved you, dear! as well as he:
Had we not been impatient, dear! and fated
    Always to disagree.

What is the use of speech? Silence were fitter:
    Lest we should still be wishing things unsaid.
Though all the words we ever spake were bitter,
    Shall I reproach you dead?

Nay, let this earth, your portion, likewise cover
    All the old anger, setting us apart:
Always, in all, in truth was I your lover;
    Always, I held your heart.

I have met other women who were tender,
    As you were cold, dear! with a grace as rare.
Think you, I turned to them, or made surrender,
    I who had found you fair?

Had we been patient, dear! ah, had you waited,
    I had fought death for you, better than he:
But from the very first, dear! we were fated
    Always to disagree.

Late, late, I come to you, now death discloses
    Love that in life was not to be our part:
On your low lying mound between the roses,
    Sadly I cast my heart.

I would not waken you: nay! this is fitter;
    Death and the darkness give you unto me;
Here we who loved so, were so cold and bitter,
    Hardly can disagree.

Extreme Unction

For Lionel Johnson

Upon the eyes, the lips, the feet,
   On all the passages of sense,
The atoning oil is spread with sweet
   Renewal of lost innocence.

The feet, that lately ran so fast
   To meet desire, are soothly sealed;
The eyes, that were so often cast
   On vanity, are touched and healed.

From troublous sights and sounds set free;
   In such a twilight hour of breath,
Shall one retrace his life, or see,
   Through shadows, the true face of death?

Vials of mercy! Sacring oils!
   I know not where nor when I come,
Nor through what wanderings and toils,
   To crave of you Viaticum.

Yet, when the walls of flesh grow weak,
   In such an hour, it well may be,
Through mist and darkness, light will break,
   And each anointed sense will see.

Villanelle of the Poet's Road

Wine and woman and song,
   Three things garnish our way:
Yet is day over long.

Lest we do our youth wrong,
   Gather them while we may:
Wine and woman and song.

Three things render us strong,
   Vine leaves, kisses and bay;
Yet is day over long.

Unto us they belong,
  Us the bitter and gay,
Wine and woman and song.

We, as we pass along,
  Are sad that they will not stay;
Yet is day over long.

Fruits and flowers among,
  What is better than they:
Wine and woman and song?
  Yet is day over long.

Saint Germain-en-Laye
(1887-95)

Through the green boughs I hardly saw thy face,
They twined so close: the sun was in mine eyes;
And now the sullen trees in sombre lace
Stand bare beneath the sinister, sad skies.

O sun and summer! Say in what far night,
The gold and green, the glory of thine head,
Of bough and branch have fallen? Oh, the white
Gaunt ghosts that flutter where thy feet have sped,

Across the terrace that is desolate,
And rang then with thy laughter, ghost of thee,
That holds its shroud up with most delicate,
Dead fingers, and behind the ghost of me,

Tripping fantastic with a mouth that jeers
At roseal flowers of youth the turbid streams
Toss in derision down the barren years
To death the host of all our golden dreams.

To his Mistress

There comes an end to summer,
  To spring showers and hoar rime;
His mumming to each mummer
  Has somewhere end in time,
And since life ends and laughter,
  And leaves fall and tears dry
Who shall call love immortal,
  When all that is must die?

Nay, sweet, let's leave unspoken
  The vows the fates gainsay,
For all vows made are broken,
  We love but while we may.
Let's kiss when kissing pleases,
  And part when kisses pall,
Perchance, this time tomorrow,
  We shall not love at all.

You ask my love completest,
  As strong next year as now,
The devil take you, sweetest,
  Ere I make aught such vow.
Life is a masque that changes,
  A fig for constancy!
No love at all were better,
  Than love which is not free.

Libera Me

Goddess the laughter-loving, Aphrodite befriend!
Long have I served thine altars, serve me now at the end,
Let me have peace of thee, truce of thee, golden one, send.

Heart of my heart have I offered thee, pain of my pain,
Yielding my life for the love of thee into thy chain;
Lady and goddess be merciful, loose me again.

All things I had that were fairest, my dearest and best,
Fed the fierce flames on thine altar: ah, surely, my breast
Shrined thee alone among goddesses, spurning the rest.

Blossom of youth thou hast plucked of me, flower of my days;
Stinted I nought in thine honouring, walked in thy ways,
Song of my soul pouring out to thee, all in thy praise.

Fierce was the flame while it lasted, and strong was thy wine,
Meet for immortals that die not, for throats such as thine
Too fierce for bodies of mortals, too potent for mine.

Blossom and bloom hast thou taken, now render to me
Ashes of life that remain to me, few though they be,
Truce of the love of thee, Cyprian, let me go free.

Goddess, the laughter-loving, Aphrodite, restore
Life to the limbs of me, liberty, hold me no more
Having the first-fruits and flower of me, cast me the core.

Venite Descendamus

Let be at last; give over words and sighing,
    Vainly were all things said:
Better at last to find a place for lying,
    Only dead.

Silence were best, with songs and sighing over;
    Now be the music mute;
Now let the dead, red leaves of autumn cover
    A vain lute.

Silence is best: for ever and for ever,
    We will go down and sleep,
Somewhere beyond her ken, where she need never
    Come to weep

Let be at last: colder she grows and colder;
    Sleep and the night were best;
Lying at last where we can not behold her,
    We may rest.

A Last Word

Let us go hence: the night is now at hand;
The day is overworn, the birds all flown;
And we have reaped the crops the gods have sown;
Despair and death; deep darkness o'er the land,
Broods like an owl; we cannot understand
Laughter or tears, for we have only known
Surpassing vanity: vain things alone
Have driven our perverse and aimless band.
Let us go hence, somewhither strange and cold,
To Hollow Lands where just men and unjust
Find end of labour, where's rest for the old,
Freedom to all from love and fear and lust.
Twine our torn hands! O pray the earth enfold
Our life-sick hearts and turn them into dust.

Colloque Sentimental

AFTER PAUL VERLAINE: II

Into the lonely park all frozen fast,
Awhile ago there were two forms who pasesd.

Lo, and their lips fallen and their eyes dead,
Hardly shall a man hear the words they said.

Into the lonely park, all frozen fast,
There came two shadows who recall the past.

'Dost thou remember our old ecstasy?'—
'Wherefore should I possess that memory?'—

'Doth thine heart beat at my sole name alway?
Still dost thou see my soul in visions?' 'Nay!'—

'They were fair days of joy unspeakable,
Whereon our lips were joined?'—'I cannot tell.'—

'Were not the heavens blue, was not hope high?'—
'Hope has fled vanquished down the darkling sky.'—

So through the barren oats they wandered,
And the night only heard the words they said.

Spleen

AFTER PAUL VERLAINE: III

Around were all the roses red,
The ivy all around was black.

Dear, so thou only move thine head,
Shall all mine old despairs awake!

Too blue, too tender was the sky,
The air too soft, too green the sea.

Always I fear, I know not why,
Some lamentable flight from thee.

I am so tired of holly-sprays
And weary of the bright box-tree,

Of all the endless country ways;
Of everything alas! save thee.

WILLIAM THEODORE PETERS
(d. 1904)

An American-born poet and actor, Peters lived for a number of years in London. A particular friend of Dowson (who wrote a poem commemorating Peters' 'Renaissance Cloak'), he composed the Epilogue to the stage version of Dowson's poetic play *The Pierrot of the Minute*, which he produced for the Primrose League at Chelsea Town Hall on 22 November 1892.

He was a 'permanent guest' of the Rhymers' Club, but removed to Paris in the late 'nineties where he contributed to an American magazine *The Quartier Latin*, dying of starvation in that city in 1904, as R. H. Sherard relates (*Twenty Years in Paris*, 1905).

He wrote children's songs, a pastoral masque, and a volume of poetical conceits described as 'a harking back ... to the ancient form of the versified epigram' (Bernard Muddiman: *The Men of the Nineties*, 1920).

Epilogue To
The Pierrot of the Minute

Spoken in the character of Pierrot

THE sun is up, yet ere a body stirs,
A word with you, sweet ladies and dear sirs
(Although on no account let any say
That *Pierrot* finished Mr. Dowson's play).

One night, not long ago, at Baden-Baden,—
The birthday of the Duke,—his pleasure garden
Was lighted gaily with *feu d'artifice*,
With candles, rockets, and a centre-piece
Above the conversation house, on high,
Outlined in living fire against the sky,
A glittering *Pierrot*, radiant, white,
Whose heart beat fast, who danced with sheer delight,
Whose eyes were blue, whose lips were rosy red,

Whose *pompons* too were fire, while on his head
He wore a little cap, and I am told
That rockets covered him with showers of gold.
'That our applause, you well deserve to win it,'
They cried: 'Bravo! the *Pierrot* of the minute!'

What with applause and gold, one must confess,
That *Pierrot* had 'arrived', achieved success,
When, as it happened, presently, alas!
A terrible disaster came to pass.
His nose grew dim, the people gave a shout,
His red lips paled, both his blue eyes went out.
There rose a sullen sound of discontent,
The golden shower of rockets was all spent;
He left off dancing with a sudden jerk,
For he was nothing but a firework.
The garden darkened and the people in it
Cried, 'He is dead,—the *Pierrot* of the minute!'

With every artist it is even so;
The artist, after all, is a *Pierrot*—
A *Pierrot* of the minute, *naif*, clever,
But art is back of him, She lives for ever!

Then pardon my Moon Maid and me, because
We craved the golden shower of your applause!
Pray shrive us both for having tried to win it,
And cry, 'Bravo! The *Pierrot* of the minute!'

To the Café aux Phares de l'Ouest, Quartier Montparnasse

The painted ship in the paste-board sea
    Sails night and day.
Tomorrow it will be as far as it was yesterday
    But underneath, in the Café,
    The lusty crafts go down,
And one by one, poor mad souls drown—
While the painted ship in the paste-board sea
    Sails night and day.

LIONEL PIGOT JOHNSON
(1867-1902)

Lionel Johnson was born on 15 March 1867 at Broadstairs, Kent, and was educated at Winchester and New College, Oxford. His parents had been Anglican, but on St. Alban's Day, 1891, he made his submission to the Roman Church. In London he led an essentially bachelor existence, passing his days in literary journalism and the habit of solitary drinking which largely contributed to his death, following a stroke, on 4 October 1902.

Johnson's critical writing is as important as his verse in that it provides what the traditionalist often lacks: a show of reason in addition to instinct. Writing of his poems Ezra Pound has remarked on their 'feeling of neatness [and] inherited order' ('Lionel Johnson', *Literary Essays of Ezra Pound*, 1954). Ian Fletcher (*The Complete Poems of Lionel Johnson*) comments that the sonnet 'The Destroyer of a Soul' 'is supposed to have been addressed to Wilde, and the soul is that of Lord Alfred Douglas' and describes the final poem in the present selection, 'A Decadent's Lyric', as an 'imitation of Symons' less wholesome love lyrics.'

By the Statue of King Charles at Charing Cross

To William Watson

SOMBRE and rich, the skies;
Great glooms, and starry plains.
Gently the night wind sighs;
Else a vast silence reigns.

The splendid silence clings
Around me: and around
The saddest of all kings
Crowned, and again discrowned.

Comely and calm, he rides
Hard by his own Whitehall:
Only the night wind glides:
No crowds, nor rebels, brawl.

Gone, too, his Court: and yet,
The stars his courtiers are:
Stars in their stations set;
And every wandering star.

Alone he rides, alone,
The fair and fatal king:
Dark night is all his own,
That strange and solemn thing.

Which are more full of fate:
The stars; or those sad eyes?
Which are more still and great:
Those brows; or the dark skies?

Although his whole heart yearn
In passionate tragedy:
Never was face so stern
With sweet austerity.

Vanquished in life, his death
By beauty made amends:
The passing of his breath
Won his defeated ends.

Brief life, and hapless? Nay:
Through death, life grew sublime.
Speak after sentence? Yea:
And to the end of time.

Armoured he rides, his head
Bare to the stars of doom:
He triumphs now, the dead,
Beholding London's gloom.

Our wearier spirit faints,
Vexed in the world's employ:
His soul was of the saints;
And art to him was joy.

King, tried in fires of woe!
Men hunger for thy grace:
And through the night I go,
Loving thy mournful face.

Yet, when the city sleeps;
When all the cries are still:
The stars and heavenly deeps
Work out a perfect will.

1889

The Precept of Silence

I know you: solitary griefs,
Desolate passions, aching hours!
I know you: tremulous beliefs,
Agonized hopes, and ashen flowers!

The winds are sometimes sad to me;
The starry spaces, full of fear:
Mine is the sorrow on the sea,
And mine the sigh of places drear.

Some players upon plaintive strings
Publish their wistfulness abroad:
I have not spoken of these things,
Save to one man, and unto God.

1893

Mystic and Cavalier

To Herbert Percy Horne

Go from me: I am one of those, who fall.
What! hath no cold wind swept your heart at all,
In my sad company? Before the end,
    Go from me, dear my friend!

Yours are the victories of light: your feet
Rest from good toil, where rest is brave and sweet.
But after warfare in a mourning gloom,
    I rest in clouds of doom.

Have you not read so, looking in these eyes?
Is it the common light of the pure skies,
Lights up their shadowy depths? The end is set:
    Though the end be not yet.

When gracious music stirs, and all is bright,
And beauty triumphs through a courtly night;
When I too joy, a man like other men:
    Yet, am I like them, then?

And in the battle, when the horsemen sweep
Against a thousand deaths, and fall on sleep:
Who ever sought that sudden calm, if I
    Sought not? Yet, could not die.

Seek with thine eyes to pierce this crystal sphere!
Canst read a fate there, prosperous and clear?
Only the mists, only the weeping clouds:
    Dimness, and airy shrouds.

Beneath, what angels are at work? What powers
Prepare the secret of the fatal hours?
See! the mists tremble, and the clouds are stirred!
    When comes the calling word?

The clouds are breaking from the crystal ball,
Breaking and clearing: and I look to fall.
When the cold winds and airs of portent sweep,
    My spirit may have sleep.

O rich and sounding voices of the air!
Interpreters and prophets of despair:
Priests of a fearful sacrament! I come,
    To make with you mine home.

1889

The Dark Angel

Dark Angel, with thine aching lust
To rid the world of penitence:
Malicious Angel, who still dost
My soul such subtile violence!

Because of thee, no thought, no thing,
Abides for me undesecrate:
Dark Angel, ever on the wing,
Who never reachest me too late!

When music sounds, then changest thou
Its silvery to a sultry fire:
Nor will thine envious heart allow
Delight untortured by desire.

Through thee, the gracious Muses turn
To Furies, O mine Enemy!
And all the things of beauty burn
With flames of evil ecstasy.

Because of thee, the land of dreams
Becomes a gathering place of fears:
Until tormented slumber seems
One vehemence of useless tears.

When sunlight glows upon the flowers,
Or ripples down the dancing sea:
Thou, with thy troop of passionate powers,
Beleaguerest, bewilderest, me.

Within the breath of autumn woods,
Within the winter silences:
Thy venomous spirit stirs and broods,
O Master of impieties!

The ardour of red flame is thine,
And thine the steely soul of ice:
Thou poisonest the fair design
Of nature, with unfair device.

Apples of ashes, golden bright;
Waters of bitterness, how sweet!
O banquet of a foul delight,
Prepared by thee, dark Paraclete!

Thou art the whisper in the gloom,
The hinting tone, the haunting laugh:
Thou art the adorner of my tomb,
The minstrel of mine epitaph.

I fight thee, in the Holy Name!
Yet, what thou dost, is what God saith:
Tempter! should I escape thy flame,
Thou wilt have helped my soul from Death:

The second Death, that never dies,
That cannot die, when time is dead:
Live Death, wherein the lost soul cries,
Externally uncomforted.

Dark Angel, with thine aching lust!
Of two defeats, of two despairs:
Less dread, a change to drifting dust,
Than thine eternity of cares.

Do what thou wilt, thou shalt not so,
Dark Angel! triumph over me:
Lonely, unto the Lone I go;
Divine, to the Divinity.

1893

Bagley Wood

To Percy Addleshaw

The night is full of stars, full of magnificence:
Nightingales hold the wood, and fragrance loads the dark.
Behold, what fires august, what lights eternal! Hark,
What passionate music poured in passionate love's defence!
Breathe but the wafting wind's nocturnal frankincense!
Only to feel this night's great heart, only to mark
The splendours, and the glooms, brings back the patriarch,
Who on Chaldæan wastes found God through reverence.
Could we but live at will upon this perfect height,
Could we but always keep the passion of this peace,
Could we but face unshamed the look of this pure light,
Could we but win earth's heart, and give desire release:
Then were we all divine, and then were ours by right
These stars, these nightingales, these scents: then shame
      would cease.

1890

The Destroyer of a Soul

To———

I hate you with a necessary hate.
First, I sought patience: passionate was she:
My patience turned in very scorn of me,
That I should dare forgive a sin so great,
As this, through which I sit disconsolate;
Mourning for that live soul, I used to see;
Soul of a saint, whose friend I used to be:
Till you came by! a cold, corrupting, fate.

Why come you now? You, whom I cannot cease
With pure and perfect hate to hate? Go, ring
The death-bell with a deep, triumphant toll!
Say you, my friend sits by me still? Ah, peace!
Call you this thing my friend? this nameless thing?
This living body, hiding its dead soul?

1892

The Classics

To Ion Thynne

Fain to know golden things, fain to grow wise,
Fain to achieve the secret of fair souls:
His thought, scarce other lore need solemnize,
Whom Virgil calms, whom Sophocles controls:

Whose conscience Æschylus, a warrior voice,
Enchaunted hath with majestics of doom:
Whose melancholy mood can best rejoice,
When Horace sings, and roses bower the tomb:

Who, following Caesar unto death, discerns
What bitter cause was Rome's, to mourn that day:
With austere Tacitus for master, learns
The look of empire in its proud decay:

Whom dread Lucretius of the mighty line
Hath awed, but not borne down: who loves the flame,
That leaped within Catullus the divine,
His glory, and his beauty, and his shame:

Who dreams with Plato and, transcending dreams,
Mounts to the perfect City of true God:
Who hails its marvellous and haunting gleams,
Treading the steady air, as Plato trod:

Who with Thucydides pursues the way,
Feeling the heart-beats of the ages gone:
Till fall the clouds upon the Attic day,
And Syracuse draw tears for Marathon:

To whom these golden things best give delight:
The music of most sad Simonides;
Propertius' ardent graces; and the might
Of Pindar chaunting by the olive trees:

Livy, and Roman consuls purple swathed:
Plutarch, and heroes of the ancient earth:
And Aristophanes, whose laughter scathed
The souls of fools, and pealed in lyric mirth:

Æolian rose-leaves blown from Sappho's isle;
Secular glories of Lycean thought:
Sallies of Lucian, bidding wisdom smile;
Angers of Juvenal, divinely wrought.

Pleasant, and elegant, and garrulous,
Pliny: crowned Marcus, wistful and still strong:
Sicilian seas and their Theocritus,
Pastoral singer of the last Greek song:

Herodotus, all simple and all wise:
Demosthenes, a lightning flame of scorn:
The surge of Cicero, that never dies:
And Homer, grand against the ancient morn.

1890

Experience

To George Arthur Greene

The burden of the long gone years: the weight,
The lifeless weight, of miserable things
Done long ago, not done with: the live stings
Left by old joys, follies provoking fate,
Showing their sad side, when it is too late:
Dread burden, that remorseless knowledge brings
To men, remorseful! But the burden clings:
And that remorse declares that bitter state.

Wisdom of ages! Wisdom of old age!
Written, and spoken of, and prophesied,
The common record of humanity!
Oh, vain! The springtime is our heritage
First, and the sunlight on the flowing tide:
Then, that old truth's confirming misery.

1889

The Church of a Dream

To Bernhard Berenson

Sadly the dead leaves rustle in the whistling wind,
Around the weather-worn, gray church, low down the vale:
The Saints in golden vesture shake before the gale;
The glorious windows shake, where still they dwell enshrined;
Old Saints by long dead, shrivelled hands, long since designed:
There still, although the world autumnal be, and pale,
Still in their golden vesture the old saints prevail;
Alone with Christ, desolate else, left by mankind.

Only one ancient Priest offers the Sacrifice,
Murmuring holy Latin immemorial:
Swaying with tremulous hands the old censer full of spice,
In gray, sweet incense clouds; blue, sweet clouds mystical:
To him, in place of men, for he is old, suffice
Melancholy remembrances and vesperal.

1890

To Leo XIII

Leo! Vicar of Christ,
His voice, His love, His sword:
Leo! Vicar of Christ,
Earth's Angel of the Lord:

Leo! Father of all,
Whose are all hearts to keep:
Leo! Father of all,
Chief Shepherd of the sheep:

Leo! Lover of men,
Through all the labouring lands:
Leo! Lover of men,
Blest by thine holy hands:

Leo! Ruler of Rome,
Heir of its royal race:
Leo! Ruler of Rome,
King of the Holy Place:

Leo! Leo the Great!
Glory, and love, and fear,
Leo! Leo the Great!
We give thee, great and dear:

Leo! God grant this thing:
Might some, so proud to be
Children of England, bring
Thine England back to thee!

1892

Celtic Speech

To Dr Douglas Hyde

Never forgetful silence fall on thee,
   Nor younger voices overtake thee,
Nor echoes from thine ancient hills forsake thee;
Old music heard by Mona of the sea:
And where with moving melodies there break thee
Pastoral Conway, venerable Dee.

Like music lives, nor may that music die,
   Still in the far, fair Gaelic places:
The speech, so wistful with its kindly graces,
Holy Croagh Patrick knows, and holy Hy:
The speech, that wakes the soul in withered faces,
And wakes remembrance of great things gone by.

Like music by the desolate Land's End
   Mournful forgetfulness hath broken:
No more words kindred to the winds are spoken,
Where upon iron cliffs whole seas expend
That strength, whereof the unalterable token
Remains wild music, even to the world's end.

1887

Vinum Dæmonum

To Stephen Phillips

The crystal flame, the ruby flame
Alluring, dancing, revelling!
See them: and ask me not, whence came
   This cup I bring.

But only watch the wild wine glow,
But only taste its fragrance: then,
Drink the wild drink I bring, and so
   Reign among men.

Only one sting, and then but joy:
One pang of fire, and thou art free.
Then, what thou wilt, thou canst destroy:
   Save only me!

Triumph in tumult of thy lust:
Wanton in passion of thy will:
Cry *Peace!* to conscience, and it must
    At last be still.

I am the Prince of this World: I
Command the flames, command the fires.
Mine are the draughts, that satisfy
    This World's desires.

Thy longing leans across the brink:
Ah, the brave thirst within thine eyes!
For there is that within this drink,
    Which never dies.

1893

Te Martyrum Candidatus

To the Very Rev. John Canon O'Hanlon

Ah, see the fair chivalry come, the companions of Christ!
White Horsemen, who ride on white horses, the Knights of God!
They, for their Lord and their Lover who sacrificed
All, save the sweetness of treading, where He first trod!

These through the darkness of death, the dominion of night,
Swept, and they woke in white places at morning tide:
They saw with their eyes, and sang for joy of the sight,
They saw with their eyes the Eyes of the Crucified.

Now, whithersoever He goeth, with Him they go:
White Horsemen, who ride on white horses, oh fair to see!
They ride, where the Rivers of Paradise flash and flow,
White Horsemen, with Christ their Captain: for ever He!

1895

Nihilism

To Samuel Smith

Among immortal things not made with hands;
Among immortal things, dead hands have made:
Under the Heavens, upon the Earth, there stands
Man's life, my life: of life I am afraid.

Where silent things, and unimpassioned things,
Where things of nought, and things decaying, are:
I shall be calm soon, with the calm, death brings.
The skies are gray there, without any star.

Only the rest! the rest! Only the gloom,
Soft and long gloom! The pausing from all thought!
My life, I cannot taste: the eternal tomb
Brings me the peace, which life has never brought

For all the things I do, and do not well;
All the forced drawings of a mortal breath:
Are as the hollow music of a bell,
That times the slow approach of perfect death.

1888

Walter Pater

Gracious God rest him! he who toiled so well
    Secrets of grace to tell
Graciously; as the awed rejoicing priest
    Officiates at the feast,
Knowing, how deep within the liturgies
    Lie hid the mysteries.
Half of a passionately pensive soul
    He showed us, not the whole:
Who loved him best, they best, they only, knew
    The deeps they might not view;
That which was private between God and him;
    To others, justly dim.
Calm Oxford autumns and preluding springs!
    To me your memory brings
Delight upon delight, but chiefest one:
    The thought of Oxford's son,
Who gave me of his welcome and his praise,
    When white were still my days;

Ere death had left life darkling; nor had sent
    Lament upon lament:
Ere sorrow told me, how I loved my lost,
    And bade me base love's cost.
Scholarship's constant saint, he kept her light
    In him divinely white:
With cloistral jealousness of ardour strove
    To guard her sacred grove,
Inviolate by wordly feet, nor paced
    In desecrating haste.
Oh, sweet grove smiling of that wisdom, brought
    From arduous ways of thought;
Oh, golden patience of that travailing soul,
    So hungered for the goal,
And vowed to keep, through subtly vigilant pain,
    From pastime on the plain,
Enamoured of the difficult mountain air
    Up beauty's Hill of Prayer!
Stern is the faith of art, right stern, and he
    Loved her severity.
Momentous things he prized, gradual and fair,
    Births of a passionate air:
Some austere setting of an ancient sun,
    Its midday glories done,
Over a silent melancholy sea
    In sad serenity:
Some delicate dawning of a new desire,
    Distilling fragrant fire
On hearts of men prophetically fain
    To feel earth young again:
Some strange rich passage of the dreaming earth,
    Fulfilled with warmth and worth.
Ended, is service: yet, albeit farewell
    Tolls the faint vesper bell,
Patient beneath his Oxford trees and towers
    He still is gently ours:
Hierarch of the spirit pure and strong,
    Worthy Uranian song.
Gracious God keep him: and God grant to me
    By miracle to see
That unforgettably most gracious friend,
    In the never-ending end!

1902

Lambeth Lyric

Some seven score Bishops late at Lambeth sat,
Gray-whiskered and respectable debaters:
Each had on head a well-strung curly hat;
   And each wore gaiters.

And when these prelates at their talk had been
Long time, they made yet longer proclamation,
Saying: 'These creeds are childish! both Nicene,
   And Athanasian.

'True, they were written by the Holy Ghost;
So, to re-write them were perhaps a pity.
Refer we their revision to a most
   Select Committee!

'In ten years' time we wise Pan Anglicans
Once more around this Anglo Catholic table
Will meet, to prove God's word more weak than man's,
   His truth, less stable.'

So saying homeward the good Fathers go;
Up Mississippi [*sic*] some and some up Niger.
For thine old mantle they have clearly no
   More use, Elijah!

Instead, an apostolic apron girds
Their loins, which ministerial fingers tie on:
And Babylon's songs they sing, new tune and words,
   All over Zion.

The Creeds, the Scriptures, all the Faith of old,
They hack and hew to please each bumptious German,
Windy and vague as mists and clouds that fold
   Tabour and Hermon.

Happy Establishment in this thine hour!
Behold thy bishops to their sees retreating!
'Have at the Faith!' each cries: 'good bye till our
   Next merry meeting!'

1888

Victory

To George Moore

Down the white steps, into the night, she came;
Wearing white roses, lit by the full moon:
And white upon the shadowy lawn she stood,
Waiting and watching for the dawn's first flame,
Over the dark and visionary wood.
Down the white steps, into the night, she came;
Wearing white roses, lit by the full moon.

Night died away: and over the deep wood
Widened a rosy cloud, a chilly flame:
The shadowy lawn grew cold, and clear, and white.
Then down she drew against her eyes her hood,
To hide away the inexorable light.
Night died away: and over the deep wood
Widened a rosy cloud, a chilly flame.

Then back she turned, and up the white steps came,
And looked into a room of burning lights.
Still slept her loveless husband his brute sleep,
Beside the comfortless and ashen flame:
Her lover waited, where the wood was deep.
She turned not back: but from the white steps came,
And went into the room of burning lights.

1888

A Decadent's Lyric

Sometimes, in very joy of shame,
Our flesh becomes one living flame:
And she and I
Are no more separate, but the same.

Ardour and agony unite;
Desire, delirium, delight:
And I and she
Faint in the fierce and fevered night.

Her body music is: and ah,
The accords of lute and viola!
When she and I
Play on live limbs love's opera!

LORD ALFRED BRUCE DOUGLAS
(1870-1945)

Lord Alfred Douglas (or 'Bosie' as he was known) was born at Ham Hall near Worcester, on 22nd October 1870, and was the third son of John Sholto Douglas—the 'screaming scarlet Marquess', as Wilde called him.

Educated at Winchester, he met Wilde in 1891 while he was still at Magdalen College, Oxford, a relationship which was to lead to Wilde's disgrace and imprisonment in 1895. Both parties wrote their respective accounts of this friendship: Wilde in his *De Profundis* (not published in unexpurgated form until it appeared in 1961), and Lord Alfred in three autobiographical works (see Bibliography).

Bosie's beauty was undeniable: 'You are the incarnation of all lovely things,' Wilde had written to him in August 1894 (*The Letters of Oscar Wilde*, 1962) while the poet Olive Custance, his future wife, addressed him as 'Prince Charming'. His temperament, inherited in part from his father, was anything but easy, however, and he was involved in many lawsuits. Received into the Roman Church when forty-one, he died at Monk's Farm, Lancing, on 20 March 1945.

A master of the sonnet form, Lord Alfred was, at his best, a fine lyrical minor poet.

A note by the author in *The Complete Poems of Lord Alfred Douglas*, 1928, locates and dates the poem 'A Song' as 'Crabbet Park, 1894', and tells us that it was 'Part of my "Prize Poem" written for the "Crabbet Club"'. 'The Dead Poet' was 'written about Oscar Wilde a year after his death'. In his *Sonnets* (1935 ed.) Douglas tells us that 'My Soul is like a Silent Nightingale' was written 'in my villa at Posilipo', and that the title *A Triad of the Moon* (of which this sonnet was the third) 'was suggested by Oscar Wilde'.

A Song

STEAL from the meadows, rob the tall green hills,
  Ravish my orchard's blossoms, let me bind
A crown of orchard flowers and daffodils,
  Because my love is fair and white and kind.

To-day the thrush has trilled her daintiest phrases,
  Flowers with their incense have made drunk the air,
God has bent down to gild the hearts of daisies,
  Because my love is kind and white and fair.

To-day the sun has kissed the rose-tree's daughter,
  And sad Narcissus, Spring's pale acolyte,
Hangs down his head and smiles into the water,
  Because my love is kind and fair and white.

The Travelling Companion

Into the silence of the empty night
I went, and took my scornèd heart with me,
And all the thousand eyes of heaven were bright;
But Sorrow came and led me back to thee.

I turned my weary eyes towards the sun,
Out of the leaden East like smoke came he.
I laughed and said, 'The night is past and done';
But Sorrow came and led me back to thee.

I turned my face towards the rising moon,
Out of the south she came most sweet to see,
She smiled upon my eyes that loathed the noon;
But Sorrow came and led me back to thee.

I bent my eyes upon the summer land,
And all the painted fields were ripe for me,
And every flower nodded to my hand;
But Sorrow came and led me back to thee.

O Love! O Sorrow! O desired Despair!
I turn my feet towards the boundless sea,
Into the dark I go and heed not where,
So that I come again at last to thee.

1897

The Dead Poet

I dreamed of him last night, I saw his face
All radiant and unshadowed of distress,
And as of old, in music measureless,
I heard his golden voice and marked him trace
Under the common thing the hidden grace,
And conjure wonder out of emptiness,
Till mean things put on beauty like a dress
And all the world was an enchanted place.

And then methought outside a fast locked gate
I mourned the loss of unrecorded words,
Forgotten tales and mysteries half said,
Wonders that might have been articulate,
And voiceless thoughts like murdered singing birds.
And so I woke and knew that he was dead.

Paris, 1901

'My Soul is like a Silent Nightingale'

A TRIAD OF THE MOON: III

My soul is like a silent nightingale
Devising sorrow in a summer night.
Closed eyes in blazing noon put out the light
And Hell lies in the thickness of a veil.
In every voiceless moment sleeps a wail,
And all the lonely darknesses are bright,
And every dawning of the day is white
With shapes of sorrow fugitive and frail.

My soul is like a flower whose honey-bees
Are pains that sting and suck the sweets untold,
My soul is like an instrument of strings;
I must stretch these to capture harmonies,
And to find songs like buried dust of gold,
Delve with the nightingale for sorrowful things.

1897

THEODORE WRATISLAW
(1871-1933)

Theodore Wratislaw was born at Rugby in 1871, of a family descended from a Count of Bohemia. He attended Rugby School and later became a solicitor.

By 1893 he had published two books of verse and determined to assay the profession of letters. He contributed to *The Savoy*, wrote a poetic drama *The Pity of Love*, and edited Plato's *Republic*. In 1895, however, he entered the Civil Service, writing nothing after 1900 save a lyric composed at Swinburne's grave in 1923.

Wratislaw's poems seem largely influenced by the metropolitan, artificial and erotic imagery of Arthur Symons's two volumes *Silhouettes*, 1892, and *London Nights*, 1895.

Eρος δ'αὖτε

Crimson nor yellow roses, nor
The savour of the mounting sea
Are worth the perfume I adore
That clings to thee.

The languid-headed lilies tire,
The changeless waters weary me.
I ache with passionate desire
Of thine and thee.

There are but these things in the world—
Thy mouth of fire,
Thy breasts, thy hands, thy hair upcurled,
And my desire!

The Epitaph

IN FORM OF A BALLADE
WHICH VILLON MADE FOR HIMSELF AND HIS COMPANIONS
WHEN EXPECTING TO BE HANGED WITH THEM

Brothers who yet are living, mortal men,
Speak not of us with wrath and bitter tongue,
Since if your souls for us are filled with pain
The more will God's grace fall your hearts among.
You see us here upon the gibbets hung:
The flesh that we too much did glorify
Has long been putrid and devoured: and dry
As dust and ashes now our bleached bones be.
Let no man then our hideous shapes decry,
But pray that God may show us all mercy.

Brothers, speak not, we pray you, with disdain
Of us poor five or six by law upstrung.
It is not every man who has his brain
Clear and well-seated, as has oft been sung.
Make ye then intercession for our wrong
To him whose death from Hell our souls did buy,
Saving us from the flames that never die,
That fresh may flow the fount of His pity.
We are dead: let none to vex our spirits try,
But pray that God may show us all mercy.

Our bodies have been washed and drenched by rain,
Dried up and blackened by the sun; a throng
Of ravens and of crows our eyes have ta'en
And pluckt the brows and beards whereto they clung.
Never are we at rest, forever swung
By every wind that shifts and passes by,
Pecked by the sharp beaks of the crow and pye
And dinted like a thimble, as you see,
Have naught to say to them that with us vie,
But pray that God may show us all mercy.

Prince Jesus, Lord who reignest in the sky,
Grant that to Hell's fierce mouth we draw not nigh
Toward such a place no love or wish have we.
Men, mock not us because we hang so high,
But pray that God may show us all mercy.

Odour

So vague, so sweet a long regret!
So sweet, so vague a dead perfume
That lingers lest regret forget,
A memory from an old-world tomb
Where vainly sunshine gleams and vainly raindrops fret,
And dying summer's wind-breath goes
So lightly over petals of the fallen rose.

Autumnal starlight, scents of hay
Beneath the full September moon,
And then, ah then! the sighing tune
That fades and yet is fain to stay:
Ah! weep for pleasures dead too soon,
While like the love-song of an ancient day
The distant music of the perfume dies away!

AUBREY BEARDSLEY

The Three Musicians

ALONG the path that skirts the wood,
  The three musicians wend their way,
Pleased with their thoughts, each other's mood,
  Franz Himmel's latest roundelay,
The morning's work, a new-found theme, their breakfast
    and the summer day.

One's a soprano, lightly frocked
  In cool white muslin that just shows
Her brown silk stockings gaily clocked,
  Plump arms and elbows tipped with rose,
And frills of petticoats and things, and outlines as the
    warm wind blows.

Beside her a slim, gracious boy
  Hastens to mend her tresses' fall,
And dies her favour to enjoy,
  And dies for *reclame* and recall
At Paris and St Petersburgh, Vienna and St James's
    Hall.

The third's a Polish Pianist
  With big engagements everywhere,
A light heart and an iron wrist.
  And shocks and shoals of yellow hair,
And fingers that can trill on sixths and fill beginners
    with despair.

The Ballad of a Barber

Here is the tale of Carrousel,
The barber of Meridian Street,
He cut, and coiffed, and shaved so well,
That all the world was at his feet.

The King, the Queen, and all the Court,
To no one else would trust their hair,
And reigning belles of every sort
Owed their successes to his care.

With carriage and with cabriolet
Daily Meridian Street was blocked,
Like bees about a bright bouquet
The beaux about his doorway flocked.

Such was his art he could with ease
Curl wit into the dullest face;
Or to a goddess of old Greece
Add a new wonder and a grace.

All powders, paints, and subtle dyes,
And costliest scents that men distill,
And rare pomades, forgot their price
And marvelled at his splendid skill.

The curling irons in his hand
Almost grew quick enough to speak,
The razor was a magic wand
That understood the softest cheek.

Yet with no pride his heart was moved;
He was so modest in his ways!
His dainty task was all he loved,
And now and then a little praise.

An equal care he would bestow
On problems simple or complex;
And nobody had seen him show
A preference for either sex.

How came it then one sunny day,
Coiffing the daughter of the King,
He lengthened out the least delay
And loitered in his hairdressing?

The Princess was a pretty child,
Thirteen years old, or thereabout.
She was as joyous and as wild
As spring flowers when the sun is out.

Her gold hair fell down to her feet
And hung about her pretty eyes;
She was as lyrical and sweet
As one of Schubert's melodies.

Three times the barber curled a lock,
And thrice he straightened it again;
And twice the irons scorched her frock,
And twice he stumbled in her train.

His fingers lost their cunning quite,
His ivory combs obeyed no more;
Something or other dimmed his sight,
And moved mysteriously the floor.

He leant upon the toilet table,
His fingers fumbled in his breast;
He felt as foolish as a fable,
And feeble as a pointless jest.

He snatched a bottle of Cologne,
And broke the neck between his hands;
He felt as if he was alone,
And mighty as a king's commands.

The Princess gave a little scream,
Carrousel's cut was sharp and deep;
He left her softly as a dream
That leaves a sleeper to his sleep.

He left the room on pointed feet;
Smiling that things had gone so well.
They hanged him in Meridian Street.
You pray in vain for Carrousel.

PROSE POEMS
AND CAMEOS

The Disciple

WHEN Narcissus died the pool of his pleasure changed from a cup of sweet waters into a cup of salt tears, and the Oreads came weeping through the woodland that they might sing to the pool and give it comfort.

And when they saw that the pool had changed from a cup of sweet waters into a cup of salt tears, they loosened the green tresses of their hair and cried to the pool and said, 'We do not wonder that you should mourn in this manner for Narcissus, so beautiful was he.'

'But was Narcissus beautiful?' said the pool.

'Who should know that better than you?' answered the Oreads. 'Us did he ever pass by, but you he sought for, and would lie on your banks and look down at you, and in the mirror of your waters he would mirror his own beauty.'

And the pool answered, 'But I loved Narcissus because, as he lay on my banks and looked down at me, in the mirror of his eyes I saw ever my own beauty mirrored.'

The Master

Now when the darkness came over the earth Joseph of Arimathea, having lighted a torch of pinewood, passed down from the hill into the valley. For he had business in his own home.

And kneeling on the flint stones of the Valley of Desolation he saw a young man who was naked and weeping. His hair was the colour of honey, and his body was as a white flower, but he had wounded his body with thorns and on his hair had he set ashes as a crown.

And he who had great possessions said to the young man who was naked and weeping, 'I do not wonder that your sorrow is so great, for surely He was a just man.'

And the young man answered, 'It is not for Him that I am

weeping, but for myself. I too have changed water into wine, and I have healed the leper and given sight to the blind. I have walked upon the waters, and from the dwellers in the tombs I have cast out devils. I have fed the hungry in the desert where there was no food, and I have raised the dead from their narrow houses, and at my bidding, and before a great multitude of people, a barren fig-tree withered away. All things that this man has done I have done also. And yet they have not crucified me.'

The Artist

ONE evening there came into his soul the desire to fashion an image of *The Pleasure that abideth for a Moment*. And he went forth into the world to look for bronze.

But all the bronze of the whole world had disappeared, nor anywhere in the whole world was there any bronze to be found, save only the bronze of the image of *The Sorrow that endureth for Ever*.

Now this image he had himself, and with his own hands, fashioned, and he had set it on the tomb of the one thing he had loved in life. On the tomb of the dead thing he had most loved had he set this image of his own fashioning, that it might serve as a sign of the love of man that dieth not, and a symbol of the sorrow of man that endureth for ever. And in the whole world there was no other bronze save the bronze of this image.

And he took the image he had fashioned, and set it in a great furnace, and gave it to the fire.

And out of the bronze of the image of *The Sorrow that endureth for Ever* he fashioned an image of *The Pleasure that abideth for a Moment*.

ERNEST DOWSON

Absinthia Taetra

GREEN changed to white, emerald to an opal: nothing was changed.

The man let the water trickle gently into his glass, and as the green clouded, a mist fell away from his mind.

Then he drank opaline.

Memories and terrors beset him. The past tore after him like a panther and through the blackness of the present he saw the luminous tiger eyes of the things to be.

But he drank opaline.

And that obscure night of the soul, and the valley of humiliation, through which he stumbled were forgotten. He saw blue vistas of undiscovered countries, high prospects and a quiet, caressing sea. The past shed its perfume over him, to-day held his hand as it were a little child, and to-morrow shone like a white star: nothing was changed.

He drank opaline.

The man had known the obscure night of the soul, and lay even now in the valley of humiliation; and the tiger menace of the things to be was red in the skies. But for a little while he had forgotten.

Green changed to white, emerald to an opal: nothing was changed.

The Princess of Dreams

POOR legendary princess! In her enchaunted tower of ivory, the liberator thought that she awaited him.

For once in a dream he had seen, as they were flowers de luce, the blue lakes of her eyes, had seemed to be enveloped in a tangle of her golden hair.

And he sought her through the countless windings of her forest for many moons, sought her through the morasses,

sparing not his horse nor his sword. On his way he slew certain
evil magicians and many of his friends, so that at his journey's
end his bright sword was tarnished and his comeliness swart
with mud. His horses he had not spared: their bones made a white
track behind him in the windings of the forest: but he still bore
her ransom, all the costly, graceful things stored in a cypress
chest: massed pearls and amethysts and silks from Samarcand,
Valance of Venice, and fine tapestry of Tyre. All these he brought
with him to the gates of her ivory tower.

Poor legendary princess.

For he did not free her and the fustian porter took his treasure
and broke his stained sword in two.

And who knows where he went, horseless and disarmed,
through the morasses and the dark windings of her forest under
the moonless night, dreaming of those blue lakes which were
flowers de luce, her eyes? Who knows? For the fustian porter
says nothing, being slow of wit.

But there are some who say that she had no wish to be freed,
and that those flowers de luce, her eyes, are a stagnant, dark pool,
that her glorious golden hair was only long enough to reach her
postern gate.

Some say, moreover, that her tower is not of ivory and that
she is not even virtuous nor a princess.

MAX BEERBOHM

'L'Oiseau Bleu'

A PAINTING ON SILK BY CHARLES CONDER

OVER them, ever over them, floats the Blue Bird; and they, the
ennuyées and the *ennuyants*, the *ennuyantes* and the *ennuyés*, these
Parisians of 1830, are lolling in a charmed, charming circle, whilst
two of their order, the young Duc de Belhabit et Profil-Perdu
with the girl to whom he has but recently been married, move
hither or thither vaguely, their faces upturned, making vain
efforts to lure down the elusive creature. The haze of very early
morning pervades the garden which is the scene of their faint
aspiration. One cannot see very clearly there. The ladies' fur-
belows are blurred against the foliage, and the lilac-bushes loom
through the air as though they were white clouds full of rain.
One cannot see the ladies' faces very clearly. One guesses them,
though, to be supercilious and smiling, all with the curved lips
and the raised eyebrows of Experience. For, in their time, all
these ladies, and all their lovers with them, have tried to catch
this same Blue Bird, and have been full of hope that it would
come fluttering down to them at last. Now they are tired of trying,
knowing that to try were foolish and of no avail. Yet it is pleasant
for them to see, as here, others intent on the old pastime. Perhaps
—who knows?—some day the bird will be trapped . . . Ah, look!
Monsieur le Duc almost touched its wing! Well for him, after all,
that he did not more than that! Had he caught it and caged it,
and hung the gilt cage in the boudoir of Madame la Duchesse,
doubtless the bird would have turned out to be but a moping,
drooping, moulting creature, with not a song to its little throat;
doubtless the blue colour is but dye, and would soon have faded
from wings and breast. And see! Madame la Duchesse looks a
shade fatigued. She must not exert herself too much. Also, the
magic hour is all but over. Soon there will be sunbeams to dispel
the dawn's vapour; and the Blue Bird, with the sun sparkling
on its wings, will have soared away out of sight. *Allons!* The
little rogue is still at large.

HUBERT CRACKANTHORPE

Pleasant Court

JUNE 28

IT IS known only to the inhabitants of the quarter. To find it, you must penetrate a winding passage, wedged between high walls of dismal brick. Turn to the right by the blue-lettered advertisement of Kop's Ale, and again to the left through the two posts, and you come to Pleasant-court. And when you are there, you can go no farther; for at the far end there is no way out.

There are thirteen houses in Pleasant-court—seven on the one side, and six on the other. They are alike, every one; low-walled as country cottages; built of blackish brick, with a six-foot plot before each, and slate roofs that glimmer wanly on the wet, winter mornings.

But winter is not the season to see Pleasant-court at its best. The drain-sluice is always getting choked, so that pools of mud and brown water loiter near the rickety fence that flanks each six-foot enclosure; and, at Christmas-time, 'most everyone is a bit out,' and young Hyams in the Walworth-road stacks half his back shop with furniture from Pleasant-court; and all day long the children of the lodger at No. 5 never stop squalling with chapped faces, and the 'Lowser's' wife makes much commotion at nights, threatening to 'settle' her husband, and sending her four children to clatter about the pavement.

In the summer, however, everyone smartens up, and by the time that sultry June days have come, Pleasant-court attempts a rural air. On the left-hand side a jaded creeper pushes its grimy greenery under the windows; some of the grass plots grow quite bushy with tough, wizened stalks; and the geranium pots at No. 7 strike flaming specks of vermilion.

Last March the 'Lowser' and his wife and his four children moved over to Southwark; the lodger at No. 5 is in work again; and now the quiet of seclusion is restored to Pleasant-court.

The children sprawl the afternoon through on the hot alley floor; Mrs. Hodgkiss hangs her washing to bulge and flap across the court, like a line of white banners; and on the airless evenings, the women, limp, with their straggling hair, and loose, bedraggled skirts, lean their bare, fleshy elbows over the fence, lingering to gossip before they go to dinner.

And on Saturday nights, the inhabitants of Pleasant-court troop out to join the rumble and the rattle of the Walworth-road, and to swell the life that shuffles down its pavement, past the flaring naphtha lights, the stall-keepers bawling in the gutter, and every shop ablaze with gross jets of gas.

In Normandy

SEPTEMBER 30

A MAUVE sky, all subtle; a discreet rusticity, daintily modern, femininely delicate; a whole finikin arrangement of trim trees, of rectangular orchards, of tiny, spruce houses, tall-roofed and pink-faced, with white shutters demurely closed. Here and there a prim farmyard; a squat church-spire; and bloused peasants jogging behind rotund white horses, along a straight and gleaming road. In all the landscape no trace of the slovenly profusion of the picturesque; but rather a distinguished reticence of detail, fresh, coquettish, almost dapper.

Paris in October

OCTOBER 4

PARIS in October—all white and a-glitter under a cold, sparkling sky, and the trees of the boulevards trembling their frail, russet leaves; garish, petulant Paris; complacently content with her sauntering crowds, her monotonous arrangements in pink and white and blue; ever busied with her own publicity, her tiresome, obvious vice, and her parochial modernity coquetting with cosmopolitanism . . .

In St. James's Park

A SULLEN glow throbs overhead; golden will-o'-wisps are threading their shadowy groupings of gaunt-limbed trees; and the dull, distant rumour of feverish London waits on the still, night air. The lights of Hyde Park corner blaze like some monster, gilded constellation, shaming the dingy stars; and across the East there flares a sky-sign—a gaudy, crimson arabesque . . .

And all the air hangs draped in the mysterious, sumptuous splendour of a murky London night. . . .

REVIEWS

OSCAR WILDE

Mr. Pater's Imaginary Portraits

Pall Mall Gazette, June 11, 1887.

To CONVEY ideas through the medium of images has always been the aim of those who are artists as well as thinkers in literature, and it is to a desire to give a sensuous environment to intellectual concepts that we owe Mr. Pater's last volume. For these Imaginary, or, as we should prefer to call them, Imaginative Portraits of his, form a series of philosophic studies in which the philosophy is tempered by personality, and the thought shown under varying conditions of mood and manner, the very permanence of each principle gaining something through the change and colour of the life through which it finds expression. The most fascinating of all these pictures is undoubtedly that of Sebastian Van Storck. The account of Watteau is perhaps a little too fanciful, and the description of him as one who was 'always a seeker after something in the world, that is there in no satisfying measure, or not at all,' seems to us more applicable to him who saw Mona Lisa sitting among the rocks than the gay and debonair *peintre des fêtes galantes*. But Sebastian, the grave young Dutch philosopher, is charmingly drawn. From the first glimpse we get of him, skating over the water-meadows with his plume of squirrel's tail and his fur muff, in all the modest pleasantness of boyhood, down to his strange death in the desolate house amid the sands of the Helder, we seem to see him, to know him, almost to hear the low music of his voice. He is a dreamer, as the common phrase goes, and yet he is poetical in this sense, that his theorems shape life for him, directly. Early in youth he is stirred by a fine saying of Spinoza, and sets himself to realize the ideal of an intellectual disinterestedness, separating himself more and more from the transient world of sensation, accident and even affection, till what is finite and relative becomes of no interest to him, and he feels that as nature is but a thought of his, so he himself is but a passing thought of God. This conception, of the power of a mere metaphysical abstraction over the mind of one so fortunately endowed for the reception of the sensible world, is exceedingly delightful, and

Mr. Pater has never written a more subtle psychological study, the fact that Sebastian dies in an attempt to save the life of a little child giving to the whole story a touch of poignant pathos and sad irony.

Denys l'Auxerrois is suggested by a figure found, or said to be found, on some old tapestries in Auxerre, the figure of a 'flaxen and flowery creature, sometimes well-nigh naked among the vine-leaves, sometimes muffled in skins against the cold, sometimes in the dress of a monk, but always with a strong impress of real character and incident from the veritable streets' of the town itself. From this strange design Mr. Pater has fashioned a curious mediæval myth of the return of Dionysus among men, a myth steeped in colour and passion and old romance, full of wonder and full of worship, Denys himself being half animal and half god, making the world mad with a new ecstasy of living, stirring the artists simply by his visible presence, drawing the marvel of music from reed and pipe, and slain at last in a stage-play by those who had loved him. In its rich affluence of imagery this story is like a picture by Mantegna, and indeed Mantegna might have suggested the description of the pageant in which Denys rides upon a gaily-painted chariot, in soft silken raiment and, for head-dress, a strange elephant scalp with gilded tusks.

If *Denys l'Auxerrois* symbolizes the passion of the senses and *Sebastian Van Storck* the philosophic passion, as they certainly seem to do, though no mere formula or definition can adequately express the freedom and variety of the life that they portray, the passion for the imaginative world of art is the basis of the story of *Duke Carl of Rosenmold*. Duke Carl is not unlike the late King of Bavaria, in his love of France, his admiration for the *Grand Monarque* and his fantastic desire to amaze and to bewilder, but the resemblance is possibly only a chance one. In fact Mr. Pater's young hero is the precursor of the *Aufklärung* of the last century, the German precursor of Herder and Lessing and Goethe himself, and finds the forms of art ready to his hand without any national spirit to fill them or make them vital and responsive. He too dies, trampled to death by the soldiers of the country he so much admired, on the night of his marriage with a peasant girl, the very failure of his life lending him a certain melancholy grace and dramatic interest.

On the whole, then, this is a singularly attractive book. Mr. Pater is an intellectual impressionist. He does not weary us with any definite doctrine or seek to suit life to any formal creed. He is always looking for exquisite moments and, when he has found them, he analyses them with delicate and delightful art and then passes on, often to the opposite pole of thought or feeling, knowing that every mood has its own quality and charm and is justified by its mere existence. He has taken the sensationalism of Greek philosophy and made it a new method of art criticism. As for his style, it is curiously ascetic. Now and then, we come across phrases with a strange sensuousness of expression, as when he tells us how Denys l'Auxerrois, on his return from a long journey, 'ate flesh for the first time, tearing the hot, red morsels with his delicate fingers in a kind of wild greed,' but such passages are rare. Asceticism is the keynote of Mr. Pater's prose; at times it is almost too severe in its self-control and makes us long for a little more freedom. For indeed, the danger of such prose as his is that it is apt to become somewhat laborious. Here and there, one is tempted to say of Mr. Pater that he is 'a seeker after something in language, that is there in no satisfying measure, or not at all.' The continual preoccupation with phrase and epithet has its drawbacks as well as its virtues. And yet, when all is said, what wonderful prose it is, with its subtle preferences, its fastidious purity, its rejection of what is common or ordinary! Mr. Pater has the true spirit of selection, the true art of omission. If he be not among the greatest prose writers of our literature he is, at least, our greatest artist in prose; and though it may be admitted that the best style is that which seems an unconscious result rather than a conscious aim, still in these latter days when violent rhetoric does duty for eloquence and vulgarity usurps the name of nature, we should be grateful for a style that deliberately aims at perfection of form, that seeks to produce its effect by artistic means and sets before itself an ideal of grave and chastened beauty.

Imaginary Portraits. By Walter Pater, M.A., Fellow of Brasenose College, Oxford.

RICHARD LE GALLIENNE
(1866-1947)

Richard Le Gallienne was born in Liverpool on 20 January 1866, and was the eldest son of a brewery manager. He was educated at Liverpool College and articled to a firm of accountants in that city. Failing an accountancy examination, he came to London and was soon established as a reviewer writing for many papers and reader for John Lane's firm The Bodley Head. The story of these years was told by Le Gallienne in his reminiscences *The Romantic Nineties*, 1926, a valuable and charming source-book of impressions concerning the literary figures of that decade. The two-volume selection he made of his reviews (*Retrospective Reviews: A Literary Log*, 1896) are an important source of contemporary opinion. They show the process of acclimatization by which Walter Pater's aesthetics were ultimately reaching the man in the street.

In 1898 he left England for the United States where he resided till after the First War, returning then to live in Paris and finally settling with his third wife in Mentone.

With sympathies originally Unitarian, Le Gallienne was one of the men of the 'nineties who showed no Catholic inclinations, repudiating the Faith of that Church in a little pamphlet *The Beautiful Life of Rome*, 1900. Poet, critic and essayist, he popularized for a newspaper readership the exclusive fin-de-siècle ideal. As a go-between Le Gallienne is important.

John Gray: 'Silverpoints'

IN WHAT does decadence consist? In a self-conscious arrangement of 'coloured' vowels, in a fastidious distribution of accents, resulting in new and subtler harmonies of verse—say some. In the choice for themes of disease and forbidden things generally—say others. For my part, while I see that both characteristics mark the modern decadent school, I do not think that either is the starting-point of that school. In regard to the first, are we to say that in proportion as language becomes more and more the perfected instrument of expression, the more it develops literary means to literary ends, it is decadent? Surely such a perfection is

in the direction of growth, not decadence. On such a definition
Virgil and Tennyson were decadents, and, moreover, it implies
that the great old poets sang like a bird on bough, without a
thought of style. But did they? Chaucer, so 'frank and hale,'
certainly did not, for one. The second definition would make
decadents of Rabelais and Swift. The real core of decadence is to
be found in its isolated interests. Its effects are gained by regarding
life as of but one or two dimensions. Its recent development
almost entirely confines its outlook on life to the colour-sense.
It puts men and dead game on the same basis—of colour. As I
have remarked elsewhere, M. Huysmans is taken with the effects
of colour on a tippler's nose, Gautier with the same effects in a
beggar's rags, but each ignores the humanity of both. Shakespeare could jest about Falstaff's nose, but he gave us the rest of
him as well—how much! Decadence, therefore, it seems to me,
comes of the decadent regarding his theme *in vacuo*, isolated
from its various relations—of morality, of pity, of humour, of
religion. Judged from this standpoint, Mr. Gray's poems are
not so decadent as he would have us suppose. They are luxurious
to the last degree, they are subtly cadenced as the song the sirens
sang, they will dwell over-unctuously on many forbidden
themes—'many whisper things I dare not tell'—they are each
separately dedicated to every more or less decadent poet of Mr.
Gray's acquaintance, and their *format*, an adaptation of the
Aldine italic books, is of a far-sought deliciousness. But in spite
of his neo-Catholicism and his hot-house erotics, Mr. Gray
cannot accomplish that gloating abstraction from the larger life
of humanity which marks the decadent.

Maybe he will accomplish it in time, but such a picture as this,
a picture of trawling at night, entitled 'Wings in the Dark,' makes
one hope he will not. I have not space for the whole poem:

> Full-winged and stealthy like a bird of prey,
> All tense the muscles of her seemly flanks;
> She, the coy creature that the idle day
> Sees idly riding in the idle ranks.
>
> Backward and forth, over the chosen ground,
> Like a young horse, she drags the heavy trawl,
> Tireless; or speeds her rapturous course unbound,
> And passing fishers through the darkness call
>
> Deep greeting, in the jargon of the sea.
> Haul upon haul, flounders and soles and dabs,
> And phosphorescent animalculæ,
> Sand, seadrift, weeds, thousands of worthless crabs.

> Low on the mud the darkling fishes grope,
> Cautious to stir, staring with jewel eyes;
> Dogs of the sea, the savage congers mope,
> Winding their sulky march Meander-wise.
>
> Suddenly all is light and life and flight,
> Upon the sandy bottom, agate strewn.
> The fishers mumble, waiting till the night
> Urge on the clouds, and cover up the moon.

The reader will not fail to note here the simplicity of the means and the richness of the impression; he will notice, too, such cunning effects as the repetition 'idle' in the first verse, and the curious predominance of the letter 'r' throughout.

Though frankly a disciple of modern French poets, Mr. Gray's verses remind one more, in their quaint deliciousness, of certain old English poets, of Crashaw especially; and a certain affinity to the work of Mr. Bridges corroborates this. The wind of Provence also blows sweetly through his verses. But to whatever school he may now, or eventually, belong, he has a gift of epithet, of dainty colour and subtle rhythm, such as distinguish his *Silverpoints* from any recent English poetry. He has a very great deal in common with the typical decadent, his book is full of affectation, but it is strongly marked by genuine individuality as well. Here is another fascinating verse taken at random:

> The shadows lie mauven beneath the trees,
> And purple stains, where the finches pass,
> Leap in the stalks of the deep, rank grass.
> Flutter of wing, and the buzz of bees,
> Deepen the silence, and sweeten ease.

And in illustration of what I have said of that hopeful sign of Mr. Gray's not being quite able to isolate himself from human interests, here is one verse more:

> In every kiss I call you mine,
> Tell me, my dear, how pure, how brave
> Our child will be! What velvet eyne,
> What bonny hair our child will have!

Is not this absurdly domestic in a decadent? Really Mr. Gray must check these natural impulses.

Arthur Symons: 'Silhouettes'

'PARIS, May, 1892.' Thus Mr. Symons dates his dedication to a lady of his acquaintance. That mere superscription means much. Viewed symbolically there is in it a world of pathos. There is always pathos when any one yearns towards a particular class of life, or centre, as it seems, of 'tone,' with a feeling that there is the ideal state, to be outside of which is to be 'provincial,' *borné*, and other dreadful things. It is the dairymaid's superstition of the 'gentleman,' the parvenu's of the 'upper ten,' the outcast's of 'society.' What 'Budmouth' in Mr. Hardy's *Return of the Native* was to Eustacia Vye, Paris is to Mr. Symons and many young men of the same school. Had Mr. Symons lived earlier he would doubtless have dated his preface from Alexandria. To be 'in the movement' at all costs, in contradistinction to being 'of the centre,' is the aim of these ardent young men. Looking through Mr. Symons's 'contents' his titles prove no less characteristic: 'Pastel,' 'Morbidezza,' 'Maquillage,' 'Nocturne,' 'The Absinthe Drinker,' 'From Paul Verlaine.' But, for all that, he is much simpler than he supposes, and there are in his book many delicate and beautiful things. His poems, indeed, look much slighter than they are. Fragile they seem, and often are, but sometimes it is with the seeming fragility of wrought iron. They are full of careful observation, and a strenuous art which has measured its form by its matter to a word. To this more self-conscious art, they sometimes add the unbidden charms of passion and song. In this poem of 'Emmy' we have also an unwonted touch of pity:

> Emmy's exquisite youth, and her virginal air,
>   Eyes and teeth in the flash of a musical smile,
> Come to me out of the past, and I see her there
>   As I saw her once for a while.
>
> Emmy's laughter rings in my ears, as bright,
>   Fresh, and sweet as the voice of a mountain brook;
> And still I hear her telling us tales that night
>   Out of Boccaccio's book.
>
> There, in the midst of the villainous dancing-hall
>   Leaning across the table over the beer,
> While the music maddened the whirling skirts of the ball,
>   As the midnight hour drew near.

There with the women, haggard, painted and old,
  One fresh bud in a garland withered and stale,
She, with her innocent voice and her clear eyes, told
  Tale after shameless tale.

And ever the witching smile, to her face beguiled,
  Paused, and broadened, and broke in a ripple of fun,
And the soul of a child looked out of the eyes of a child,
  Or ever the tale was done.

O my child, who wronged you first, and began
  First the dance of death that you dance so well?
Soul for soul: and I think the soul of a man
  Shall answer for yours in hell.

Let us quote another impression with a fresher atmosphere:

Night, and the down by the sea
  And the veil of rain on the down:
And she came through the mist and the rain to me
  From the safe warm lights of the town.

The rain shone in her hair,
  And her face gleamed in the rain:
And only the night and the rain were there
  As she came to me out of the rain.

These poems have both strength and charm. Many other poems
prove that Mr. Symons has a genuine gift of impressionism.
Mr. Whistler and M. Verlaine are evidently the dominant
influences with him at present, as Browning, and perhaps Mr.
Meredith, were in his first book. *Silhouettes* is a marked artistic
advance on *Night and Days*, but Mr. Symons's next volume will
be more crucial. It will be all the better if he will let himself go a
little more, and not keep so self-conscious an eye upon his art,
which by this time may safely be trusted to act instinctively.

Lionel Johnson: 'Poems'

To—shall we say?—the professional lovers of Thomas Hardy,
to those who merely collect his first editions as some collect
book-plates, Mr. Lionel Johnson's *Art of Thomas Hardy* was, I

believe, a disappointment. As criticism, I am bound to admit, it
fell short—it was too busied with the methods of criticism in
general, curiously forgetting their particular application to Mr.
Hardy. Yet for those who are able to take a book for what it is,
independent of what it professes to, or ought to, be, Mr. Lionel
Johnson's book on Mr. Hardy was far from being a disappointment. Its learning alone, so irritating, it would seem—to the
learned?—I confess, no little impressed and delighted me. It was
like spending an afternoon in the Bodleian. But it was not
merely its old-world love of learning that made the book memorable; it was the poetry one felt behind the prose, poetry that
enriched the book with many passages of solemn eloquence and
vivid description. However, one had not to wait for Mr. Johnson's
prose to know that he was a poet. His contributions to the *Book
of the Rhymers' Club* attracted attention among those who care
to keep a sympathetic eye upon 'the homely slighted shepherd's
trade.' At a time when it was the fashion for the young poet to be
lawlessly 'modern' both in theme and style, it was refreshing to
find a very young poet deliberately singing the old ideals, and
following the old great traditions—a poet who believed not only
in God and King Charles, but in Homer and Shakespeare, Dante
and Milton, a literary Catholic believing devoutly in the apostolic
succession of all really great writers, loving that one unchangeable
literary ideal, which, as Sainte-Beuve has said, is 'new and
ancient, easily contemporaneous with every age.'

The spontaneous impulse one felt was a little low in vitality.
Had there never been poets before him, it is very unlikely that
Mr. Johnson would have been a poet at all. But then he is not the
first poet begotten of poets, and such poets, if seldom or never
great, our sophisticated tastes are often apt to consider more
delightful than the great. The subtle echo of the voices of the
great has a charm which those voices themselves sometimes fail
to exercise. Such, Mr. Churton Collins has somewhat narrowly
decided, is largely the charm of Tennyson, and Mr. Lionel
Johnson's poetry is thus 'rich with sweets from every muse's
hive.' His volume is like an old garden, every flower awaking
charming reminiscences of unforgotten, half-forgotten, and
perhaps quite forgotten, poets, the whole invested with an antique
dignity, and steeped in the sentiment of antiquity. The passion
for the past has seldom, if ever, in our day found so devout an
expression. Every poem seems to whisper to us 'the old was best'
—'the old was best'—and we put down the volume firmly determined to join the Legitimist League to-morrow. And surely that
cause which was so fruitful an inspirer of unselfish ideals, and of
so much noble poetry in its day and since, has seldom found

expression so moving, yet so dignified, as in Mr. Johnson's lines to the statue of King Charles I at Charing Cross:

> Comely and calm, he rides
> Hard by his own Whitehall:
> Only the night wind glides:
> No crowds, nor rebels, brawl.
>
> Gone, too, his Court: and yet,
> The stars his courtiers are:
> Stars in their stations set;
> And every wandering star.
>
> Alone he rides, alone,
> The fair and fatal king:
> Dark night is all his own,
> That strange and solemn thing.
>
> Which are more full of fate:
> The stars; or those sad eyes?
> Which are more still and great:
> Those brows; or the dark skies?

Such a poem as this, apart from its value as poetry, is a touching witness of the constancy of the human heart.

Among Mr. Lionel Johnson's new poems the one which fascinates me most is that upon an old drawing, from which I quote these two haunting verses:

> Not in the crystal air of a Greek glen,
> Not in the houses of imperial Rome,
> Lived he, who wore this beauty among men:
> No classic city was his ancient home.
> What happy country claims his fair youth then,
> Her pride? and what his fortunate lineage?
> Here is no common man of every day,
> This man, whose full and gleaming eyes assuage
> Never their longing, be that what it may:
> Of dreamland only he is citizen,
> Beyond the flying of the last sea's foam.
>
> Set him beneath the Athenian olive trees,
> To speak with Marathonians: or to task
> The wise serenity of Socrates;
> Asking what other men dare never ask.

Love of his country and his gods? Not these
The master thoughts, that comfort his strange heart,
When life grows difficult, and the lights dim:
In him is no simplicity, but art
Is all in all, for life and death, to him:
And whoso looks upon that fair face, sees
No nature there: only a magic mask.

Among the many lost causes which Mr. Johnson loves to
celebrate is the old Irish literature, and he has a touching
apostrophe to the 'Celtic Speech,' of which I quote the fine
opening verse—the poem being appropriately dedicated to Dr.
Douglas Hyde:

Never forgetful silence fall on thee,
    Nor younger voices overtake thee,
Nor echoes from thine ancient hills forsake thee;
Old music heard by Mona of the sea:
And where with moving melodies there break thee
Pastoral Conway, venerable Dee.

ARTHUR SYMONS

In 1899 Symons dedicated his book *The Symbolist Movement in Literature* to Yeats 'both as an expression of deep personal friendship and because you, more than anyone else, will sympathize with what I say in it, being yourself the chief representative of that movement in your country.'

Mr W. B. Yeats

I

MR YEATS is the only one among the younger English poets who has the whole poetical temperament, and nothing but the poetical temperament. He lives on one plane, and you will find in the whole of his work, with its varying degrees of artistic achievement, no unworthy or trivial mood, no occasional concession to the fatigue of high thinking. It is this continuously poetical quality of mind that seems to me to distinguish Mr Yeats from the many men of talent, and to place him among the few men of genius. A man may indeed be a poet because he has written a single perfect lyric. He will not be a poet of high order, he will not be a poet in the full sense, unless his work, however unequal it may be in actual literary skill, presents this undeviating aspect, as of one to whom the act of writing is no more than the occasional flowering of a mood into speech. And that, certainly, is the impression which remains with one after a careful reading of the revised edition of Mr Yeats' collected poems and of his later volume of lyrics, 'The Wind among the Reeds.' The big book, now reissued with a cover by a young artist of subtle and delicate talent, Miss Althea Gyles, contains work of many kinds; and, among mainly lyrical poems, there are two plays, 'The Countess Cathleen,' and 'The Land of Heart's Desire.' 'The Countess Cathleen' is certainly the largest and finest piece of work which Mr Yeats has yet done. Its visionary ecstasy is firmly embodied in persons whose action is indeed largely a spiritual action, but action which has the lyrical movement of great drama. Here is poetry which is not only heard, but seen; forming a picture, not less than moving to music. And here it is the poetry which makes the drama, or I might say equally the drama which makes the poetry; for the finest writing is always part of the dramatic action, not a hindrance to it, as it is in almost all the poetical plays of this century. In the long narrative poem contained in the same volume, 'The Wanderings of Oisin,' an early work, much rewritten, a far less mature skill has squandered lyrical poetry with a romantic prodigality. Among the lyrics in other parts of the book there are a few which Mr Yeats has never excelled in a felicity which seems almost a matter of mere luck; there is not a lyric which has not some personal quality of beauty; but we must turn to the later volume to find the full extent of his capacity as a lyric poet.

In the later volume, 'The Wind among the Reeds,' in which symbolism extends to the cover, where reeds are woven into a net to catch the wandering sounds, Mr Yeats becomes completely master of himself and of his own resources. Technically the verse is far in advance of anything he has ever done, and if a certain youthful freshness, as of one to whom the woods were still the only talkers upon earth, has gone inevitably, its place has been taken by a deeper, more passionate, and wiser sense of the 'everlasting voices' which he has come to apprehend, no longer quite joyously, in the crying of birds, the tongues of flame, and the silence of the heart. It is only gradually that Mr Yeats has learnt to become quite human. Life is the last thing he has learnt, and it is life, an extraordinarily intense inner life, that I find in this book of lyrics, which may seem also to be one long 'hymn to intellectual beauty.'

The poems which make up a volume apparently disconnected are subdivided dramatically among certain symbolical persons, familiar to the readers of 'The Secret Rose,' Aedh, Hanrahan, Robartes, each of whom, as indeed Mr Yeats is at the trouble to explain in his notes, is but the pseudonym of a particular outlook of the consciousness, in its passionate, or dreaming, or intellectual moments. It is by means of these dramatic symbols, refining still further upon the large mythological symbolism which he has built up into almost a system, that Mr Yeats weaves about the simplicity of moods that elaborate web of atmosphere in which the illusion of love, and the cruelty of pain, and the gross ecstasy of hope, became changed into beauty. Here is a poet who has realised, as no one else, just now, seems to realise, that the only excuse for writing a poem is the making of a beautiful thing. But he has come finally to realise that, among all kinds of beauty, the beauty which rises out of human passion is the one most proper to the lyric; and in this volume, so full of a remote beauty of atmosphere, of a strange beauty of figure and allusion, there is a 'lyrical cry' which has never before, in his pages, made itself heard with so penetrating a monotony.

There are love-poems in this book which almost give a voice to that silence in which the lover forgets even the terrible egoism of love. Love, in its state of desire, can be expressed in verse very directly; but that 'love which moves the sun and the other stars,' love to which the imagination has given infinity, can but be suggested, as it is suggested in these poems, by some image, in which for a moment it is reflected, as a flame is reflected in trembling water. 'Aedh hears the cry of the sedge,' for instance; and this is how the sedge speaks to him:

> I wander by the edge
> Of this desolate lake
> Where wind cries in the sedge:
> *Until the axle break*
> *That keeps the stars in their round*
> *And hands hurl in the deep*
> *The banners of East and West*
> *And the girdle of light is unbound,*
> *Your head will not lie on the breast*
> *Of your beloved in sleep.*

By such little, unheard voices the great secret is whispered, the secret, too, which the whole world is busy with.

> O sweet everlasting Voices be still;
> Go to the guards of the heavenly fold
> And bid them wander obeying your will
> Flame under flame, till Time be no more;
> Have you not heard that our hearts are old,
> That you call in birds, in wind on the hill,
> In shaken boughs, in tide on the shore?
> O sweet everlasting Voices be still.

To a poet who is also a mystic there is a great simplicity in things, beauty being really one of the foundations of the world, woman a symbol of beauty, and the visible moment, in which to love or to write love songs is an identical act, really as long and short as eternity. Never, in these love songs, concrete as they become through the precision of their imagery, does an earthly circumstance divorce ecstasy from the impersonality of vision. This poet cannot see love under the form of time, cannot see beauty except as the absolute beauty, cannot distinguish between the mortal person and the eternal idea. Every rapture hurries him beyond the edge of the world and beyond the end of time.

The conception of lyric poetry which Mr Yeats has perfected in this volume, in which every poem is so nearly achieved to the full extent of its intention, may be clearly defined; for Mr Yeats is not a poet who writes by caprice. A lyric, then, is an embodied ecstasy, and an ecstasy so profoundly personal that it loses the accidental qualities of personality, and becomes a part of the universal consciousness. Itself, in its first, merely personal stage, a symbol, it can be expressed only by symbol; and Mr Yeats has chosen his symbolism out of Irish mythology, which gives him the advantage of an elaborate poetic background, new to modern poetry. I am not sure that he does not assume in his readers too ready an acquaintance with Irish tradition, and I am not sure that his notes, whose delightfully unscientific vagueness renders them by no means out of place in a book of poems, will do quite all that is needed in familiarising people's minds with that tradition. But after all, though Mr Yeats will probably regret it, almost everything in his book can be perfectly understood by any poetically sensitive reader who has never heard of a single Irish legend, and who does not even glance at his notes. For he has made for himself a poetical style which is much more simple, as it is much more concise, than any prose style; and, in the final perfecting of his form, he has made for himself a rhythm which is more natural, more precise in its slow and wandering cadence, than any prose rhythm. It is a common mistake to suppose that poetry should be ornate and prose simple. It is prose that may often allow itself the relief of ornament; poetry, if it is to be of the finest quality, is bound to be simple, a mere breathing, in which individual words almost disappear into music. Probably, to many people, accustomed to the artificiality which they mistake for poetical style, and to the sing-song which they mistake for poetical rhythm, Mr Yeats' style, at its best, will seem a little bare, and his rhythm, at its best, a little uncertain. They will be astonished, perhaps not altogether pleased, at finding a poet who uses no inversions, who says in one line, as straightforward as prose, what most poets would dilute into a stanza, and who, in his music, replaces the aria by the recitative. How few, it annoys me to think, as I read over this simple and learned poetry, will realise the extraordinary art which has worked these tiny poems, which seem as free as waves, into a form at once so monumental and so alive! Here, at last, is poetry which has found for itself a new form, a form really modern, in its rejection of every artifice, its return to the natural chant out of which verse was evolved; and it expresses, with a passionate quietude, the elemental desires of humanity, the desire of love, the desire of wisdom, the desire of beauty.

II

I have said that Mr Yeats is the only one among the younger English poets who has the whole poetical temperament, and nothing but the poetical temperament. He is also the only one who combines a continuously poetical substance with continuous excellence of poetical technique. Celtic, if you will, in the quality of his imagination, he has trained that imagination to obey him, as the Celtic imagination rarely obeys those who are for the most part possessed by it. Seeming to many to be the most spontaneous of writers, he is really the most painstaking, the most laboriously conscientious. He makes his visible pictures out of what has come to him invisibly, in dreams, in the energetic abandonment of meditation; but he rarely falls into the error of most mystical poets, who render their visions literally into that other language of ordinary life, instead of translating them freely, idiom for idiom. His verse, lyric and dramatic, has an ecstasy which is never allowed to pass into extravagance, into rhetoric, or into vagueness. Though he has doubtless lost some of the freshness, the fairy quality, of his early work, that freshness and that fairy quality have been replaced by an elaborately simple art, which becomes more and more accomplished, and, in the best sense, precise. The grace of youth is bound to fade out of poetry as it fades out of faces; and all we can hope is that, as in life, the first grey hairs may bring with them some of the grey wisdom of experience, so, in art, time may strengthen what is strong and bring conscious mastery instead of the unconsciousness of early vigour. Mr Yeats could not again become so simple, so joyous, so untouched by human things, as to write another such poem as 'The Lake-Isle of Innisfree'; but he can write now with a deeper and more passionate sense of beauty, more gravely, with a more remote and yet essentially more human wisdom. And his verse, though he has come to play more learned variations upon its rhythms, has become more elaborately simple, more condensed, nearer in form to what is most like poetry in being most like prose. It is the mistake of most writers in verse to form for themselves a purely artificial kind of rhythm, in which it is impossible to speak straight. Open 'Herod,' for instance, at random, and read:

> Herod shall famous be o'er all the world,
> But he shall kill that thing which most he loves.

Now there, in a purely prosaic statement, are two inversions, which turn what might have been at all events the equivalent of good prose into what is only the parody of poetry. Take one of the most beautiful and imaginative passages out of 'The Shadowy Waters,' and read:

> The love of all under the light of the sun
> Is but brief longing, and deceiving hope,
> And bodily tenderness; but love is made
> Imperishable fire under the boughs
> Of chrysoberyl and beryl and chrysolite
> And chrysoprase and ruby and sardonyx.

Is there a word or a cadence in these lines which could not have been used equally well in prose, or in conversation; and yet, can it be denied that those lines are exquisite verse, moving finely to their own music? To get as far from prose, or from conversation, as possible: that is the aim of most writers of verse. But really, the finest verse is that verse which, in outward form and vocal quality, is nearest to dignified prose or serious conversation. Turn to some passage in Shakespeare in which poetical subtlety seems to refine upon speech to its last possibility of expression; the words of Troilus, for instance, as he waits for Cressida in the orchard:

> I am giddy; expectation whirls me round.
> The imaginary relish is so sweet
> That it enchants my sense: what will it be
> When that the watery palate tastes indeed
> Love's thrice repured nectar? Death, I fear me,
> Swooning destruction, or some joy too fine,
> Too subtle potent, tuned too sharp in sweetness,
> For the capacity of my ruder powers:
> I fear it much; and I do fear besides,
> That I shall lose distinction in my joys;
> As doth a battle, when they charge on heaps
> The enemy flying.

In all Shakespeare there is not a passage fuller of the substance of poetry or finer in the technique of verse; yet might not every word have been said in prose, word for word, cadence for cadence, with the mere emphasis of ordinary conversation? And Mr Yeats has never failed to realise, not only that verse must be as simple and straightforward as prose, but that every line must be packed with poetical substance, must be able to stand alone, as a fine line of verse, all the more because it challenges at once the standards of prose and of poetry. If it has so simple a thing to say as this:

> No, no, be silent,
> For I am certain somebody is dead:

it must say it with the same weight, the same gravity, as if it had to say:

> Her eyelids tremble and the white foam fades;
> The stars would hurl their crowns among the foam
> Were they but lifted up.

It was the error of Browning, it is the error of many who have learnt of him everything but his genius, to realise only that verse must be like speech, without realising that it must be like dignified speech. Browning has written the most natural, the most vocal, verse of any modern poet; but he has, only too often, chosen the speech of the clubs and of the streets, rather than the speech of those who, even in conversation, use words reverently.

Whether or not Mr Yeats is, or may become, a great dramatist, one thing is certain: he, and he alone among English poets since Shelley, has the dramatic sense and the speech of the dramatist. His plays may seem to lack something of the warmth of life; but they are splendidly centred upon ideas of life, and they speak, at their best, an heroic language which is the intimate language of the soul. When Seanchan, in 'The King's Threshold,' dying of hunger, says to the Chamberlain:

> You must needs keep your patience yet awhile,
> For I have some few mouthfuls of sweet air
> To swallow before I am grown to be as civil
> As any other dust;

when he says to the cripples:

> What bad poet did your mothers listen to
> That you were born so crooked?

we hear the note of great dramatic speech, in which poetry is content to seem simpler than prose. We hear the same speech, not more imaginative, but more elaborate, in 'On Baile's Strand,' when Cuchullain speaks to his sword, and calls it

> This mutterer, this old whistler, this sand-piper,
> This edge that's grayer than the tide, this mouse
> That's gnawing at the timbers of the world;

and, more elaborately yet, but speech always, when he says:

> I think that all deep passion is but a kiss
> In the mid battle, and a difficult peace
> 'Twixt oil and water, candles and dark night,
> Hill-side and hollow, the hot-footed sun
> And the cold sliding slippery-footed moon,
> A brief forgiveness between opposites
> That have been hatreds for three times the age
> Of this long 'stablished ground.

We feel the instinct or sure science of the dramatist, his essential property, more than words, in the great discovery of Cuchullain that the man he has killed is his own son. Cuchullain is sitting on a bench beside a blind man and a fool, and the blind man cries out to the fool: 'Somebody is trembling. Why are you trembling, fool? the bench is shaking, why are you trembling? Is Cuchullain going to hurt us? It was not I who told you, Cuchullain.' And the blind man says: 'It is Cuchullain who is trembling. He is shaking the bench with his knees.' As a stage effect, and an effect which is greater drama than any words could be, greater than the fine words which follow, it would be hard to invent anything more direct, poignant, and inevitable.

We have often to complain, in reading poetical plays, that so far as there is poetry and so far as there is drama, the poetry at the best is but an ornament to the drama, no structural part of it. Here, on the other hand, both grow together, like bones and flesh. And, while it has usually to be said that the characters of poetical drama speak too much, here condensation is carried as far as it can be carried without becoming mere baldness. Each thing said is a thing which had to be said, and it is said as if the words flowered up out of a deep and obscure soil, where they had been germinating for a long time in the darkness. The silences of these plays are like the pauses in music; we have the consciousness, under all the beauty and clearness and precision of the words we hear, of something unsaid, something which the soul broods over in silence. The people who speak seem to think or dream long before speaking and after speaking; and though they have legendary names, and meet fantastically on a remoter sea than that which the Flying Dutchman sails over, or starve on the threshold of king's palaces that poetry may be honoured, or fight and die ignorantly and passionately among disasters which it is their fate to bring upon themselves, they are human as a disembodied passion is human, before it has made a home or a prison for itself

among circumstances and within time. Their words are all sighs,
they come out of

> that sleep
> That comes with love,

and out of

> the dreams the drowsy gods
> Breathe on the burnished mirror of the world
> And then smooth out with ivory hands and sigh.

They are full of weariness and of ecstasy, remembering human
things, and mortality, and that dreams are certainly immortal,
and that perhaps there may be a love which is also immortal.
They speak to one another not out of the heart or out of the mind,
but out of a deeper consciousness than either heart or mind, which
is perhaps what we call the soul. There is wisdom in these plays
as well as beauty; but indeed beauty is but half beauty when it is
not the cloak of wisdom, and wisdom, if it is not beautiful, is but
a dusty sign-post, pointing the way ungraciously.

1900, 1904.